THE CIVIL WAR
VIRGINIA

THE CIVIL WAR ——
VIRGINIA

Chester G. Hearn

SALAMANDER

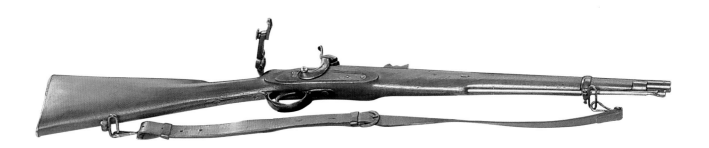

A SALAMANDER BOOK

Published by Salamander Books
The Chrysalis Building
Bramley Road
London W10 6SP
United Kingdom

An imprint of **Chrysalis** Books Group plc

ISBN 1 84065 558 5

10 9 8 7 6 5 4 3 2 1

All correspondence concerning the content of this volume should be addressed to Salamander Books.

Credits
Editor: Shaun Barrington
Editorial Consultant: Angus Konstam
Designer: John Heritage
Picture Researcher: Rebecca Sodergren
Production: Don Campaniello
Reproduction: Anorax Imaging Ltd
Printed and bound in Malaysia

Additional captions
Page 1: Virginia state seal flag, unit unknown, proudly boasting *Sic Semper Tyrannis* ("Ever Thus to Tyrants") beneath the figure of "Liberty."
Page 2: Henry Kelly of the 1st Virginia Cavalry, poses with his Colt Revolving Carbine and Colt Navy .36 Revolver.
Page 3: Snare drums and bugle of the Confederacy.
Page 4: Calisher and Terry cavalry carbine, with ramrod stowed, and leather strap. This firearm was owned by Major General J. E. B. Stuart.

CONTENTS

LET ME TELL YOU WHAT IS COMING

In the year 1860 the Commonwealth of Virginia represented in area, resources, and in population one of the leading states of the Union, just as she had since colonial and revolutionary days. Virginia produced some of America's most notable statesmen, and many of them participated in the formation of the Constitution of the United States. A majority of the members of Congress were either natives of Virginia or the sons or grandsons of those who had been born within her borders – borders that stretched east to west from the Atlantic Ocean to the Ohio River.

At the falls of James River stood Richmond, the commonwealth's capital, third in size among southern cities. Established in 1737, the city grew to a population in 1860 of 38,000 whites, free blacks, and slaves. Richmond's mercantile economy linked the crop-producing Piedmont to the commercial world and brought prosperity to its citizens. The city led the South in the manufacture of flour, meal, tobacco, and iron, and became the home of the Tredegar Iron Works, the South's only factory for making cannon and railroad rails. Virginia, being 68,000 square miles in size, was the largest state east

"You have chosen to inaugurate civil war, and, having done so, we will meet it in a spirit as determined as the administration has exhibited toward the South."

VIRGINIA GOVERNOR JOHN LETCHER TO SECRETARY OF WAR SIMON CAMERON, 15 APRIL 1861.

of the Mississippi and among the most centrally located. Her tidal rivers and estuaries reached from rich farmlands 150 miles inland to ports along Chesapeake Bay. Western Virginians could barge their goods all the way down the Ohio and Mississippi rivers to New Orleans, the South's largest city. Of all the southern states, Virginia was among the most self-sufficient, having every variety of soil, large deposits of iron, lead, zinc and copper, a wide belt of gold-bearing quartz, coal deposits, railroads, canals, and an industrial base greater than any state in the antebellum South. By 1860 some eleven and a half million acres were being actively farmed and another 20 million acres lay as yet unimproved within the boundaries of the 86,000 farmsteads and ranches. According to the census that year, 641 of them were more than one thousand acres.

In 1860, Virginia did not have a public school system but did have schools in every neighborhood throughout the commonwealth, and the state paid tuition for those who needed financial assistance. Her colleges and universities ranked among the best in the nation.

The Virginia Military Institute had the reputation for being the "West Point of the South," and many considered Thomas Jefferson's University of Virginia the leading institution of higher learning in the United States. Young men throughout the nation attended the medical college in Richmond. Even slaves received an education, sometimes in trade schools and sometimes on plantations. Many of them became skilled mechanics, blacksmiths, some wagonmakers, shoemakers, and other craftsmen. In 1860, Virginia's general assembly reported the value of the commonwealth's real estate at $374,989,889. Slave property totaled $313,148,275 and represented Virginia's second greatest asset.

Slaveholders believed that such assets must be protected. In the view of state government, the economy of the commonwealth depended upon a stable slave population.

Below: *The Tredegar Ironworks in Richmond was the largest ironworks and gun foundry in the Confederacy, making the Virginian capital a city of great strategic importance.*

Virginia's military population – white men between the ages of 18 and 45 – numbered 196,587. There were also 490,865 slaves and 52,128 slaveholders, making Virginia the largest slave-holding state in the Union. About 50,000 of the arms-bearing population lived in western Virginia, where slaveholding was not popular, and two years later the region would separate from the commonwealth and establish the state of West Virginia.

Is there ever a starting point for war? The genesis of the conflict can perhaps be traced to 1859 when a fanatical abolitionist by the name of John Brown attempted to capture the United States armory and arsenal at Harpers Ferry, Virginia.

John Brown's Raid

Fifty-five-year-old John Brown, after a life of failed enterprises, decided that he was an abolitionist. With the evils of slavery constantly to the fore in all his thinking, he left his homestead in North Elba, New York, and in August 1855 transported five of his sons to Osawatomie, Kansas, to help make the territory safe for antislavery settlers. After proslavery adherents burned the free-state community of Lawrence, Brown and his sons and followers dragged five proslavery settlers from their homes and hacked them to death with broadsword by the banks of the Pottawatomie Creek. During the next three years "Old Brown of Osawatomie," now a hunted murderer, hatched a plan to seize the Federal arsenal at Harpers Ferry, arm the slaves, foment insurrection, and carry the war of abolition into the farming communities of Virginia.

Brown believed that God had chosen 1859 as the time for him to rid the country of the stain of slavery. His efforts were supported and financed by the "Secret Six," wealthy men of New York and Massachusetts who believed in his cause and encouraged it. During the summer he changed his name to Isaac Smith, grew a long silvery beard, and assumed the persona of the prophet Elijah. He rented a farm

Above left: *Virginia governor John Letcher, a man with some momentous decisons to make in the coming months.*

Above: *A slave holding pen in Alexandria, Virginia after its seizure by Union troops in April 1861. Amid the terror and the courage of the War, it is easy to lose sight of what was perhaps its primum mobile, the evil of slavery.*

in Maryland across the Potomac River from Harpers Ferry and with several of his sons began recruiting whites and former slaves to serve as cadre for his army. Only 21 volunteers, among them five blacks, responded to his call.

On the night of 16 October Brown's platoon crossed the Potomac, stopped the eastbound Baltimore and Ohio train, and seized the undefended armory, arsenal, and rifle works, all of which were separated from each other. Brown took possession of the armory fire-engine building and sent a detachment of followers into the countryside to take hostages and round up recruits. His men captured a few white farmers in their bedclothes, among them a descendant of George Washington, and commandeered their slaves, horses, and carriages. Elsewhere, no slaves responded to Brown's call.

Instead of attracting reinforcements, Brown's invasion angered the townspeople. They promptly armed themselves with rusty muskets and squirrel guns. Paul Revere-type riders circulated through the county raising militia companies from nearby Charles Town, Jefferson, Shepherdstown, and Martinsburg. The volunteer units, under the command of Colonel Robert W. Baylor, quickly recaptured the rifle works, cleared the arsenal, and surrounded the armory engine-house, which served as Brown's fort. During the daylong skirmish on 17 October, three Harpers Ferry locals and four raiders were killed, and sharpshooters mortally wounded two of Brown's sons.

During the day President James Buchanan learned of the raid through a Baltimore and Ohio relay office. He conferred by telegraph with Virginia Governor Henry A. Wise and ordered Lieutenant Colonel Robert E. Lee to take a detachment of marines from Washington, D.C., and put down the insurrection. Late afternoon Lee departed on special Baltimore and Ohio trains with Lieutenant James Ewell Brown "Jeb" Stuart and Lieutenant Israel Green's marines to recover Federal property.

On 18 October, as daylight flooded the Potomac valley, Lee sent Stuart through the armory gate to demand Brown's surrender. Brown cracked open the door of the engine-house and told Stuart, in so many

Below: The abolitionist John Brown (1800-59) was seen as a crusading hero by some and a dangerous zealot by others.

words, to come and get him. Stuart retired, gave the signal, and Green's marines stormed the engine-house, battered down the door, killed two raiders, wounded Brown, and in less than two minutes ended the affair. Green lost one young marine during the exchange of musket fire, and in a burst of anger bent his sword trying to disembowel Brown.

Buchanan wanted to try the prisoners in Federal court, but Governor Wise insisted that the trial be held in state court before Brown succumbed to his wounds. Wise wanted to make a public statement about abolitionists inspiring slave insurrection and got his way. In a hurried trial at nearby Charles Town, Brown and his survivors were convicted of treason, murder, and insurrection.

On 2 December 1859, John Brown calmly walked to the gallows that still smelled of fresh-cut

lumber. With crows calling from nearby fields and the Virginia militia standing at attention, Charles Town's sheriff gave the nod and old John Brown went to his death. Brown's execution brought together for the first time dozens of witnesses dressed in militia uniforms who would one day become distinguished field and cavalry officers in the Confederate Army.

As John Brown lay "a'mouldering in his grave," (a stirring melody that later became "The Battle Hymn of the Republic") enraged southerners pointed their fingers at Republicans for instigating a slave insurrection and financing the attempt. In the North, abolitionists adopted Brown's prediction that the sin of slavery would "never be purged away, but with blood." The rift between North and South was growing. Southerners swore that if a Republican won the 1860 presidential election, they would secede.

Above: *Following the seizure of the Harper's Ferry (now Harpers Ferry without the apostrophe) arsenal by John Brown and his armed supporters in October 1859, state and federal troops commanded by Robert E. Lee stormed the arsenal, and Brown was captured. In this print a party of citizen soldiers under the command of Captain Alburtis are engaging the insurgents before the government troops arrived.*

John Brown did not start the Civil War, but he hurried it along, and in April 1861, Harpers Ferry would again become a center of attention.

VIRGINIA REACTS

On 1 December 1859, one day before the execution of John Brown, the Virginia general assembly met at the suggestion of Governor Wise to reorganize the militia, add more volunteer companies, collect munitions of war, and improve the state's defenses. The people, though almost unanimously in favor of the Union, nonetheless seconded the action because of the growing antislavery agitation emanating from the North.

Congress convened on 5 December, three days after the execution of Brown, and the House of Representatives argued for two months over the selection of a speaker. The wrangling concerned three topics: slavery, states-rights, and secession. On 1 February 1860 the House finally elected a Republican, William Pennington of New Jersey, and this produced a sympathetic decision in Richmond.

On 1 January 1860 Virginia elected John Letcher governor, but he had to wait until 26 May to be inaugurated. For the next five months Wise continued to serve as governor. The politics of the two men were distinctly at odds. Wise advocated secession if a Republican became president, but Letcher had won the election because he held pro-Union views. Wise continued to promote armament and encouraged the general assembly to invite Colonel Lee, who had recently squelched the Harpers Ferry raid, to come to Richmond and give advice on organizing the Virginia militia. Lee, a native of Virginia and a relative of George Washington, lived in Arlington, but he was also an officer in the U.S. Army and had sworn allegiance to the United States.

Above right: John Brown was hanged in Charlestown, Virginia on 2nd December 1859. According to one legend he stopped to kiss the baby of a slave woman on the steps of the town jail before mounting the wagon that transported him to the gallows.

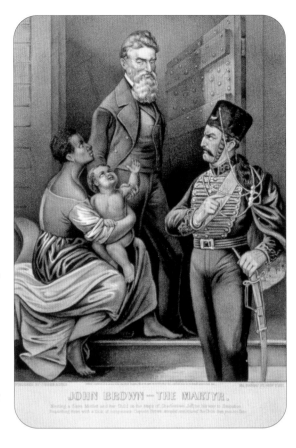

JOHN BROWN — THE MARTYR.

Lee demurred, leaving the matter of militia building in the governor's hands. Wise understood Letcher's pro-Union position, and though a lame duck governor, he began cementing his relationship with the commonwealth's militia.

THE ELECTION OF 1860

In early 1860 the people of the country were already in heated debate over the national election, still eleven months away. Congress and the legislatures of the states were in session discussing the same four subjects: slavery, states-rights, secession, and who would succeed James Buchanan of Pennsylvania as president and John C. Breckinridge of Kentucky as vice president.

Upon these issues the people divided and subdivided. Three parties emerged to elect candidates for the office of president and vice president.

In Virginia, choosing delegates to national conventions became a strained and stormy struggle. On 16 February the Democrat party in Virginia met in Richmond and after a discordant session appointed delegates, who themselves could not agree on the vital questions of the day, and sent them to the national convention. On 28 February the Constitutional Union party in Virginia, composed of Whigs and those opposed to secession, met in Richmond and elected delegates to their own national convention. Republicans were conspicuously absent as a political party, and those with Republican views fell in with the Constitutionalists.

On 23 April Virginia delegates went to the Democratic convention in Charleston, South Carolina, and became involved in rancorous debate. Instead of nominating candidates, the conventioneers split into two dissenting groups over the issue of slavery. The northern Democrats met in Baltimore and nominated Popular Sovereignty champion Stephen A. Douglas of Illinois as their candidate for

president and Herschel V. Johnson, of Georgia, for vice president. Southern Democrats, predominantly states-rights and proslavery men but not radical secessionists, put forward the names of John Breckinridge for president and Joseph Lane of Oregon for vice president.

On 9 May the Constitutional Union party met in Baltimore, adopted a compromise platform espousing "the Union, the Constitution and the enforcement of the laws," and nominated Tennessee's John Bell for president and the popular Edward Everett of Massachusetts as his running mate.

North and South watched intently when in mid-May the fledgling Republican Party met in Chicago to select its presidential candidate. From the Deep South's viewpoint, all Republicans were abolitionists. Some in Virginia felt the same way. Southerners, however, were wrong to label the party as abolitionist. The majority of Republicans cared little either way about slavery where it existed, and most Virginians, in contrast to their southern neighbors,

Left: A satire showing the four presidential candidates in the election of 1860; Abraham Lincoln (Republican), John Bell (Constitutional Union), John C. Breckinridge (Southern Democrat) and Stephen A. Douglas (Northern Democrat). The candidates tear apart a map of the U.S.

Below: *The Southern Democrat candidate for the presidential elections of 1860 was John C. Breckinridge (1821-75), a Senator from Kentucky. When the war began he became a general in the Confederate Army, and later served as Confederate Secretary of War. The caricature is the work of a Northern opponent of the Senator and of his anti-abolitionist views.*

seemed to understand this difference. On 18 May Republicans nominated Abraham Lincoln of Illinois president and Hannibal Hamlin of Maine as his running mate. The Republican platform downplayed the slavery issue but many southerners could not shake the notion that duplicity was involved, so they all waited with high emotions for the outcome of the national election in November.

For the next five months a fierce political contest raged throughout the Union. Virginia remained circumspect, waiting for the results. On 6 November Lincoln and Hamlin tallied 1,866,452 votes, not one

of them coming from the southern states. Douglas came in second with 1,376,957 votes, Breckinridge followed with 849,781 votes, and Bell trailed with 588,879 votes. Had the Democrats not split, they would have carried the popular vote, but Lincoln would have still won the electoral vote even if the Constitutional Union vote had been swung to the Democrats. Lincoln, though a minority president, owed no part of his victory to the division of his political adversaries.

Virginians listened when Lincoln pledged to not interfere with southern institutions, but the pro-

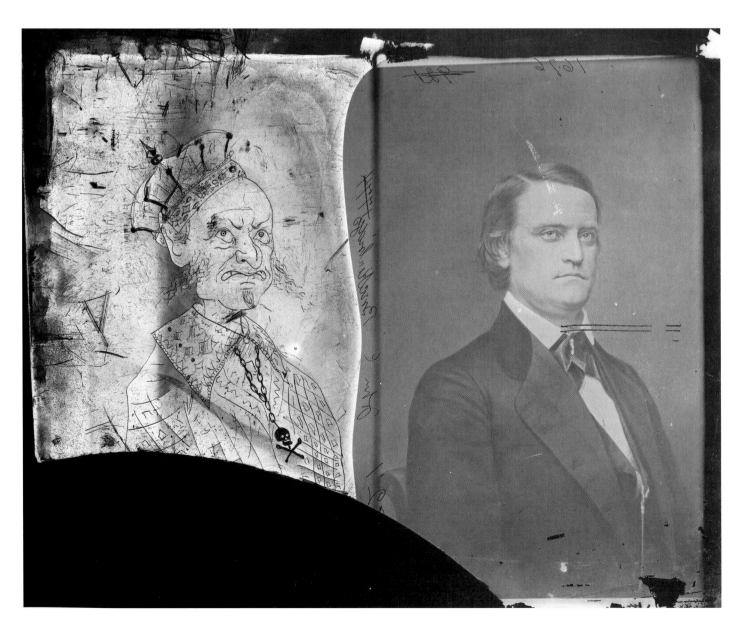

secessionists doubted whether the president could keep his word. What worried southerners most was the Republican platform advocating high tariffs and costly infrastructure improvements that favored northern states.

THE UNION UNRAVELS

On 3 December, after several southern states called conventions to discuss secession, President Buchanan delivered a message to Congress arguing against the right of secession. But he also expressed his opinion that Congress had no right to coerce a state choosing to secede by deterring it with military might. The House of Representatives appointed a select committee of thirty-three to study the matter with the objective of recommending ways to perpetuate the Union. Before meaningful discussions began, Howell Cobb of Georgia resigned as secretary of the treasury, Major Robert Anderson transferred the Federal garrison from Fort Moultrie to Fort Sumter in Charleston harbor, and John B. Floyd of Virginia resigned as secretary of war. On 20 December South Carolina passed an ordinance of secession, occupied all the Federal forts in Charleston harbor but Sumter, captured the U.S. Revenue cutter William Aiken, and sent three commissioners to Washington to treat with President Buchanan as representatives of an independent state.

Secession of the South occurred so swiftly that neither Congress nor Virginians could keep pace with the sudden exodus. By 1 February, five weeks before Lincoln's inauguration, seven states of the Deep South seceded, seized all Federal property within their boundaries, and sent state troops to garrison the holdings. Four states, including Virginia, remained tenuously within the Union, waiting for developments to determine their future.

WASHINGTON PEACE CONFERENCE

On 7 January 1861, Virginia Governor Letcher convened an extra session of the general assembly to discuss the deteriorating political condition of the country and the impact on the commonwealth. A week later the general assembly ordered an election on 4 February to choose delegates for a state convention on the subject of determining whether any ordinances should be issued changing Virginia's relations with the Union. Virginians chose levelheaded delegates and men largely without regard to political affiliation. They met and decided that the course of the state should be determined by popular vote. They also decided that Virginia should abstain from hostile action toward states in secession while at the same time restraining any action between North and South that might jeopardize reunification.

Southern states sent their ablest men to the convention to urge Virginians to join the secession movement. Virginia delegates gave the visitors a respectful hearing but promised no alliances. If Virginia joined the Confederacy, the delegates feared that the commonwealth would become the battleground for a fierce and protracted civil war, and the burden would fall more heavily on Virginia than any other state.

The delegates sought a solution, and on 19 January the general assembly passed a resolution inviting other states to meet in Washington's Villard Hotel for a peace conference in the hope of healing the nation's grievances. Virginia formed the conference around some of her most distinguished men, ex-President John Tyler, William C. Rives, and James A. Seddon. When discussion began on 4 February, Lincoln predicted that nothing would come of it. With the slave states outnumbered two-to-one, their representatives wavered between spats of wary

defensiveness and belligerence. The seven proposals emanating from the conference pleased no one. General Winfield Scott scornfully called the gathering a "collection of visionaries and fanatics." The Senate and House rejected the proposals, substantiating Lincoln's prediction.

Virginia delegates returned to Richmond and placed before the general assembly the unsuccessful results of the convention. No one expected a solution, but Virginians still clung to thin threads of hope. Perhaps, they thought, the newly inaugurated president might find a way to secure peace. On 8 April the general assembly sent three of their most distinguished members – Alexander H.H. Stuart, William B. Preston, and George W. Randolph – to confer with President Lincoln and ask what course he intended to pursue with the recently formed Confederate States of America. Lincoln met with them on 12-13 April and said that he intended to preserve the Union at all costs. On 12 April South Carolina attacked the Federal garrison at Fort Sumter and two days later forced the evacuation of U.S. troops. The arrival of Virginia's emissaries at the White House really could not have occurred at a worse time.

CALL TO ARMS

On 15 April President Lincoln issued a call for 75,000 militia apportioned among the states to serve for three months to "suppress" the seven southern states bonded together in rebellion. Lincoln made it clear that "the first service assigned will . . . be to repossess the forts, places, and property which have been seized from the Union." Simon Cameron, Lincoln's secretary of war, dutifully informed Governor Letcher that Virginia's quota consisted of three militia regiments totaling 2,340 infantry and riflemen and directed them to rendezvous at Staunton, Wheeling, and Gordonsville.

Letcher replied the same day, writing, "I have only to say that the militia of Virginia will not be furnished to the powers at Washington for any such use or purpose . . . Your object is to subjugate the

Southern States, and a requisition made upon me for such an object . . . will not be complied with. You have chosen to inaugurate civil war, and, having done so, we will meet it in a spirit as determined as the administration has exhibited toward the South."

The governor turned the issue of Virginia's status over to the same convention of delegates that had been meeting periodically since 4 February. On 17 April, after two days of heated debate, delegates adopted Virginia's Secession Ordinance by a vote of 88 to 55. Passage of the Ordinance required ratification by the voters of the commonwealth, and 23 May was designated voting day. No one really doubted the outcome. Virginia would certainly secede, but for strategic reasons the delegates on 17 April chose to delay the announcement of the Ordinance for a further two days. Virginia had few arms to fight a war and no factories to make them, but ex-Governor Wise had a plan and enough influence with the militia to solve the problem without troubling himself about the possible consequences.

THE WISE CONSPIRACY

Having always been a states-rights man, Wise fully agreed with South Carolina's capture of Fort Sumter and became incensed when learning of Lincoln's demand for Virginia militia to fight his southern friends. Though Letcher, by law, commanded the Virginia militia, Wise maintained a closer connection with many of the officers. One day before the passage of the Secession Ordinance, Wise concocted a scheme to capture the Federal armory and arsenal at Harpers Ferry before Lincoln could raise enough troops to hold it. Earlier he had advocated taking Virginia out of the Union but keeping her neutral until all Federal property could be seized. Letcher and most delegates considered such a deceit to be

dishonorable and rejected the scheme, so Wise proceeded without them and arranged a secret meeting at Richmond's Exchange Hotel to promote his plan.

Wise needed a legman. He took Nat Tyler, the editor of the *Richmond Enquirer*, into his confidence and used him to arrange a meeting with several of the militia commanders, one being Captain John Imboden. Meanwhile, Imboden met Wise on the street. Wise gave him the names of militia commanders he wanted brought to the hotel "to confer about a military matter."

At 7:00 P.M. Imboden arrived at the hotel with Captains Turner and Richard Ashby of Fauquier County, Captain Oliver R. Funsten of Clarke County, and Captain John A. Harman of Staunton. Wise also

Above: When Abraham Lincoln (1809-1865) was elected the 16th President of the United States in 1861 he reaffirmed his refusal to compromise over his strong views on preserving the Union. This led to the secession of eleven Southern states from the Union and set the country on the road to war. This early portrait dates from around 1847 during his time in Congress.

succeeded in luring armory superintendent Alfred M. Barbour into the conspiracy because Barbour was both a Virginian, a convention delegate, and in Richmond. Had a roster of attendees been kept during John Brown's execution, all the principle members of Wise's plot would have been on it. Wise still hoped to win Letcher's approval and sent a committee of three to urge the governor's approval. Letcher rejected the scheme as an act of treason, so Wise proceeded without him. After hanging John Brown for raiding Harpers Ferry eighteen months ago, Wise now planned to launch his own raid.

Ignoring Letcher's rejection, Wise contacted Colonel Edmund Fontaine of the Virginia Central Railroad and John S. Barbour of the Orange and Alexandria and the Manassas Gap Railroads and asked their support in transporting militia troops to Harpers Ferry. Both men agreed providing the

Secession Ordinance passed and Governor Letcher supported the attack. Late that night Wise took his committee to the governor's home, woke him up, and explained the plan in detail. Letcher agreed to the raid if the convention passed the Ordinance in the morning.

Wise did not bother going to bed and spent the night writing instructions to any delegates who supported him. He then instructed Imboden,

Harman, and the Ashbys to leave in the morning, assemble their commands, and wait for his orders. He also sent Superintendent Barbour back to Harpers Ferry with instructions to recruit the support of armory employees.

When the convention met in the morning, Wise appeared at the head table. He drew a pistol from his coat, placed it next to his watch, and stretched a point by stating that 2,000 troops under the

Left: Harpers Ferry, sited on the junction of the Potomac and Shenandoah Rivers became a town of great strategic importance due to its arsenal and its position as the gateway to Virginia's lush Shenandoah Valley. When Virginia seceded from the Union the contents of the arsenal and its manufacturing equipmnt were transported to Richmond, where they would be used to arm the fledgling Confederate army.

command of Major General Kenton Harper were on the way to Harpers Ferry with orders to take possession of the Federal armory, arsenal, and rifle works. With half the convention stupefied and the other half cheering, the ex-governor condemned Letcher for inaction. Wise declared that with Lincoln in the White House, war was inevitable, and the convention must not allow the Federal government to squeeze the commonwealth into submission while delegates wasted time in debate. He also said that a Massachusetts regiment of 1,000 infantry was on the road to Harpers Ferry and if Virginians occupied the town quickly, then the armory's guards would flee without firing a shot.

At first, Wise made little progress. Delegates who joined the convention faction known as "cooperationists" declared the Harpers Ferry raid "unauthorized and illegal." The convention turned into a near riot with men at each other's throats. A hush settled over the hall when word arrived that Letcher had decided to support the raid. Debate came to a halt, and on the afternoon of 17 April the Secession Ordinance passed. Wise put the pistol back in his pocket and walked to the street. He had fired a shot without pulling the trigger.

HARPERS FERRY MISCHIEF

On the morning of 17 April, Captains Imboden, Funsten, Harman, and the Ashby brothers disembarked from trains and were met by throngs of people gathered at the stations demanding to know who authorized the mobilization of the militia. At Staunton, Imboden merely replied that he was acting on the governor's orders, though he had received no word and the convention had not yet voted. During the afternoon Letcher wired General Harper to take command of the militia and proceed to Harpers

Ferry. Harper set out for Winchester, leaving instructions to put the Augusta militia on trains and meet him there.

Meanwhile, Barbour returned to Harpers Ferry with James A. Seddon, who would one day become the Confederacy's fourth secretary of war. Mildly intoxicated and dead tired, Barbour shuffled into the

Right: Two soldiers from the 22nd New York Volunteer Regiment on garrison duty in Harpers Ferry in 1861. Union troops seized the town, but were too late to prevent Virginians from spiriting the arsenal away to safety.

armory with the awkward mission of telling his Federal employees that the armory would soon belong to Virginia and promised them excellent wages if they agreed to work for the state. Many workers were Unionists and revolted. Men poured into the streets, someone shouted "treason," and fist-fights erupted on the Ferry Lot. Barbour retreated into the Wager House hotel just as the morning train from Baltimore pulled into the station and deposited Captain Charles Kingsbury, the new armory superintendent, on the dock. Barbour grabbed Kingsbury, hurriedly transferred responsibility for the armory to him, retreated from the mob, and holed up in a nearby building.

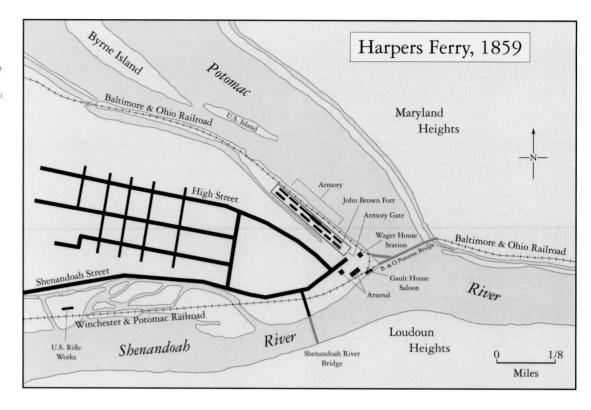

After hearing Barbour's incredulous announcement, First Lieutenant Roger Jones, commanding 42 guards from the U.S. Mounted Rifles, wired Washington for reinforcements. He then recruited a few armory workers and by nightfall his force numbered sixty. Rumors spread that large bands of uniformed troops had been seen approaching from the south, so Jones picketed all the roads leading into the Ferry. He already knew that Harpers Ferry, ringed by hills and high bluffs, could not be defended.

One of the units was Imboden's artillerymen, who had been seen rolling six guns off a train at Strasburg. Imboden started down the Shenandoah Valley, writing later, "The people generally received us coldly. The war spirit that bore them up through four years of trial and privation had not yet been aroused." On the afternoon of 18 April, Imboden loaded his Staunton Artillery on a waiting train at Winchester. During the day ten militia units passed through the town, including the West Augusta Guards, the Monticello Guards, and the Albemarle

Rifles. When the train pulled into Charles Town, Imboden found Colonel William Allen's Jefferson Guards and the mounted companies of Funsten and the Ashbys waiting for him.

At 9:00 P.M. Jones wired Washington that several companies of Virginia militia had been observed at Halltown, four miles away. He expected to be attacked within the hour. Nobody received the message in the war department because Ashby's riders had stolen down the Potomac after dark and cut the telegraph wires.

At nightfall Harman's militia arrived at Bolivar Heights, a village overlooking Harpers Ferry. Harman expected to confront Massachusetts infantry but observed only a few pickets that promptly fled back to town.

He noticed smoke rising above the town and feared that Federal troops had torched the Ferry. Jones had no malicious design toward the town, but at 10:00 P.M. he set fire to the arsenal in an effort to destroy 15,000 muskets and rifles neatly boxed in

wooden crates. Other workmen stacked combustibles in the armory, struck matches, and disappeared.

Jones put his men in marching order and started across the Potomac Bridge. Believing the fast-approaching Virginia militia would arrive at any moment, angry townspeople waving squirrel guns started in pursuit. Halfway across the bridge Jones paused and formed a skirmish line. Two kegs of powder exploded in the arsenal. The sound rumbled down the valley and out across the Charles Town pike. A reddish glow settled above the town. The mob rushed back to Harpers Ferry, and the militia sprinted toward the town to save it. There they found Ashby's cavalry dousing the fire in the arsenal. Jones recalled his skirmish line and continued his withdrawal toward Carlisle Barracks, Pennsylvania.

On the morning of 19 April Barbour, Seddon, and General Harper assessed the remains of the arsenal and armory and reported minimal damage. There were tons of arms to salvage, more than 300 machines to pack with the shafting and belting to run them. The only train to Richmond was the Baltimore and Ohio that ran through Maryland. General Harper wired Richmond for help, and for the next two weeks the Ferry remained vulnerable to counterattack, but none came.

MIDNIGHT AT NORFOLK

Governor Letcher considered the ability to produce small arms only part of the commonwealth's needs. Having taken action against Harpers Ferry, he now

Below: Both sides used a variety of different firearms during the war, but the North achieved a general standardization of armament as the war progressed. These examples of Union longarms include: a US Army Model 1842 smoothbore musket with its bayonet (top); the same weapon converted into a rifled musket (center left), and a model 1841 "Mississippi" rifled musket.

decided to do the same with the Gosport Navy Yard at Norfolk, where the Federal government maintained a stockpile of cannon. On 18 April he gave the assignment to General William B. Taliaferro, who was considered a harsh disciplinarian and unpopular among his troops.

Commandant Charles S. McCauley, USN, commanded the yard, which also happened to be the Union's most important naval base. Reinforcements were on the way, but McCauley panicked, and soon after dark on 19 April he ordered the cannon spiked and the torch applied to base facilities. He also ordered five ships set afire, one skeletonized, and four scuttled, including the powerful steamer Merrimack. Only three vessels escaped, more so from McCauley's firebrands than Taliaferro's militia.

Many of the broken and charred ships settled in the shallow Elizabeth River and were salvable. McCauley failed to destroy the dry dock and ship-building equipment, leaving Virginia with the means of creating her own navy.

On 21 April Virginia militia marched into the smoldering yard and commandeered 1,200 cannon that would eventually find their way into forts across the Confederacy. Taliaferro also rescued 2,800 barrels of gunpowder that McCauley, had he not been in such a hurry, could have used to blow the entire base to pieces.

Virginians began fortifying Norfolk and the neighboring town of Portsmouth with some of the guns left behind by McCauley. Over time the Merrimack would be resurrected and become the

Below: *As the war progressed the US Army Model 1861 "Springfield" rifled musket (center right) became the most common Union infantry weapon, although other weapons continued to be manufactured, such as the 3rd Type Justice rifled musket, produced by the P.S. Justice Company of Philadelphia (bottom right).*

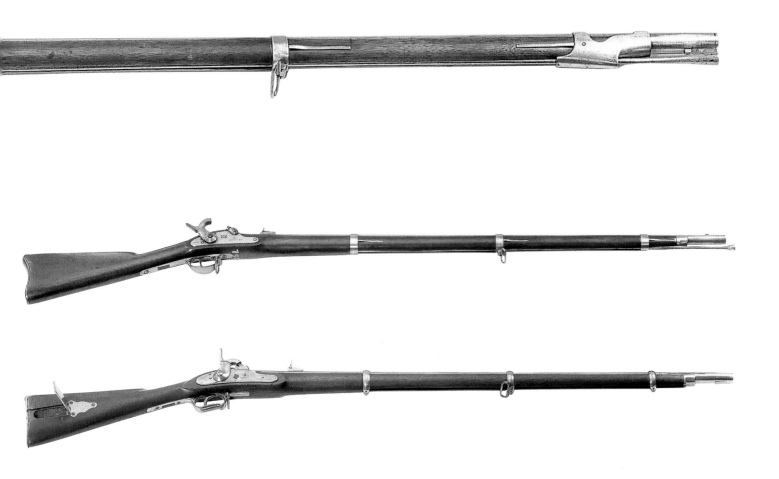

Confederacy's first ironclad. A joyful *Richmond Daily Enquirer* reporter remarked: "We have material enough to build a Navy of iron-plated ships."

The loss of Norfolk and its naval stores would have far-reaching consequences and marked the first of many humiliating defeats eventually suffered by the Union.

April 15 and the six days that followed marked the beginning of war in Virginia. There was no formal declaration.

LEE'S DILEMMA

On 18 April, one day after the Virginia convention passed the Secession Ordinance, Lincoln authorized General Winfield Scott to offer Colonel Robert E. Lee field command of the U.S. Army. Lee's responsibilities entailed the invasion of Virginia. Lee had good reason to consider the offer. He lived in comfort with his wife in a magnificent mansion at Arlington, across the river from Washington. He opposed slavery and secession, but he was a devoted Virginian and on 20 April resigned his commission. Two days later the Virginia convention appointed him major general in command of the military and naval forces of the commonwealth. Lee accepted the post, knowing that he would have to mobilize forces for the defense of Virginia against the powers of the nation to which he had sworn fidelity. No decision could have been more difficult. Had he accepted Lincoln's offer, the Civil

Below: As it became the Confederate capital, the defense of Richmond was vital to the Southern cause. Although the main Confederate army protected it from the north, the city remained vulnerable to an amphibious attack through the Tidewater region to the east. This is exactly what happened in the spring of 1862.

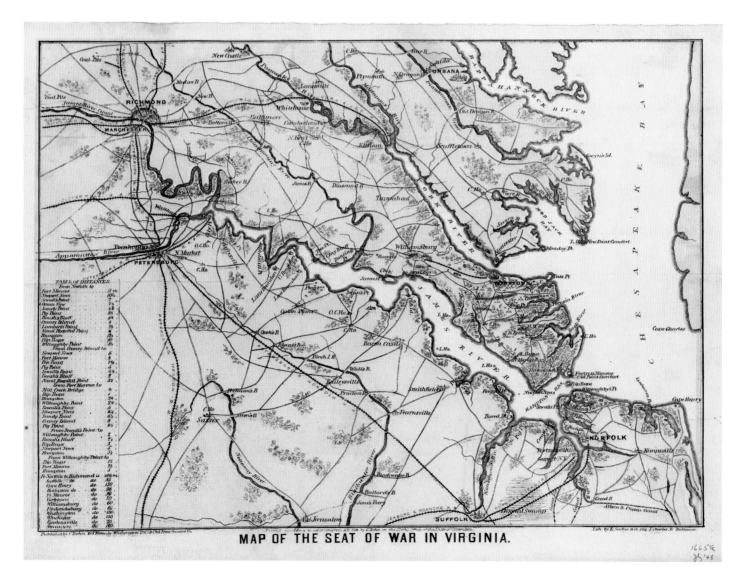

MAP OF THE SEAT OF WAR IN VIRGINIA.

War might well have ended much sooner and with far less bloodshed.

Those early events and decisions in Virginia set the stage for a protracted conflict, and Lee would push it to the limit of the South's endurance.

TIMELINES:

1737: The city of Richmond is established

25 June 1788: Virginia enters the Union as the tenth state.

16 October 1859: John Brown raids the Federal armory and arsenal at Harpers Ferry.

18 October 1859: Colonel Robert E. Lee captures Brown's raiders.

1 December 1859: Governor Henry A. Wise urges Virginia's mobilization of militia.

2 December 1859: John Brown is executed at Charles Town, Virginia.

1 January 1860: John Letcher is elected Virginia's governor.

23 April 1860: Democrats split over the choice of presidential candidates. Later, northern Democrats nominate Stephen Douglas: southern Democrats nominate John Breckinridge.

9 May 1860: Constitutional Union Party nominates John Bell for president.

18 May 1860: Republican Party nominates Abraham Lincoln for president.

6 November 1860: Abraham Lincoln wins the national presidential election.

20 December 1860: South Carolina secedes.

7 January 1861: Governor Letcher convenes extra session of general assembly to study the secession movement.

9 January 1861: Mississippi secedes.

10 January 1861: Florida secedes.

11 January 1861: Alabama secedes.

19 January 1861: Georgia secedes.

26 January 1861: Louisiana secedes.

1 February 1861: Texas secedes.

4-27 February 1861: Virginia sends delegates to the Washington Peace Conference.

12 April 1861: South Carolina forces attack Fort Sumter.

14 April 1861: Major Robert Anderson evacuates Fort Sumter.

15 April 1861: President Lincoln calls for 75,000 troops.

15 April 1861: Governor Letcher rejects Lincoln's call for Virginia troops with a clear promise of armed resistance.

17 April 1861: Virginia passes Secession Ordinance.

18 April 1861: Colonel Robert E. Lee is offered command of the Union army.

18 April 1861: U.S. troops evacuate Harpers Ferry.

19-20 April 1861: The Union navy burns the Gosport Navy Yard at Norfolk, Virginia.

20 April 1861: Lee resigns his commission in the U.S. Army.

22 April 1861: The Virginia convention appoints Lee major general in command of Virginia's army and navy.

Below: *The Hardee hat was favored by Union artillerymen and some northern infantry units during the first years of the Civil War, was actually designed by William J. Hardee, who served the Confederate cause as a general.*

1861
IT IS HIGH NOON

In April 1861, when General Lee took command of the military and naval forces of Virginia, he possessed excellent insight into the Union's strategy for suppressing the commonwealth. He expected the Orange & Alexandria Railroad to be struck, threatening the Virginia Central. He also expected Fort Monroe overlooking Hampton Roads to be vigorously held by Union forces, thereby controlling access to the James River and ultimately to Richmond. To the west he expected the Cumberland Valley and the Shenandoah Valley to be targeted, in an attempt to divide eastern Virginia from western Virginia and isolate pro-Union Wheeling and Parkersburg from Richmond. To defend so large an area required thousands of state troops at every portal from the Potomac River and Chesapeake Bay to the Ohio River.

As volunteers reported for duty, Lee mixed raw recruits with militia and deployed them for defense at Norfolk to garrison the navy yard. He put them in front of Washington at Alexandria, at Harpers Ferry in the Potomac Valley, below Charleston in the Kanawha Valley, and he placed intermediate forces and observation posts in between. Western

> *"Martial music is heard everywhere, day and night, and all the trappings and paraphernalia of war's decorations are in great demand."*
>
> JOHN B. JONES, A REBEL WAR CLERK'S DIARY

Virginians did not share the state convention's enthusiasm for war. On 21 April citizens of Monongahela County met and resolved to support the Union despite the stand taken by the remainder of the state. In the weeks to come, the action of Monongahelans gathered momentum.

HARPERS FERRY BEFORE THE WAR

Harpers Ferry enjoyed a long history, dating back to 1747 when architect Robert Harper settled at the confluence of the Potomac and Shenandoah rivers and decided to go into the ferry business. Before Harper arrived, Peter Stephens farmed the hillsides and referred to the plot beside the river as "The Hole," which is exactly how it looked from the cliffs and bluffs that surrounded it.

In 1794 George Washington owned property in the area and chose the fast-flowing-water site for the new national armory. In 1819 John Hall, who invented a breech-loading rifle, moved to the Ferry from Maine and built Hall's Rifle Works beside the Shenandoah. The armory and rifle works attracted hundreds of skilled mechanics from the North, and

Harpers Ferry soon became one of Virginia's most prosperous industrial towns. The town also became an important connecting point with the Chesapeake and Ohio Canal, which skirted Maryland Heights on the other side of the Potomac.

In 1836 Virginia and Maryland built a 900-foot bridge with six spans across the Potomac so passengers on the Baltimore and Ohio Railroad would not have to ferry across the river to connect with Wheeling. After the connection, Virginia added the 32-mile long Winchester and Potomac spur that connected the granary of the lower Shenandoah with the markets of Baltimore and Washington.

The small, compact town spread up the hillside and along the Shenandoah, eventually spilling into Bolivar Heights after the population reached about 2,000. By 1859 Harpers Ferry had become as much a railroad town as an arms-producing town. Passengers entering the town by rail could step off the platform and go directly into the Wager House or the Potomac Restaurant. The popular Gault House Saloon operated beside the Winchester and Potomac tracks and offered a variety of intoxicants and female entertainment. On the hill overlooking the armory and on property rented from the U.S. government, a few bawdy houses looked down upon the workmen in the armory.

Nobody who lived in the town much cared for it. The streets were dirty, pestilence rampaged through town during the summer months, pigs rooted the alleys, the rivers occasionally flooded, and when it rained hard, runoff swept off the hill and into the buildings and stores that cluttered Shenandoah Street. No saloonkeeper could pass a night without clubbing a drunk who wanted to start a fight.

By summer's end, 1861, the industrial base of Harpers Ferry and the bridges that fed the town would lie in ruins. Only one armory building

Left: Both sides relied on railroads to supply their armies in Virginia, and therefore engines, rolling stock, and track became prime targets for cavalry or guerrilla raids. This train was photographed on the Orange & Alexandria Railroad near Union Mills, Virginia in 1864.

survived the war: the engine-house, otherwise known as John Brown's Fort.

PROFESSOR JACKSON AT HARPERS FERRY

During April 1861 Lee would not rest until all the contents of Harpers Ferry armory and arsenal were moved to safety. When General Harper appeared incapable of handling the job, Lee detached Colonel Thomas J. Jackson from his post at the Virginia Military Institute and sent him to the Ferry with instructions to get the machinery to Richmond using whatever means possible. Jackson, a professor of artillery and physics, was perhaps better known for

his eccentricities. He had lived in poverty throughout his childhood, and despite having developed peculiar personal habits, he graduated from West Point in July 1842, 17th in a class of 59. Lee became acquainted with Jackson during the Mexican War and remembered that he fought well at Veracruz, Cerro Gordo, and Chapultapec.

Lee wanted a commanding figure at Harpers Ferry. Jackson had been there during John Brown's execution in 1859 and was familiar with the area's rugged topography. Jackson was also a West Point trained disciplinarian with a talent for improvising. He stood six feet tall and weighed 175 pounds, but his most distinguishing features were his oversized

Left: *The personal campaigning baggage of General Robert E. Lee. These include a camp bed and blanket used by the general during the Siege of Petersburg (1864), and a table from his winter headquarters near Orange Courthouse (1864-65). The pen lying on the table was the one he used to sign the surrender document at Appomattox Courthouse in April 1865.*

and shipped all the machinery, shafting, and belting from the armory to an old musket factory in Richmond.

Jackson took special interest in the double-tracked line of the Baltimore and Ohio Railroad, which passed regularly through Harpers Ferry carrying passengers and coal from western Virginia to Washington. Lee authorized the destruction of the Potomac Bridge, over which the trains rolled, but Jackson had a better idea. He blocked the outbound track on one side of the Ferry and the inbound track on the other side, stacking up 400 engines and cars for miles. With all train traffic stopped, Virginians tore up tracks and began shuttling engines and cars onto the Winchester and Potomac. Most of the rolling stock made its way to the Virginia Central and provided the Confederacy with enough rail transportation to keep men and munitions rolling through the South for another four years.

RICHMOND: CAPITAL OF THE CONFEDERACY

On 4 February 1861, the same day that the Washington Peace Conference assembled, delegates from the secession states convened in Montgomery, Alabama, to form the Southern Confederacy. On 16 March delegates adopted a provisional constitution, selected Jefferson Davis of Mississippi president, Alexander Stephens of Georgia vice president, confirmed Stephen R. Mallory as secretary of the navy, organized a government, adopted the Stars and Bars as the Confederate flag, authorized an army, and prepared for war. Not everyone agreed with the constitution, but nobody had the time to perfect it.

On 27 April the Virginia convention invited the Confederate government to move from Montgomery to Richmond. The citizens of the Old Dominion had not yet voted to secede, though they finally did on 23

Above: When the Confederates were forced to withdraw from the northern part of Virginia they did what they could to destroy the railroad tracks behind them. In this photograph Union engineers inspect damage to the Orange & Alexandria Railroad between Bristoe Station and the Rappahannock River.

feet, a broad, lined brow, intense blue eyes, and a long list of odd habits such as sucking on lemons.

When in late April Jackson arrived at Harpers Ferry, he began by sending most of the militia generals home. He retained a cadre of competent line officers, organized militia units into regiments, and dismissed everyone who refused to sign the new enlistment rolls. General Harper became a colonel, General Harman a lieutenant colonel, and Colonel Baylor a major. During the reorganization Jeb Stuart arrived. He took command of one regiment of cavalry, and Captain Turner Ashby took the other. After converting the militia into a Virginia brigade of 7,700 infantry, artillery, and cavalry, Jackson commandeered the Winchester and Potomac Railroad

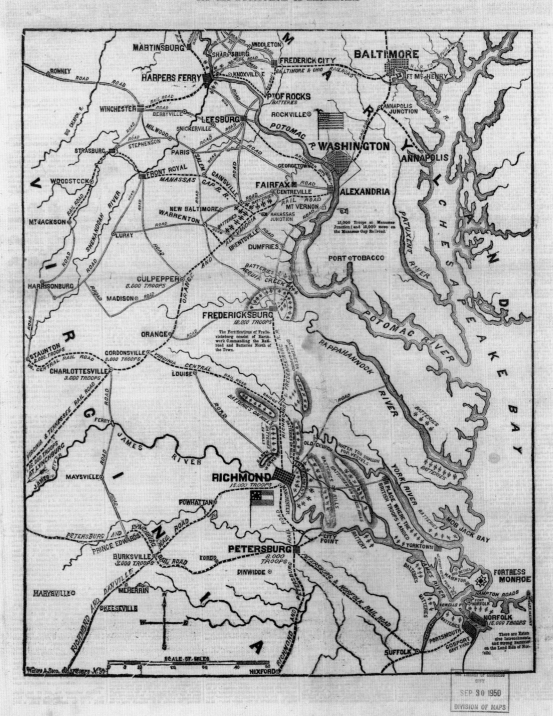

THE NEW YORK HERALD.

WHOLE NO. 9047.   MORNING EDITION—MONDAY, JUNE 17, 1861.   PRICE TWO CENTS

THE SEAT OF WAR IN VIRGINIA.

Positions of the Rebel Forces, Batteries, Intrenchments and Encampments in Virginia---The Fortification for the Protection of Richmond.

Left: This newspaper map, printed a month before the Battle of First Manassas (Bull Run) outlines the strategic situation in June 1861. Beauregard's Confederate army was grouped around Manassas, while McDowell's Union army was encamped near Washington D.C. Interestingly the newspaper greatly overestimated the strength of Confederate forces, and placed Johnston's Confederate army at Fredericksburg rather than in the Shenandoah valley.

35

May by a vote of 97,000 for and 32,000 against. Three days before the statewide vote, the provisional government under President Davis agreed that the capital should be moved to Richmond because of the city's proximity to the Federal capital. As the Confederate government began dismantling its offices in Montgomery, a human flood of bureaucrats, agents, civilian workers, outlanders, and thousands of soldiers began transforming old Richmond into a burgeoning city that would serve as a magnet for the Union army. The 100 miles that separated Richmond from Washington would become the bloodiest corridor in America.

Confederate clerk John B. Jones watched as the once quiet town swelled from a prewar population of 38,000 to numbers that defied counting. Jones wrote, "Every hour there are arrivals of organized companies from the country. The precincts of the city will soon be a series of encampments."

Every sort of undesirable character followed behind the influx of troops, including spies, counterfeiters, pickpockets, and thugs. With saloons and gambling houses through the city crime and prostitution became rampant. By summer the tobacco warehouses became hospitals, and Union soldiers began filling the prisons.

By year's end, earthworks, fortifications, rifle pits, and heavy artillery crowned the city's outskirts. War brought false prosperity to everyone. Christopher G. Memminger, secretary of the treasury, raised $27 million in specie. Most of it came from the sale of bonds or the seizure of funds in

Below: Fort Monroe on the eastern tip of Virginia's tidewater peninsula remained in Union hands after Virginia seceded, and served as a strategically important base for both the Union army and the navy.

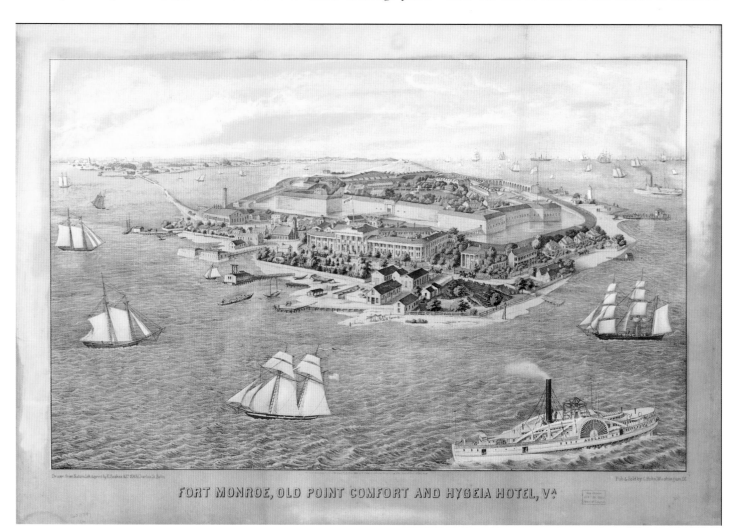

FORT MONROE, OLD POINT COMFORT AND HYGEIA HOTEL, VA.

Federal customhouses and banks operated by northern investors. Almost all the specie went to Europe to pay for arms and munitions, leaving the people with no medium of exchange but paper money unsupported by gold. By the end of 1861, the people of Richmond felt the early bite of runaway inflation.

CONTRABAND OF WAR

President Lincoln could never decide upon the best way to utilize 43-year-old Major General Benjamin F. Butler, but the powerful politician and attorney from Massachusetts had raised militia companies and wanted to glean from the war two personal objectives – wealth and an opportunity to become president. Lincoln turned Butler over to General Scott and told him to put the wily Massachusetts general where he

would do no harm. Because Fort Monroe overlooked Hampton Roads and was strategically located to disrupt Confederate blockade running, Scott put Butler there. Butler had already irritated Marylanders by invading Baltimore, but Scott did not care if he irritated Virginians. Butler invited a few trusted friends to join his command, knowing they would help fill his pockets with graft.

Slaves from local farms began descending upon the fort looking for sanctuary. Three of the fugitives came from Colonel Charles K. Mallory's nearby plantation. Major John B. Cary of the Virginia Artillery called upon Butler and asked what the general intended to do with Colonel Mallory's slaves. Butler replied that he had put them to work in the fort. Cary demanded that they be returned in compliance with fugitive slave laws. Butler decided to practice a

Above: Fort Monroe provided a relatively safe haven for runaway slaves from nearby Hampton during the first months of the war. After the declaration by Union General Benjamin F. Butler that the fugitives could be treated as war contraband many more arrived.

THE FREEDOM FORT

Slaves operated their own system of communication, and General Benjamin F. Butler's emancipation of three slaves made sensational news in Virginia's Tidewater region. On rivers like the York and the James, information passed by slaves could travel a hundred miles in a few days. The news that General Butler refused to return fugitives on the pretext that their labors for the enemy made them legitimate "contraband of war" gave Virginia slaves new hope. Soon scores of runaways began passing through the pickets posted around Fort Monroe. They came by land, river, and sea, some on old scows, oyster boats, canoes, and rafts where bloodhounds could not follow.

On 27 May, three days after Butler's contraband decree, sixty-seven fugitives applied for work at the fort. By the end of July the number had swelled to a thousand men, women, and children. They called their new home Fort Freedom.

Above: *The fugitive slaves at Fort Monroe were set to work improving the field defenses around Hampton and Newport News, while the Union government decided what to do with them.*

Butler turned them over to his quartermaster, who entered them on the payroll and gave them tasks consistent with their skills. Most of the men did heavy work. They dug earthworks, expanded the perimeter of the fort, and unloaded supply ships. Others became servants, some became guides, and women became cooks and clothes washers. Butler fed and clothed them, deducting small amounts from their wages for the upkeep of dependents. The general went a step farther and established Fort Freedom School with day classes for children and evening sessions for adults.

As the refugee population grew, families moved into the nearby ruins of Hampton, which Confederates had destroyed to keep the Federals from enjoying its conveniences. Butler's engineers helped lay out the town, and the freedmen did the rest. When asked to name the streets, they decided upon Lincoln, Union, Freedom, and Liberty.

Butler was looking into the future. Someday (perhaps) all his fugitives would be voters.

little law and said, "I am under no constitutional obligation to a foreign country, which Virginia now claims to be."

"But you say we cannot secede," Clay argued, "and so you cannot consistently detain the Negroes."

Butler replied, "But you say you have seceded, so you cannot consistently claim them. I shall hold them as contraband of war." Butler suggested that if the colonel wanted his slaves, he should come to the fort and there take the oath of allegiance to the United States.

Butler's "contraband" policy spread like a whirl-wind through the Tidewater area, and Fort Monroe became a haven for runaways. At first Lincoln remained circumspect about the general's policy of emancipation. The Republicans endorsed it, even though it came from a Democrat, and the term contraband became an overnight appellation for slaves on the run. Scott feared an uncontrollable exodus of slaves from the South and tried to discourage Butler from continuing the practice, but the general seldom listened to advice when he knew the voters were on

PHILIPPI, WEST VIRGINIA.
SCENE OF THE FIRST BATTLE OF THE REBELLION, FOUGHT JUNE 3RD 1861.

his side. Lincoln ruled that the secession of the South abrogated the old slave laws and wryly labeled the general's action "Butler's fugitive slave law." It enabled escaped slaves to obtain paying jobs building fortifications and working as personal servants for Union officers.

The term contraband in reference to escaped slaves disappeared after the passage of the Confiscation Acts, the first of which appeared on 6 August 1861.

Above: *In June 1861 Philippi in Barbour County, Virginia (now West Virginia) was the scene of one of the first skirmishes of the war, where the heavily outnumbered Confederate garrison was forced to withdraw in an engagement dubbed "the Philippi Races".*

Left: *A satirical cartoon depicting attempts to recruit volunteers for the Confederate cause during the spring of 1861.*

VOLUNTEERING DOWN DIXIE.

FIRST BLOOD

Union General Winfield Scott's fourth line of invasion had as its objective the capture of Richmond by way of the Tidewater, in particular the James and York rivers. His call for action developed into the first land battle of the Civil War near a small Virginia town called Big Bethel, which lay eight miles inland from Hampton. The two principal characters involved were General Butler and Virginia native Colonel John B. "Prince John" Magruder, who unofficially called his small command the Confederate Army of the Peninsula. Magruder's nickname came from his courtly manner, amusing theatrical behavior, and by his hosting lavish parties. The Richmond Dispatch called him "The picture of the Virginia gentleman, the frank and manly representative of the chivalry of the dear Old Dominion." This pleased Magruder, who enjoyed attention equally as much as Butler.

Magruder had fortified Big Bethel with a howitzer and 1,400 troops. Butler believed he could capture the garrison and open the way for a larger force to attack Richmond. He detached 4,400 blueclads supported by artillery from Fort Monroe to execute a simple pincers movement. Before daybreak on 10 June, two green militia units marched out on different roads, and when they reached the rendezvous mistook each other for the enemy and opened fire. Magruder heard the commotion and sent four under-strength regiments down the road to investigate. In a poorly managed attack the Federals fell back in disorder after losing 76 men, among them Major Theodore Winthrop of Butler's staff, who was "shot while standing on the fence and flourishing his sword." Magruder lost eleven men. The lopsided Confederate victory was mainly due to Colonel Daniel H. Hill's superior tactics, but the skirmish made Magruder look good. On 17 June he became a brigadier general. Butler, however, displayed his incompetence as a field commander and lost his job to 72-year-old John E. Wool.

OPERATIONS IN WESTERN VIRGINIA

Governor Letcher and General Lee both anticipated trouble with the pro-Union element in western Virginia. Colonel George D. Porterfield, commanding Virginia volunteers at Grafton, warned there would be fighting and asked for 1,000 muskets. Lee dipped into the Harpers Ferry mother lode and filled Porterfield's requisitions.

Left: *General George B. McClellan (1826-85), known as "Little Mac."*

Below: *Young men like this Union cavalry trooper from West Virginia had some hard choices to make. This mountainous region opposed secession, and loyalties were deeply divided. McClellan's victories secured the region for the Union cause, and West Virginia became a state in its own right in June 1863.*

Below: Rosecrans led a brigade by a mountain path to seize the Staunton-Parkersburg Turnpike in Pegram's rear. A two-hour fight saw the Confederates split in two. Half escaped to Beverly. Pegram and the rest surrendered.

In mid-May 35-year-old Major General George B. McClellan, commanding Ohio volunteers, received orders at his Cincinnati headquarters to reinforce Union regiments at Wheeling and Parkersburg. On 26 May he ordered Benjamin F. Kelley, a railroad agent and colonel of the Wheeling Union Regiment, to move to Grafton and wait for reinforcements from Parkersburg. Kelley actually had two units, which he renamed the 1st and 2nd Virginia Union Volunteers, though they contained few native Virginians. Porterfield, having 550 untrained and poorly armed infantry and cavalry, fell back to Philippi to await reinforcements.

On 30 May Brigadier General Thomas A. Morris, commanding an Indiana brigade, rendezvoused with Kelley and with 3,000 men and two pieces of artillery moved on Porterfield's force at Philippi. On 2 June two loyal Virginia ladies rode 34 miles on horseback to warn Porterfield, but the night was dark and stormy and his men bedded down. In the morning Morris brought up artillery without being detected, but Kelley mishandled the encirclement and after a brief skirmish Porterfield escaped to Beverly, 30 miles down the pike.

Porterfield's undisciplined force, now 1,200 strong, exhibited no enthusiasm for fighting and continued to retreat. Morris followed without encountering any determined resistance and advanced at the same rate of speed that Porterfield retreated. The Federal advance and the Confederate retreat was to go down in history as the "Philippi Races."

General Lee had seen enough of Porterfield's retrograde movements and sent Brigadier General Robert S. Garnett, an old army artillery officer, to clean out Morris' force and put down the so-called western Virginia "revolution."

Garnett arrived with fresh troops and patched together two regiments. One became the 31st Virginia: the other the 25th Virginia. Garnett detached units at Beverly and along the Parkersburg turnpike and took possession of Laurel Hill, the northeast extension of Rich Mountain. Garnett chose his position well, securing the mountain gateway to northwestern Virginia.

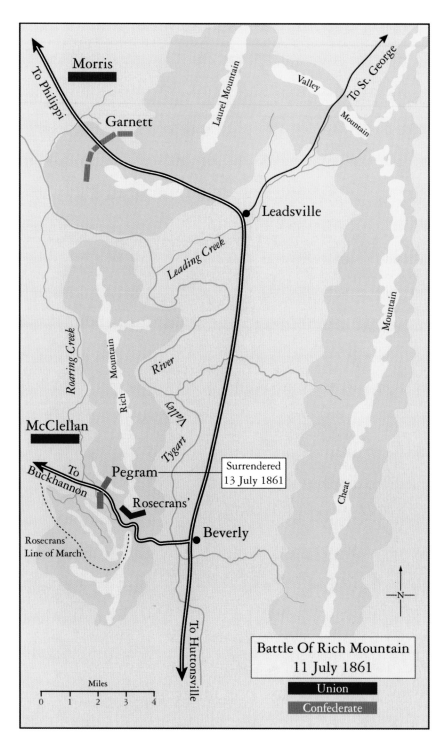

Surrendered 13 July 1861

**Battle Of Rich Mountain
11 July 1861**

Union
Confederate

In June McClellan arrived with more troops, bringing the Union force to 20,000 men from Ohio and Indiana. They fanned out and occupied the Baltimore and Ohio tracks from Wheeling to Cumberland.

Garnett placed 5,000 Confederate troops at Laurel Hill, leaving Lieutenant Colonel John Pegram with 1,000 men on Rich Mountain and 450 more at Beverly. After scouting the size of McClellan's force, Garnett decided not to take aggressive action until Lee supplied him with more troops. On 1 July Lee replied that he was sending the 44th Virginia, 12th Georgia, and 6th North Carolina. McClellan, however, had already concentrated three brigades at

Left: *The Virginian-born Brigadier-General Robert S. Garnett commanded the Confederate forces sent to quell the rebellion in western Virginia during the summer of 1861. He was killed at the Battle of Cheat Mountain in September 1861.*

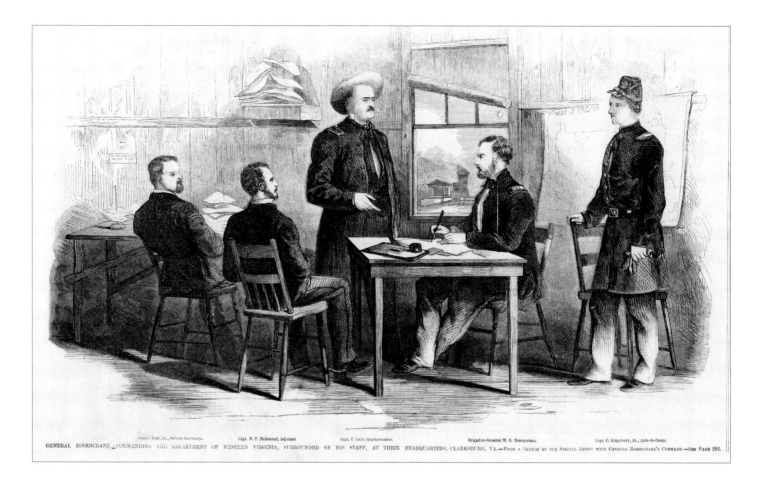

GENERAL ROSENCRANZ, COMMANDING THE DEPARTMENT OF WESTERN VIRGINIA, SURROUNDED BY HIS STAFF, AT THEIR HEADQUARTERS, CLARKSBURG, VA.—FROM A SKETCH BY OUR SPECIAL ARTIST WITH GENERAL ROSENCRANZ'S COMMAND.—SEE PAGE 293.

Above: General William S. Rosencrans (1819-98), pictured here with his staff at Clarksburg in 1861, commanded a Union brigade in western Virginia during the summer of 1862, and defeated a small Confederate force at Rich Mountain.

Far right: In May 1861 General Joseph E. Johnston (1807-91) was sent to take command of Confederate forces in the Shenandoah Valley. Two months later his troops would combine with Beauregard's army to defeat McDowell at the Battle of First Manassas.

Buckhannon and one at Philippi for an offensive. He intended to threaten Garnett at Philippi, attack Pegram on Rich Mountain with the brigades posted at Buckhannon, capture Beverly, and cut off Garnett's retreat.

On 11 July Brigadier General William S. Rosecrans' brigade led the attack on Pegram's position by filing through dense woods during a heavy rainstorm while McClellan's two brigades and artillery threatened Pegram's front.

In an action known as Rich Mountain, Rosecrans and McClellan drove Pegram back upon Garnett at Laurel Hill. Garnett, however, had already withdrawn without informing Pegram. Finding himself surrounded, Pegram surrendered to McClellan at Beverly. Two days later Garnett lost his life while commanding another retrograde movement at Carrick's Ford.

While McClellan battled Garnett in northwestern Virginia, Brigadier General Jacob D. Cox, commanding the Union "Brigade of the Kanawha," took his force up the valley of the Kanawha River and on 25 July captured Charleston. Ex-governor Henry Wise, now a Confederate brigadier general, fell back to Gauley Bridge, skirmished with Cox, and retreated to Lewisburg. Cox fortified Gauley Bridge and heard no more from Wise, mainly because the 3-day-old Union defeat at Manassas stalled action everywhere else.

The battle for northwestern Virginia ended in a Union victory and produced a political dividend that led to the dissolution of the Old Dominion. On 11 June 1861 delegates from 26 counties convened at Wheeling to discuss the possible creation of a new state. After two months they passed ordinances to withdraw from Virginia and form the new state of

Kanawha with 48 designated counties (two were added later), with its capital at Wheeling. This irregular and illegal process initiated by an unauthorized convention eventually led on 20 June 1863 to the creation of West Virginia.

About 25,000 West Virginians fought for the Union and an estimated 15,000 fought for the Confederacy.

GENERAL JOSEPH E. JOHNSTON AT HARPERS FERRY

On 15 May 1861 the Confederate government, still operating out of Montgomery, decided to send a senior military officer to Harpers Ferry and chose 54-year-old Brigadier General Joseph E. Johnston, a native of Farmville, Virginia. A graduate of West Point, Johnston was thought to be one of the brightest tacticians and most skillful engineers to resign from the Federal army and join the Confederacy. The change came as some relief to Lee, who considered Colonel Jackson too pugnacious, too secretive, and too unpredictable in his management of affairs at Harpers Ferry. Policymakers still hoped to lure Maryland into the Confederacy, but Jackson's intrusions into Maryland to dismantle the Baltimore and Ohio Railroad had undermined the efforts.

Lee failed to notify Jackson that General Johnston was coming to take command of the district. Jackson did not know Johnston, but he understood protocol. When the general arrived, Jackson demanded to see his orders. Johnston, somewhat abashed, dug through his saddlebags until he found the letter establishing his authority. An autocratic and petulant man, Johnston would never tolerate this type of abuse from a subordinate, but he knew Jackson was right. When the general produced the document, Jackson saluted and offered his services.

He knew Johnston only by reputation and considered him a competent professional soldier. The two men quickly agreed that Harpers Ferry, which Jackson had drained of its arms-making capability, offered no strategic value and mutually decided to abandon the town as soon as possible. Lee cautioned that doing so would "be depressing to the cause of the South," but he added that if a withdrawal became necessary, to "destroy all facilities for the approach or shelter of the enemy."

While waiting for developments, Johnston restructured the military organization at Harpers Ferry and assigned Jackson a brigade composed of the 2nd, 4th, 5th, 27th, and 33rd Virginia infantry regiments. In the days to come the unit would win renown as the Stonewall Brigade.

ACTION IN THE SHENANDOAH

Three weeks after General Johnston arrived at Harpers Ferry, Captain Robert L. Doyle of the 3rd Virginia, while performing outpost duty at nearby Shepherdstown, warned that "twenty or twenty-five thousand" Federals were poised to invade Virginia at the upper Potomac fords. What Doyle observed was 69-year-old Major General Robert Patterson's Pennsylvania militia composed of three-month volunteers and a few units of U.S. Regulars stationed at Chambersburg. Patterson's orders were to recapture the Ferry's arsenal and prevent enemy troops in the Shenandoah Valley from joining a larger force of Confederates camped at Manassas. Major General Patterson's command, however, was neither 25,000 strong nor prepared to fight.

Johnston used Doyle's warning as an excuse to abandon Harpers Ferry immediately, whose greater area population of 3,100 had already dwindled to about half. Lee warned Johnston, "The evacuation

would interrupt our communication with Maryland, and injure our cause in the State." Jefferson Davis was still bent on bringing Maryland into the Confederacy because doing so would force the Union to move the capital from Washington. Davis soon learned, however, that whenever Johnston decided to make a move, nothing could stop him but a direct order, and sometimes even that failed to work.

Right: The damage caused by the Confederates as they withdrew from Manassas Junction was considerable. In this photograph Union engineers and railroad officials survey the devastation caused to the Orange & Alexandria Railroad.

Jackson's demolition teams went to work, blew up the armory, arsenal, and rifle works, and left nothing of military value standing in the Ferry.

On 14 June Patterson's militia crossed the Potomac at Williamsport. He believed the first great battle of the war would be fought at Harpers Ferry and that the result would be decisive. When he reached the Ferry he found no one on the streets but a Confederate cavalry patrol. Johnston moved west to Bunker Hill, located between Martinsburg and Winchester, to await the arrival of Jackson's brigade. He sent Jeb Stuart's cavalry on wide sweeps to watch Patterson's movements, which were erratic because the general was daily receiving different instructions from Washington. When Jackson arrived, he went immediately into Martinsburg, destroyed railroad

Below: During the decades following the end of the war romanticism attached to the resistance offered by Virginians to the invading Union troops. The reality of this resistance involved guerrilla attacks on Union supply trains and outposts rather than feisty Southern belles as portrayed in this poster published in 1894.

property, organized teams of oxen to pull more engines down the pike to Winchester, and then waited. Johnston took part of his command, now called the Confederate Army of the Shenandoah, to Winchester and organized it into four brigades of 10,010 infantry, 334 cavalry, and 278 artillery. During the next two weeks, eight more regiments reported for duty.

Before leaving Martinsburg, Johnston told Jackson to avoid an engagement. Soon after he

departed, Stuart rode into Jackson's camp and reported part of Patterson's force camped at Falling Waters. Jackson decided the time had come to bloody his brigade and on 2 July took the 5th Virginia and Captain William N. Pendleton's Rockbridge Artillery on a reconnaissance. Jackson stirred up the Pennsylvania militia but found them too strong to attack. He returned to Martinsburg to demolish the stock left in the rail yard while Pendleton, with cannon named Matthew, Mark, Luke, and John, held off Patterson's cautious advance.

With clouds of black smoke curling skyward from torched coal cars, Jackson turned his back on Martinsburg and rejoined Johnston at Winchester. The Baltimore and Ohio Annual Report of 1861 blamed Jackson for the loss of 42 locomotives and tenders, 386 cars, 23 bridges embracing 127 spans with a total length of 4,713 feet, and more than 36 miles of track that had been lifted from ties and sent into the Confederacy.

On 3 July Jackson learned that he had been elevated to brigadier general. Lee wrote, "May your advancement increase your usefulness to the State."

Two weeks later the rookie general and his brigade won immortality near a small stream named Bull Run.

PRELUDE TO BULL RUN

On 2 June 1861 Brigadier General Pierre G.T. Beauregard, who, after starting the war by bombarding Fort Sumter, came to Virginia to take charge of the growing number of Confederate troops on the "Alexandria Line," 26 miles from Washington. He established his headquarters at Manassas Junction and began building a defensive perimeter behind Bull Run. The choice of Bull Run was strategic because it covered the Orange & Alexandria

"ON TO RICHMOND"

On 16 July 1861 Americans North and South vented their patriotism on the streets of their cities. Some believed it would be a quick, romantic struggle, though professional officers on both sides believed the men were still too green for offensive operations. Northern politicians lobbied Lincoln for action, pointing to success in western Virginia. They insisted that on 20 July the Confederate government must not be allowed to convene as planned in Richmond. Northern newspapers fueled the uproar, with headlines that read "On to Richmond!"

Constance Cary Harrison's homestead lay near Arlington. Tall majestic oaks once surrounded the home, but one spring afternoon while children picked wildflowers, Union lumberjacks arrived and cut down her trees for Washington's fortifications. After they left, she took a servant into the cellar and buried the family's old English silverware and heirlooms. Then she and two widowed sisters packed a few belongings and in June moved into a "cheerless inn" at Bristoe Station, the first stop beyond Manassas on the Orange and Alexandria Railroad, to be near the army. "By this time," Constance wrote, "all our kith and kin of fighting age had joined the [Virginia] volunteers."

From a room above the tracks she watched as cars filled with young soldiers clattered by. Constance recalled, "It was impossible to allow such a train to pass without running out upon the platform to salute it. Such shouts went up from sturdy throats while we stood waving hands, handkerchiefs, or the rough woolen garments we were at work upon." She noticed that most of the men were privates, most dressed in shabby clothes.

On Sundays the women drove to the army encampment near Manassas to visit "the boys," but on 17 July a rumor that enemy troops were on the march "sent an electric shock through our circle," Constance recalled. "Feminine heroism could go no farther." Early on the morning of 18 July she and others gathered by the tracks, listening to the rumble of artillery at Blackburn's Ford.

Her party of friends and servants walked the tracks, moving closer to the thump of cannon. They spent a long day of waiting and watching, and of weeping and praying. During late afternoon a very dirty soldier with his arm in a sling came limping down the tracks. Constance rushed toward him, offering bread, meat, and water. While dabbing his sweat-blackened brow, she desperately asked about her Virginia boys.

"The Virginia, marm?" the private snorted. "Why, of course. They warn't no two ways o'thinkin' 'bout that thar reg'ment. They just *kivered* tharselves with glory!"

Above: This Union smoothbore siege gun formed part of the defenses of Fort Woodbury at Arlington, Virginia during the winter of 1861-62. After the defeat at Manassas the Union army retired behind the formidable defenses surrounding Washington D.C. to regroup and prepare for a fresh offensive.

Railroad, which connected with the Virginia Central and Richmond, and the Manassas Gap Railroad, keeping lines open to General Johnston's army in the lower Shenandoah.

Excellent roads at Centreville, located three miles east of Bull Run, provided advantages for the concentration of Brigadier General Irvin McDowell's Union force. Three roads, connected to side roads, provided McDowell with many opportunities to hold the Confederate front in check while initiating swift flank movements.

McDowell had spent the past months building an army to defend Washington. Having collected a force of 34,000 men, most of them 90-day volunteers with enlistments ending, McDowell could no longer delay taking the offensive.

The tactics had been carefully crafted. General Patterson's army of 18,000 would keep General

Right: *After the Confederate withdrawal from Centreville, McDowell's Union army occupied the defensive works surrounding the town before advancing on the Confederate deployments west of Bull Run.*

MANASSAS JUNCTION, LOOKING TOWARDS BULL RUN AND CENTREVILLE, TAKEN FROM THE PARAPET OF THE FORTIFICATIONS TO THE S HEADQUARTERS OF THE REBEL GENERALS, ETC.—FROM A SKETCH BY OUR SPECIAL ARTIST

Johnston's Confederates tied down in the Shenandoah so he could not reinforce Beauregard. From Lincoln's perspective, the odds certainly looked impressive because Beauregard's Confederate army consisted of only 22,000 men. Patterson, however, stopped at Bunker Hill on 15 July and on the following day withdrew to Charles Town to cover Harpers Ferry, a town that weeks ago had lost its military importance.

On 18 July McDowell reached Centreville, but he seemed tentative over what to do next. His logistics had not kept pace with the army, and because of the inexperience of his officers and men, he postponed an attack. Instead, he dispatched a reconnaissance in force and sent one division against Brigadier General Milledge L. Bonham's command at Mitchell's Ford on Bull Run and another division against Brigadier General James Longstreet's command at Blackburn's Ford. Both Union thrusts were repulsed with minor loss on both sides, but artillery continued to duel throughout the afternoon.

The Union probe caused an immediate reaction in Richmond. Adjutant General Samuel Cooper, one of the more levelheaded members of the Confederate government, ordered Johnston to bring his 12,000 men from the Shenandoah to Manassas as quickly as possible. He also ordered Brigadier General Theophilus H. Holmes, whose 3,000-man brigade was at Aquia Creek, to reinforce Beauregard. With thousands of Confederate reinforcements converging on Manassas, the odds would suddenly change, but only if Johnston and Holmes arrived on time.

Johnston received his marching orders at midnight, 17 April, and since Patterson had already withdrawn toward Harpers Ferry, he left 2,500 men to monitor Patterson's movements and with the others started immediately for Ashby Gap and the Manassas Gap Railroad.

While waiting for McDowell to attack, and having so many roads and fords to watch, Beauregard disposed his forces over a twelve-mile front. He placed Brigadier General Jubal Early's and Holmes' brigades at Union Mills Ford on the far right flank and beside the Orange & Alexandria Bridge. Two miles upstream at McLean's Ford he deployed Brigadier General David R. Jones's command. Another mile upstream Longstreet's brigade was still

THE RAILWAY DEPOT, SHOWING THE VARIOUS FORTIFICATIONS AND
Page 366

Right: *The Battle of First Manassas (Bull Run) swirled around the Henry House. The guns in the foreground mark the site occupied by Union batteries during the climax of the battle.*

at Blackburn's Ford, and farther upstream Bonham's brigade was still at Mitchell's Ford. Brigadier General Philip St. George Cocke's men covered two fords, Ball's and Lewis', which ran between Bonham's position and Stone Bridge on the Warrenton pike. Cocke sent another detachment to cover farm fords above Stone Bridge. By then, advance units from Johnston's Shenandoah army began arriving at Manassas, and Beauregard put them in reserve behind the fords.

McDowell wasted two days performing reconnaissance, distributing supplies, and organizing a battle plan. Those crucial hours enabled Johnston and Holmes to transfer their commands to Manassas. Johnston, though the senior general present, yielded field command to Beauregard because "Borie" had made the troop dispositions and studied the area's topography.

McDowell's next mistake was putting two divisions in reserve, 11,000 men and 25 pieces of artillery, and then almost forgetting to use them. After 72 hours of muddling over tactics, McDowell put his army in motion.

BULL RUN – 21 JULY 1861

Pressed by Washington for action, McDowell finally announced that he would begin his attack on the morning of 21 July. Word spread rapidly in both directions. In Washington hundreds of sightseers dressed in finery packed lunches, climbed into carriages, and trotted to Centreville to watch the Rebels get whipped. Beauregard also read the news and put his divisions on alert.

During the night of 20-21 July, Brigadier General Daniel Tyler's division moved down the Warrenton pike and massed about two miles from Stone Bridge. Israel B. Richardson's brigade moved

southwest of Centreville toward Blackburn's Ford. McDowell took the rest of the Union army, less his reserves, seven miles northwestward to cross at Sudley Springs for the main assault on Beauregard's left flank. McDowell's plan, though he was unaware of Johnston's arrival, made good tactical sense. Richardson's feint at Blackburn Ford and Tyler's feint down the Warrenton pike was nicely designed to draw forces away from the main assault, thereby

allowing McDowell to sweep in from the north and destroy the Confederate army in a powerful flanking movement. Had Johnston's force not been on the field, McDowell's plan might have worked.

Such complicated movements by green troops strung out over a 14-mile field during daylight hours depended upon precisely executed maneuvers – otherwise it would lead to disaster. Before dawn, Confederate scouts observed the enemy concentrat-

ing along the Warrenton pike. Beauregard concluded that the Federals would attempt to turn his left flank at Stone Bridge, though it had been destroyed, and ordered brigade commanders to prepare to change position on short notice. At 5:30 A.M. General Evans reported enemy troops advancing down the pike. Beauregard grasped what he believed to be an opportunity to strike the Federal left and rear. He ordered Jones, Longstreet, and Ewell's

Above: The uniform frock coat worn by General Beauregard during his victory at First Manassas. During the first year of the war dress regulations were often ignored; he augmented his coat with non-regulation epaulettes and belt plate.

to keep his brigade commanders informed, they were all unaccustomed to managing battle maneuvers.

At the same hour, General Evans noticed that Federals on the pike were not pressing the attack but long columns of blue were marching down an unfinished railroad cut towards Sudley Springs, about twelve miles north of where Beauregard had established his command post. At 8:45 General A.P. Alexander detected the Federal movement and from Signal Hill flashed a message to Evans, "Look out for your left; you are turned."

Beauregard quickly discerned that the Federals were flanking his dispositions on the left at the time his troops were flanking the Federals on the right, but he paused to confer with Johnston before issuing new orders. On Johnston's advice Beauregard detached Bernard E. Bee and Francis S. Bartow's brigades from the Shenandoah army and shifted the troops from the unthreatened right to Henry House Hill. Beauregard then took personal command of the battle line while Johnston, his superior, assumed a staff role and fed reinforcements to pressure points on the left.

Despite McDowell's slowly executed envelopment, he succeeded in driving the grayclads onto Henry House Hill. General Jackson's brigade arrived just in time to establish a new defensive line, and it was here that he stood off repeated Union attacks and earned the nickname "Stonewall." More grayclads from the unthreatened right doubled up the hill and filled gaps in the wavering Confederate line.

During the afternoon Edmund Kirby Smith's brigade, the last of Johnston's command from the Shenandoah Valley, arrived with 1,700 fresh and rested infantry. They were six miles in the rear of the main battle, but Johnston's staff officers doubled them up Sudley Road. As the brigade turned into the woods below Bald Hill, a Federal bullet seriously

brigades to cross the fords at the first sound of heavy fire and flank the enemy, promising that the attack would be followed up by Holmes and Johnston's reserves. At 8:30 Beauregard took Johnston to a high hill overlooking the battlefield to watch the Confederate attack on the right. He expected to win a decisive victory by midday and cut off the Federal retreat to Washington. Despite Beauregard's efforts

Right: *General Pierre G.T. Beauregard (1818-93) from Louisiana commanded the troops who fired on Fort Sumter in April 1861, then took charge of the volunteer army assembling to defend Virginia from the inevitable Union invasion. Although a competent general, his career in the Confederate army was hindered by his antipathy for President Davis.*

Above: *The Battle of First Manassas (Bull Run), 21 July 1861. This sketch shows the advance of the 71st New York Volunteer Regiment of Burnside's "Rhode Island" brigade over Matthew's Hill during the opening stages of the battle.*

Right: *This stone bridge across Bull Run played little part in the battle, but became the focus of the chaotic rout of McDowell's army late in the afternoon of 21 July. The bridge was subsequently destroyed, then rebuilt.*

wounded General Smith. Colonel Arnold Elzey took command of the brigade and, aided by Beckham's Virginia artillery on the northern slope of Bald Hill, checked the Federal advance.

McDowell saw that his men had been stopped and rushed another brigade across the fords above Stone Bridge and put it position to attack across the Henry House Hill plateau. Jackson moved two Virginia batteries into position, rallied troops from other broken commands, and showed McDowell that it was useless to try to turn the flank of the Confederate army. Beauregard observed Jackson's stand on the hill, ordered his staff to raise a loud cheer, and ordered an all-out charge on McDowell's weakened left flank.

Joe Johnston, from his command post on the Confederate right, observed elements of the Federal army reeling back and ordered General Early's Virginia Brigade to move from McLean's Ford, sweep around the far left where a column of Federals were milling about in the woods, and strike the enemy's flank. Early joined Elzey and drove the enemy back upon the Warrenton pike. Jeb Stuart's cavalry joined the counterattack and galloped through two Federal batteries and a regiment of Fire Zouaves, throwing them back upon McDowell's reserves.

At 4:00 P.M. the Federal force, covered by two brigades of reserves, began an orderly withdrawal that quickly disintegrated into a rout. Federal brigades dissolved, regimental flag-bearers threw down their banners, and company commanders joined their scattered elements in a pell-mell race for the nearest ford. Thousands of fleeing blueclads filled the roads leading to Centreville. McDowell tried to

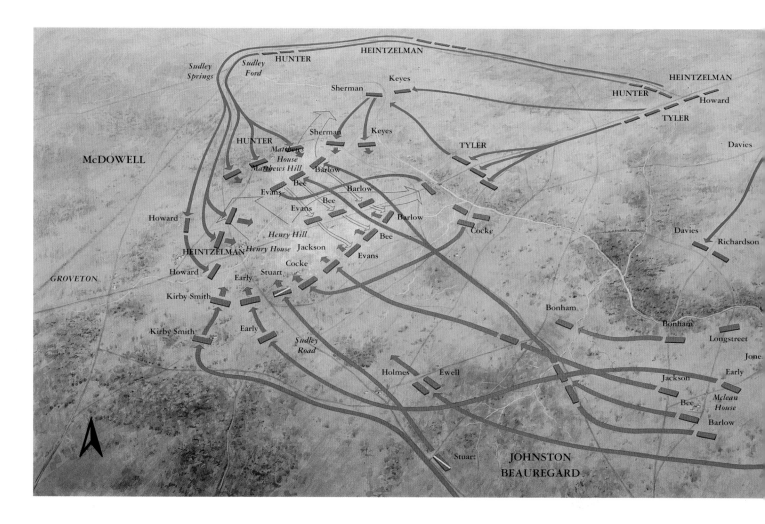

Above: *A panoramic depiction of the Battle of First Manassas (Bull Run), 21 July 1861. While McDowell pinned the Confederates along the creek with one division he sent the rest in a wide outflanking march to the east. These troops fell upon the Confederate left wing, pushing them as far west as Henry House Hill before the Confederate line rallied behind Jackson's Virginia brigade, which stood "like a stone wall." Confederate reinforcements then turned the tide of battle.*

reform his troops as they converged on the town, but they swept right past him. The confused mob threw away muskets, haversacks, canteens, ammunition boxes, and anything that would impede their flight. When Longstreet's brigade crossed Bull Run and entered abandoned Federal camps, they found pots and kettles simmering over fires, food cooking, quarters of beef hanging from trees, and long lines of wagons filled with provisions and ammunition. Longstreet's men were hungry, and instead of pursuing the Yanks, they stopped to eat.

Mixed among the congestion on the roads clattered hundreds of carriages filled with sightseers who were as anxious to get back to the defenses of Washington as the soldiers they had come to see whip the Rebels. The panic continued through the night. Hours later McDowell's army filtered through

the defenses of Washington and settled into their old camps. Beauregard could not pursue. The daylong battle had depleted his ammunition and exhausted his men. In the first major battle of the Civil War, Federals and Confederates alike fought well when taking into consideration the overall inexperience of the officers and the men. Beauregard had an advantage because he held a defensive position with shorter lines of communication. He deployed his men well and used all of them, while McDowell made the mistake of widely separating his force and holding too many units in reserve. However, had General Patterson's 18,000-man army kept Johnston occupied in the Shenandoah as planned, the war may have ended at Bull Run with a decisive victory for the North. The "on to Richmond" mentality suffered a jolt with McDowell's defeat at Bull Run.

CENTREVILLE

MILES

Holmes

Ewell

ge &
ndric R.R.

Holmes

Right: *Bull Run Creek lay between the Union army and the Confederate position around Henry House Hill. When the bridge became blocked by a logjam of fleeing troops and wagons, many Union soldiers splashed across the muddy shallows of the creek wherever they could find a safe crossing place.*

On 27 July Abraham Lincoln relieved the beleaguered general as head of the army and replaced him with Major General George B. "Little Mac" McClellan, the only man in the Union army who had distinguished himself in battle with his victories in western Virginia.

1st Bull Run	Engaged	Killed	Wounded	Missing
Union troops	28,452	418	1,011	1,216
Confederate troops	32,232	387	1,582	12

CHEAT MOUNTAIN TURNABOUT

Since 20 April 1861 General Lee had been either in command of Virginia's defenses or serving as President Davis' special military advisor. After his promotion to full general he wanted a field command, and because Union forces had embedded themselves in western Virginia, Davis believed that Lee could drive them out. General McClellan had gone to Washington, leaving Brigadier General Joseph J. Reynolds' brigade in western Virginia to guard the strategic Staunton-Parkersburg road. Lee wanted the road because it led through the heart of western Virginia.

The Parkersburg pike ran through the Tygart Valley. Two side roads connected with the pike, one at Huttonsville and the other Elkwater. The Huttonsville-Monterey road ran southeasterly, passing up Cheat Mountain and over Cheat Summit before descending and crossing Cheat River. Elkwater stood directly on the Parkersburg pike with Rich Mountain about two miles to the northwest. Reynolds had posted Colonel Nathan Kimball's

Above: *Lithograph of First Manassas printed in Chicago in 1890. One of the many heroes to emerge at First Manassas was the Confederate cavalry officer J.E.B. Stuart, who led his brigade of Virginia cavalry in a spirited charge during the final stages of the battle.*

Right: *The Battle of Cheat Mountain involved a brigade-sized Confederate assault ordered by western Virginian regional commander Major-General Robert E. Lee against an entrenched Union position on the top of Cheat Mountain, with a supporting drive up the Tygart Valley. The Confederate attack was uncoordinated, and Colonel Albert Rust who spearheaded the assault soon became convinced he was heavily outnumbered. Lee ordered a halt to the attack, and withdrew his troops.*

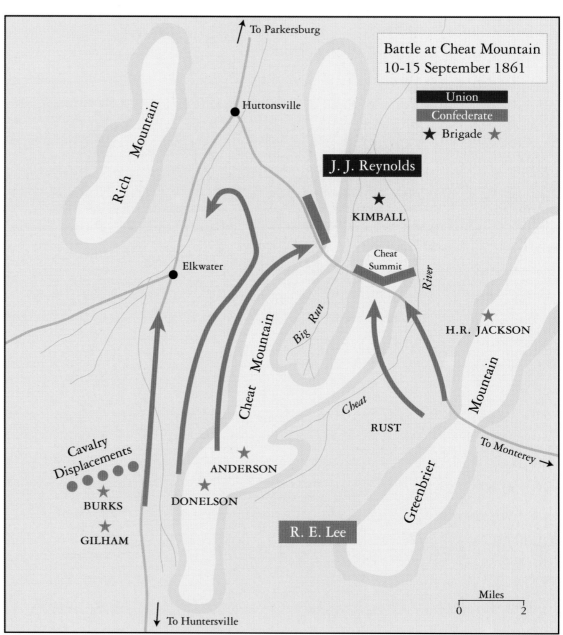

Battle at Cheat Mountain
10-15 September 1861

Union
Confederate
★ Brigade ★

To Parkersburg

Rich Mountain

Huttonsville

J. J. Reynolds

★
KIMBALL

Cheat Summit

River

Elkwater

Cheat Mountain

Big Run

★
H.R. JACKSON

Greenbrier Mountain

Cheat

RUST

To Monterey →

Cavalry Displacements

★
BURKS

★
ANDERSON

★
DONELSON

★
GILHAM

R. E. Lee

Miles
0   2

↓ To Huntersville

PROMOTION AND SELF-PROMOTION

Above: *Confederate President Jefferson Davis (1808-89) enjoyed a fractious relationship with many of his commanders, with the exception of Robert E. Lee, who continued to enjoy his Commander-in-Chief's full confidence throughout the war.*

On 31 August 1861, President Davis sent to the Confederate Senate the names of five officers for confirmation to full general. Prior to the act of 16 May 1861, the highest rank had been set at brigadier general. Adjutant General Samuel Cooper topped the list with his promotion to full general retroactive to 16 May. Albert Sidney Johnston of Kentucky came second with his rate retroactive to 30 May. Then came Robert E. Lee, ranking from 14 June, and Joe Johnston, ranking from 4 July. On that day Beauregard also received promotion to full general, retroactive to 21 July for his performance at Bull Run. The placement of fourth outraged Johnston, and he blamed President Davis for manipulating the law. He argued that he had been the most senior officer in the U.S. Army to resign and join the Confederacy, and by Confederate law he deserved to retain that seniority. Johnston had a point because he had resigned from the U.S. Army before Lee or Albert Johnston and had been the first Virginian to be named brigadier general. In Johnston's view, the right pecking order should have been himself, Cooper, Albert Johnston, Lee and Beauregard.

Unable to control his wrath, Johnston wrote a scalding 1800-word letter of protest to Davis, who was a man equally sensitive to slight. When Johnston was in the U.S. Army and Davis was secretary of war, the latter thought he had done Johnston a great favor by making him quartermaster general. By raising him to full general in the Confederate army, Davis believed he had done Johnston another favor. He could not understand Johnston's display of ill temper and fumed over the general's personal attack. Instead of engaging in a long verbal or written dispute, which Davis seldom did, he decided to rebuke Johnston with a short answer:

Sir: I have just received and read your letter of the 12th. Inst. Its language is, as you say, unusual; its arguments and statements utterly one sided, and its insinuations as unfounded as they are unbecoming.

I am, &c.   Jeff'n Davis

The controversy touched off a feud between Davis and Johnston that continued to smolder for the remainder of their lifetimes.

regiment on Cheat Summit and the rest of his own brigade in the Tygart Valley near Elkwater.

Lee reconnoitered the area and decided that Kimball's position on Cheat Summit was the weakest and could be flanked by moving up Cheat River and assaulting it from the rear. He sent Colonel Albert Rust's 2,000-man column to launch a surprise attack on Kimball, hoping that Reynolds would take the bait while another brigade under Brigadier

General Samuel R. Anderson made a deeper envelopment and cut the road behind Kimball. A third brigade under Brigadier General Henry R. Jackson would follow behind Rust and occupy Cheat Summit while three other brigades would advance up the valley to Elkwater and surround Reynolds' force. Heavy rain and cold weather, however, slowed the Confederate advance. On 12 September Lee's skirmishers drove the Federal outposts back to Elkwater,

Below: The battle flag of the 8th Virginia Volunteers was awarded to the regiment by General Beauregard following its valiant performance at the Battle of Ball's Bluff (Leesburg) in October 1861.

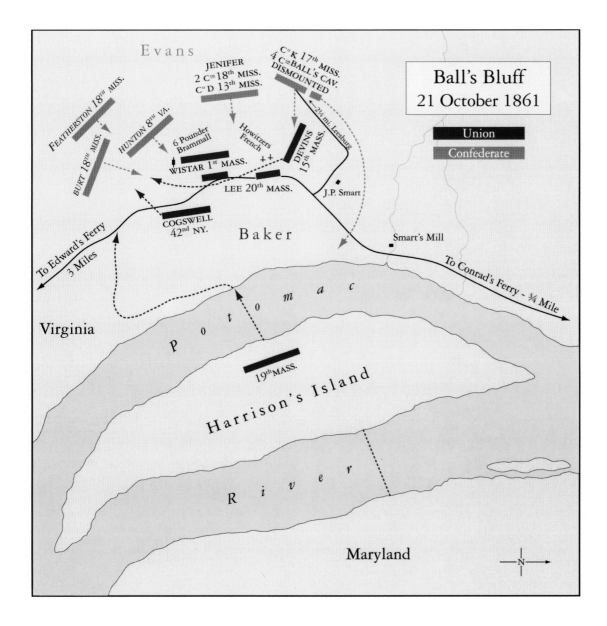

and Anderson's grayclads cut the road behind Cheat Mountain. Rust's attack, which was to signal a general advance, never materialized. This puzzled Lee, who pulled Anderson back to join with his other three brigades in an attack on Reynolds' main position on Cheat Mountain. Reconnaissance the following morning revealed that Reynolds had carefully deployed to repulse an attack, so Lee withdrew after losing about 100 men.

Douglas Southall Freeman, Lee's biographer, summed up the Cheat Mountain fiasco in six words, "[Lee's] first campaign had ended ingloriously." The reason lay in Rust's failure to deliver the first assault.

Captured Federals tricked Rust into believing that Kimball's force on Cheat Summit consisted of 4,000 entrenched blueclads when there were only 300.

THE BALL'S BLUFF "DEMONSTRATION"

After McDowell's retreat from Bull Run in July, the Federal government threw a cordon of formidable and heavily manned defenses around Washington and Alexandria. Confederate cavalry patrolled the area, but both sides remained quiescent while intensifying their efforts to gather military strength. One hot spot continued to be the upper Potomac River

Above: On October 21 1861 Brigadier-General Stone's Union brigade crossed the Potomac River near Leesburg in order to perform a reconnaissance in force of Confederate positions near Leesburg. The move was meant to demonstrate the willingness of McClellan's Army of the Potomac to take the fight to the enemy. Instead the ill-judged demonstration highlighted the inexperience of the Union army.

near Leesburg, where Harrison's Landing provided a ferrying point between Maryland and Virginia.

Brigadier General Charles P. Stone commanded a Union division near Poolesville, Maryland, with primary responsibility for patrolling the fords and watching Colonel Nathan G. Evans' Confederate brigade at Leesburg. South of Leesburg, Brigadier General George A. McCall's Union division at Dranesville was attempting to drive the Confederates out of the area and back to the Shenandoah Valley. On 20 October General McClellan, now commanding the Army of the Potomac, telegraphed McCall, ". . . a slight demonstration on your part would have the effect to move them." McCall assigned the first phase of the demonstration to Stone, that of moving Evans' force away from Leesburg.

On 21 October Stone ordered Colonel Edward D. Baker's brigade to cross the Potomac at Harrison's Island and attack Evans. Baker was actually a U.S. Senator from Oregon with no former military experience. He did not scout the enemy, nor did he secure enough boats to transport his entire force across the Potomac. He ordered those who crossed the river to scale 70-foot Ball's Bluff on the Virginia side and attack Evans' dispositions.

Evans expected the attack and moved troops from other outposts to meet it. As soon as the first elements of Baker's command came over the bluff and onto open ground, Evans' grayclads struck the disorganized Federals, whose backs were to the river, front and flank. In the disaster that followed, Baker's brigade lost 49 killed, 158 wounded, and 714 missing. Edwin M. Stanton, Union secretary of war, needed a scapegoat.

On 9 February he authorized the arrest of Colonel Stone on the recommendation of the Committee on the Conduct of the War and threw him in prison for 189 days without trial for being "unsound on the question of slavery." Stone never learned why he had been cast into jail and when released was sent to the Department of the Gulf as Major General Nathaniel P. Banks' chief of staff.

Evans and Stone never met again. Evans became a brigadier general, a wartime drunk, and a postwar high-school principal in Alabama. Colonel Stone resigned from the army, became chief of staff to the Khedive of Egypt, and lived for a decade as an Egyptian pasha.

WINTER'S INTERREGNUM

As cold, wet weather descended upon the hills and valleys of northern Virginia, men took leave and went home. Others hunkered down in winter quarters in new defensive earthworks dug by slave labor at Centreville and Manassas. Confederate cavalry patrols continued to clash with Federal patrols operating along the Potomac, but the battles of 1861 in Virginia had ended for a spell.

On 7 October 1861 Stonewall Jackson received his second star. General Johnston assigned him to the Shenandoah Valley district, and on 4 November Jackson departed from Manassas and established headquarters at Winchester. Although Jackson formed the left wing of Johnston's army, his command in many ways became independent.

The war had not touched much of Virginia. Most of the hard fighting occurred around the Old Dominion's fringes. Changes caused by war came slowly at first. Harpers Ferry, Manassas, Alexandria, western Virginia, and a small part of the Tidewater region experienced the first blows.

The greatest transformation occurred in Richmond, the new seat of the Confederate government, but not directly because of battle. Beyond Richmond small towns still slumbered. People

turned out as trains passed north filled with officers and volunteers from the Carolinas, Florida, Georgia, Alabama, Mississippi, Louisiana, and Texas. Ladies and children wearing patriotic emblems congregated at country stations. Some wore red, white, and blue and waved small Confederate flags. If a train stopped, the women passed down the platform and handed up cakes, pies, and slices of ham to volunteers complaining of empty stomachs.

Old men congregated on benches at the station or in the town square to jaw about sons and grandsons off to war. They spat tobacco juice on the ground and swore they knew more about fighting a war than Jeff Davis and the crowd from Montgomery. They placed their faith in Joe Johnston and Beauregard. Bobby Lee had let them down.

Harvests of grain, tobacco, potatoes, and root crops were already in storage, but smokehouses operated around the clock curing hams and sides of bacon, some for personal consumption and some for the Confederate quartermaster. The money was good, but everyone agreed that Confederate treasury notes

Above: *During the winter of 1861-62 Johnston's Confederate army went into well-defended winter quarters around Manassas Junction. This photograph of the outer works of the Confederate position was taken after Johnston's withdrawal the following spring.*

Far left: *Three scenes depicting the Union defeat at Ball's Bluff. The initial Union advance was halted by fire from Brigadier-General Evans' brigade (top); in the fighting that followed the northern Senator Colonel Edward D. Baker was killed (center); the battle ended in an ignoble rout as Union survivors scrambled over the bluffs and swam the Potomac to safety (bottom).*

Right: *Confederate winter quarters near Manassas Junction consisted of hastily-improvised log and earth cabins. These temporary structures were abandoned the following spring.*

Below: *The Henry House on Henry House Hill was destroyed during the Battle of First Manassas (Bull Run), and the octogenarian resident Judith C. Henry was killed. The remains of the house were photographed after Union troops reoccupied the Manassas battlefield the following spring.*

and vouchers were poor substitutes for gold. If somebody had predicted that by 1864 flour would sell for $275 a barrel, nobody would have believed it.

Optimists thought the war might be over, convinced that the Yanks had been taught a lesson. If Lincoln would not yield, then come spring Joe Johnston would fix the Federals for good. The mention of spring turned farmers thoughts to planting next year's crops and the exhausting hours of labor from dawn to dusk. Like the soldiers in their winter

quarters, Virginia's countryfolk welcomed the rest that came with cold weather.

So Virginians waited for the good news that never came. Snow fell in the Blue Ridge Mountains. Frost covered Tidewater plantations. Clouds of black smoke rose from the chimneys of Richmond and 1861 passed, without resolution; or even a clear indication of the suffering to follow.

TIMELINES: 1861

27 April: Richmond is offered as the Confederate capital.

1 May: General Lee sends Colonel Thomas J. Jackson to Harpers Ferry.

6 May: Arkansas secedes.

6 May: Jefferson Davis declares a state of war with the United States.

20 May: North Carolina secedes.

20 May: The Confederate government agrees to relocate to Richmond.

24 May: General Butler declares fugitives to be "contraband."

31 May: General Beauregard receives command of the Confederate Army of the Potomac.

8 June: Tennessee secedes.

10 June: General Butler is defeated at Big Bethel.

10-14 July: McClellan defeats Confederate forces in Western Virginia.

18-21 July: Beauregard defeats McDowell's Union army at Bull Run.

22 July: Western Virginia votes to uphold Union.

27 July: McClellan receives command of the Union army.

11 September: General Lee is defeated at Cheat Mountain.

21 October: Union forces are defeated at Ball's Bluff.

6 November: The South elects Jefferson Davis to a six-year term as president.

21 November: Judah Benjamin becomes secretary of war.

25 November: The Confederate navy begins the conversion of the USS *Merrimack* to an ironclad.

28 November: The Confederate government admits Missouri.

9 December: Tidewater planters burn cotton crops to prevent seizure by the Union.

10 December: The Confederate government admits Kentucky.

Above: *Slaves bringing in the wheat harvest near Culpeper Courthouse, Virginia. Central Virginia remained a vital source of provisions for the Confederacy during the years which followed.*

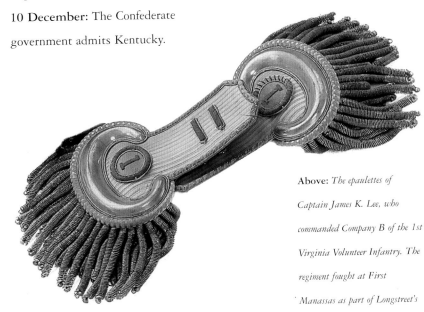

Above: *The epaulettes of Captain James K. Lee, who commanded Company B of the 1st Virginia Volunteer Infantry. The regiment fought at First Manassas as part of Longstreet's Brigade of Beauregard's Army of the Potomac.*

1862: THE MAGNITUDE OF THE DISASTER

Throughout the winter of 1862 the Union and Confederate armies in northeastern Virginia held nearly the same positions as in the autumn of 1861. General Joe Johnston's Army of Northern Virginia still occupied Manassas with its right resting on Major General Theophilus Holmes' division at Fredericksburg and its left on Stonewall Jackson's division in the lower Shenandoah Valley. Confederate pickets patrolled the Old Dominion's border from one end of the Potomac to the other and into the mountains of western Virginia.

General McClellan, hailed by the press as the "Young Napoleon," had not wasted the winter. By 1 March the Army of the Potomac had grown to 222,000 well-equipped, well-provisioned, and well-drilled men. Lincoln, having grown weary of McClellan's reluctance to advance, ordered him to do so no later than 22 February, drive back the rebel army, and press on to the capture of Richmond.

After weeks of delay McClellan finally took to the field. He sent Major General Nathaniel P. Banks' V Corps to Harpers Ferry with orders to attack Jackson's division in the Shenandoah Valley. On 24

> *"We cannot look into the future of this world at all. We cannot form an idea as to where or in what condition we may be one month hence."*
>
> BETTY HERNDON MAURY
> OF VIRGINIA

February Banks, a former governor of Massachusetts devoid of military experience, brushed away a few Confederate pickets and occupied the near-deserted town.

McClellan advanced the main elements of his army from camps around Washington to attack Johnston's Confederates at Centreville and Manassas. The Army of the Potomac slogged through the mud, reached the old Bull Run battlefield, and discovered that Johnston had abandoned the position and put his forces behind the Rappahannock River at Fredericksburg. The only vestiges of Johnston's occupation of Manassas were scores of imposing Quaker guns with their wooden snouts protruding from empty earthworks.

McClellan returned to Washington and proposed moving 120,000 troops from Alexandria down the Potomac by water to Fort Monroe and using the Peninsula as a base of operations for assaulting Richmond. He agreed to leave 18,000 men behind to defend Washington, 7,000 to occupy Manassas, and 35,000 to help Banks defeat Jackson in the Shenandoah Valley. The huge reorganization of Union forces caused another lengthy delay that was

Above: *Soldiers from the Army of the Potomac photographed with part of the army's encampment spread out below them, outside Washington D.C. during early 1862. Camps like this ringed the Union capital while General McClellan prepared his army for the 1862 spring offensive.*

unexpectedly punctuated by a clash of ironclads in Hampton Roads.

DUEL OF THE FIRST IRONCLADS

On 8 May 1861, three weeks after Virginia's militia occupied the Gosport Navy Yard, Confederate Secretary of the Navy Stephen R. Mallory, said, "I regard the possession of an iron-armored ship as a matter of first necessity. Such a vessel at this time could traverse the entire coast of the United States, prevent all blockades, and encounter, with a fair prospect of success, their entire Navy." Ten months later the Confederacy created such a ship, the CSS

Virginia. Salvage teams had pulled the torched and scuttled screw-steamer USS *Merrimack* from the bottom of the Elizabeth River and spent the better part of a year converting her into the first Confederate ironclad. The vessel could never have become a reality without Richmond's Tredegar Iron Works, the only mill in the South that was capable of producing the vessel's plates.

Mallory gave command of the *Virginia* to 60-year-old Captain Franklin Buchanan, a former U.S. Navy officer who many regarded as the quite sternest curmudgeon they had ever met. One of *Virginia's* crew remarked, "A sailor never lived with nerve sufficient to disobey him."

Buchanan was the very type of man Mallory wanted in command of the Confederacy's first ironclad. He charged Buchanan with securing Hampton Roads, the very area where McClellan intended to disembark the Army of the Potomac.

No sailor who had served on the original *Merrimack* would ever recognize her again. Workmen cut her down to the waterline and erected a 170-foot superstructure with sides sloping 35-degrees to water's edge. Four-inch wrought-iron bars crisscrossed an inner casemate built of oak 22 inches thick. When fully loaded the flat deck of the 263-foot ship went awash, giving her the appearance of a barn roof afloat.

She was armed with six 9-inch smoothbores and four rifled guns of 6- and 7-inch caliber. A cast-iron beak four feet long projected from her bow. Because of her weight, she drew 22 feet, and the two 600-horsepower engines salvaged from *Merrimack* generated about 6 knots and could barely propel her against the tide. When Buchanan steamed into Hampton Roads on 8 March, he discovered that it took thirty minutes to turn her around.

That two ironclads were being built at the same time – *Virginia* in the South and *Monitor* in the North – was one of the most remarkable coincidences of the Civil War. Unlike *Virginia*, John Ericsson's *Monitor* represented a quantum leap in

Above: *This "quaker gun" was left behind by the Confederates when the army withdrew to Fredericksburg during early March 1862. The timber barrel was fashioned and painted to look like a piece of heavy ordnance, and was designed to fool enemy scouts into believing the Confederate guns were still in place.*

71

Right: *The Florida senator Stephen Mallory (1812-73) served as the Confederate Secretary of the Navy throughout the war, and was instrumental in the development of Confederate ironclad warships such as the CSS Virginia.*

Right: *Admiral Franklin Buchanan (1800-74) flew his flag in the CSS Virginia when it sortied against the Union fleet in Hampton Roads on March 8. He was wounded during the engagement, and unable to take part in the engagement against the USS Monitor fought the following day.*

a revolving 140-ton turret amidships armed with two 11-inch smoothbores. Her decks were awash, and from a distance the vessel's 9-foot-high turret and the 4-foot-high pilothouse resembled, according to one Confederate observer, a "Yankee cheese box on a raft." When *Virginia* steamed into Hampton Roads on 8 March, Lieutenant John L. Worden, skipper of

design technology, "an ingenious adaptation of the materials at hand." He built the odd-looking creature in 101 days and on 25 February put her into commission. The 172-foot *Monitor* displaced 1,200 tons, drew 10.5 feet, lay flat in the water, and carried

the *Monitor*, was still at sea. During the morning, as the *Virginia* crawled down the Elizabeth River, men were still working on her.

Neither they nor the crew proper knew Buchanan was not on a shakedown cruise but headed for battle. He conned the ironclad straight across Hampton Roads and at 2:00 P.M. opened fire on the 50-gun USS *Congress* and the 30-gun USS *Cumberland*. Buchanan rammed *Cumberland*, which sank, and forced *Congress* to surrender. During the fight Buchanan came on deck and was hit in the leg by musket fire. Carried inside the casemate, he turned command of the vessel over to Lieutenant Catesby Jones. During the mêlée three Union steam

Left: *Union officers photographed on the deck of the USS* Monitor *while the ironclad was anchored in the James River below Drewry's Bluff, July 1862. The officer seated on the far right is Lieutenant Samuel Dana Greene, who commanded the crews of the* Monitor's *guns during the engagement, and who took over command of the ship when Captain Worden was wounded during the engagement with the CSS* Virginia.

Above: The engagement between the USS Monitor *and the CSS Virginia (rebuilt using the hull of the USS* Merrimack*) was the first clash between two ironclad warships. Although the engagement was inconclusive, the action changed the face of naval history.*

frigates ran aground, one the powerful USS *Minnesota*. Jones, however, withdrew at 5:00 P.M. with 21 dead and wounded but with good intentions of finishing off the *Minnesota* in the morning.

During the night the *Monitor*, after nearly foundering in the Atlantic, steamed into Hampton Roads and took position beside the *Minnesota*. At daylight 9 March Jones returned to Hampton Roads and observed what at first appeared to be a floating battery beside *Minnesota*, but the vessel moved toward him and started to maneuver. At 9:00 A.M. the two ironclads battled for two hours without damaging one another. Worden withdrew to renew his supply of ammunition and at 11:30 resumed the battle. Gun crews on *Virginia* concentrated their fire on *Monitor*'s pilothouse, struck the sight hole, and

blinded Worden. Both ironclads withdrew, each with slight damage, and for the next two months the two ironclads patrolled each other from afar.

When the Confederate garrison at Norfolk was forced to evacuate on 9 May, they blew up the *Virginia* because she could not navigate the James without grounding. Eight months later the *Monitor* went to sea and on 31 December 1862 foundered in a gale off Cape Hatteras. The two ironclads, though both on the bottom, revolutionized future ship design among every navy of the world.

STONEWALL JACKSON'S VALLEY CAMPAIGN

After General Jackson conducted an undistinguished winter campaign in the snow-covered mountains of western Virginia, he returned to Winchester to keep an eye on the Shenandoah Valley. On 22 February Ashby's scouts watched as General Banks V Corps moved 18,000 troops from Frederick, Maryland, to Harpers Ferry. Four days later McClellan came to the Ferry and placed elements of Banks' corps at Charles Town, Smithfield, Martinsburg, and Bunker Hill. Fine macadam roads connected the camps. Lincoln wanted to restore the use of the Baltimore & Ohio and clean the rebels out of the valley, and McClellan's dispositions were well placed to do both.

On the same day that Banks occupied Harpers Ferry, Joe Johnston removed three regiments from Jackson's command. Then on 9 March Johnston abandoned Centreville and Manassas, leaving Jackson with no supports. Based upon field returns 2 March, Banks had 30,000 men to assault Winchester. Jackson had 5,267 men in three brigades composed of 4,279 infantry, 369 artillery, and 601 cavalry. When on 11 March Banks moved on Winchester, Jackson could only fall back. Banks sent Brigadier General James Shields' division (9,000) to Strasburg, deposited Brigadier General Alpheus S. Williams' division (7,000) at Winchester,

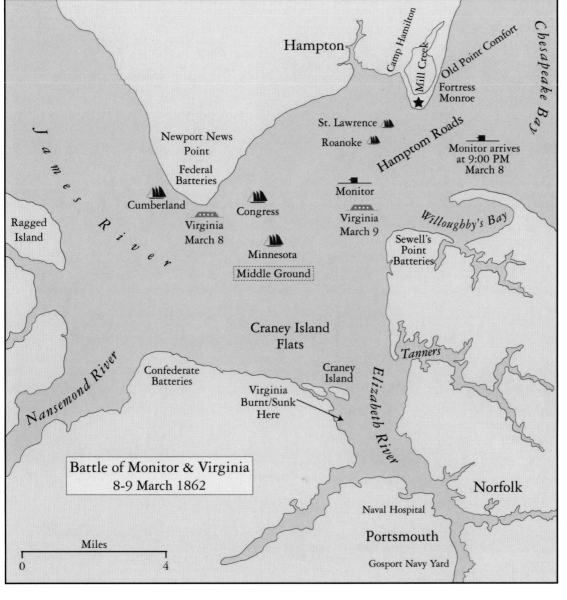

Left: *The Battle of Hampton Roads was fought over two days in 1862. On March 8 the CSS* Virginia *sortied from the Elizabeth River and destroyed the wooden-hulled warships USS* Cumberland *and USS* Congress. *After spending the night at anchor off Sewell's Point the Confederate ironclad tried to attack the stranded USS* Minnesota, *but the newly-arrived USS* Monitor *intercepted her, initiating a long but relatively bloodless engagement between the two ironclads.*

Right: General Thomas J. "Stonewall" Jackson (1824-63).

Below: The personal campaigning effects of General Jackson are now on display in the Museum of the Confederacy in Richmond, Virginia. They include his forage cap, an Adams and a Lefaucheaux revolver, his sword, and the gauntlets he wore when he was shot at the Battle of Chancellorsville.

and left Brigadier General John Sedgwick's division (7,000) at Harpers Ferry. With Jackson neutralized, Banks prepared to join McClellan for the Peninsular Campaign and let Sedgwick keep tabs on the Valley.

Jackson's task was to hold Banks in the Valley, so on 23 March he attacked Shields at Kernstown. He did not expect to defeat Shields, but the crisp fight resulted in a tactical victory for the Confederacy because it prevented Banks from reinforcing McClellan and caused a ripple effect in Washington. Secretary of War Stanton detached Brigadier Louis Blenker's division from McClellan's force and sent it to Major General John C. Frémont in western

Virginia, and McDowell's I Corps of 40,000 troops was withheld from McClellan to protect Washington. The Union army now had three scattered corps watching Jackson's small command: Banks in the Shenandoah, McDowell on the Rappahannock, and Frémont in Mountain Department of western Virginia. All three generals reported directly to Washington with no one in charge of overall operations in the Valley.

General Johnston then moved his army to oppose McClellan on the Peninsula, leaving only Richard Ewell's 8,000-man division at Gordonsville. Instead of weighting his column with Ewell's

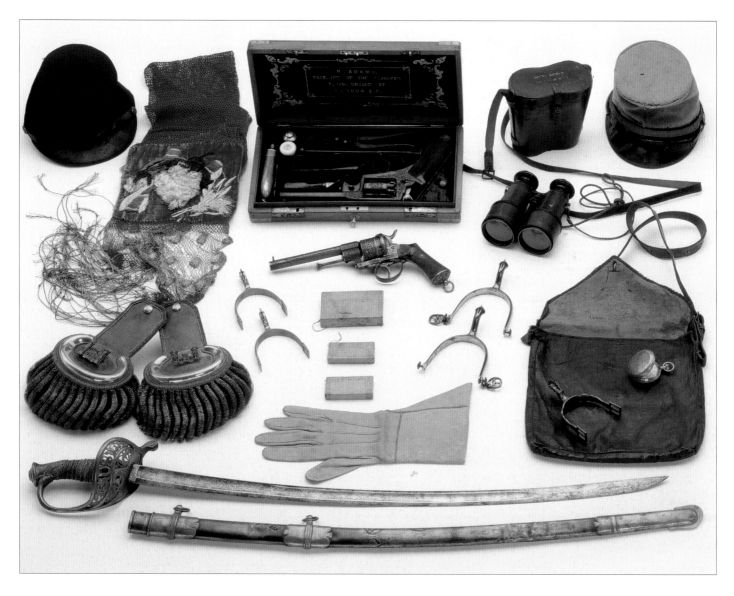

Right: *Brigadier-General Turner Ashby (1828-62) was labeled "the Knight of the Confederacy" by the press, a reflection of both his martial abilities and his chivalric nature. He served as "Stonewall" Jackson's cavalry commander in the Shenandoah Valley during the first half of 1862.*

Far left: *Turner Ashby was killed during a skirmish at Chesnut Ridge near Harrisonburg, Virginia on June 6, 1862 during the fighting which led to Jackson's decisive twin victories at Cross Keys and Port Republic. He was buried alongside his brother in Winchester, Virginia.*

Left: *Although more ornately decorated than most, this weapon is typical of the cavalry sabers used by Confederate horsemen during the war. This particular example made by Louis Heiman & Bro. belonged to Brigadier-General Archibald Gracie, who was killed at Petersburg in 1864.*

division, Jackson continued retreating up the Valley, coaxing Banks to follow. At every town Banks detached a small part of his command, and by the time he passed through Harrisonburg, large numbers of his men had been deployed in the rear.

Jackson understood the region's topography. Banks had never seen it before. Jackson wanted to keep Banks on the western side of the Massanutten Mountains and made a forced march to Swift Run Gap. There he summoned Ewell's division from Gordonsville and Brigadier General Edward Johnson's small division from western Virginia. The additions brought Jackson's strength to 17,000.

Ashby's scouts reported that Frémont's division was marching to Staunton, presumably to join Banks. A junction of Frémont and Banks would spell disaster for Jackson, so he decided to strike Frémont's column before it reached the Valley. Jackson left Ewell at Swift Run Gap, took Ashby's cavalry and Johnson's division to McDowell, and on 8 May repulsed Frémont and threw him back to Franklin.

While Jackson was at McDowell, Banks received orders to hold Strasburg with Williams' division and to send Shields' division to Fredericksburg. On 12 May Shields departed, leaving Banks with 8,000 men.

Using Ashby's cavalry to screen his movements, Jackson started towards Strasburg, turned abruptly east through the Massanuttens, joined forces with

BELLE OF THE VALLEY

During Jackson's Valley Campaign in 1862, 19-year-old Belle Boyd volunteered to fight the enemy in the only way she could and became a Confederate spy.

Danger and adventure excited Belle, and she clearly thrived on attention. She lived the life of a tomboy in Martinsburg and loved to ride horses. Her long journeys took her up and down the Valley and across farm roads that connected with the pike. She had keen eyes, a natural vivaciousness, and charm enough to gather intelligence from Federals wherever she encountered them. Belle never worried about being alone; ladies of the South would have looked with contempt upon her tendency to strike up acquaintances with soldiers by the roadside.

Her first encounter with Union soldiers occurred on 4 July 1861 when they broke into her home to raise the Stars and Stripes. One of them insulted her mother, so she drew a pistol and killed him. General Patterson placed guards around the house to watch her, but she charmed them, gathered information, and used her slave, Eliza Hopewell, to carry the intelligence to Jackson. Later, Belle moved to Front Royal, never realizing that in 1862 the area would be occupied by Federal troops. When General Shields took control of the town, Belle hid upstairs at the Stickland house (coincidentally owned by her

Above: *Mary Isabelle Boyd (1843-1900), known as "Belle" Boyd from Martinsburg, Virginia shot a Union soldier who was threatening her mother, then went on to become a spy for General Jackson and a courier for Jefferson Davis.*

family) and eavesdropped on a council of war through a knothole in the floor. She learned that Shields had been ordered east, a move that would weaken Banks' corps and open opportunities for Jackson. Belle jumped on her horse, used false papers to bluff her way through sentries, and rode 30 miles until she located Colonel Ashby and gave the information to him. She galloped back to Front Royal and returned before daylight to keep Shields from discovering her absence.

On 23 March, as Jackson's troops charged into Front Royal, Belle ignored the firing and ran through the streets looking for Jackson. She spotted an officer and shouted, "The Yankee force is very small. Tell him to charge right down and he will catch them all."

Jackson got the message and pressed the attack. That evening a courier brought her a note from the general, "I thank you, for myself and for the army, for the immense service that you have rendered your country today."

In 1863 Belle began carrying diplomatic messages abroad for President Davis. French correspondents loved to hear her tales and called her "La Belle Rebelle." Peace might have stifled her spirit had she not turned to acting and spent the remainder of her life entertaining audiences by reliving her wartime escapades.

Ewell at Luray, made another forced march to Front Royal, and on 23 May with 16,000 men struck Banks' flank.

Banks had four options. He could stay and fight Jackson at Strasburg, go west and join Frémont, go north to Winchester where he had more troops, or retreat in force to Manassas. Banks listened to his advisors and retired to Winchester.

Jackson's weary "foot cavalry" wasted time looting abandoned Union supply trains, but Ashby's cavalry broke up the feast and another forced march began. In a skillful attack on 25 May, Jackson drove Banks out of Winchester with heavy loss and pursued him down the pike to Martinsburg. On 26 May Banks crossed the Potomac at Williamsport, Maryland, leaving other elements of his command behind. Three days later Jackson concentrated his force at Halltown, four miles from Harpers Ferry.

The proximity of Confederate forces to Harpers Ferry threw Washington strategists into turmoil. With McClellan on the Peninsula and McDowell at Fredericksburg, Lincoln and Stanton put their heads together and contrived a scheme to trap Jackson in the lower Shenandoah. Stanton ordered part of McDowell's corps to move west and Frémont's corps to move east and meet at Strasburg. Banks hastily organized another force to assail Jackson from the north.

On 30 May Jackson became aware of the three-prong effort to encircle him and began withdrawing to Winchester. While on the way, a courier hailed Jackson's train and informed him that advanced elements of Shields' division were already at Front Royal. At that moment, McDowell's Corps and Frémont's Corps were closer to Strasburg than Jackson's division, some elements of which were 38 miles away. Jackson said nothing of the situation to his subordinates, but he sent Ashby's cavalry down

one road to check Frémont's advance and an infantry brigade down another road to check Shields' advance. By noon on 1 June Jackson had his entire force of 15,000 troops, 2,000 prisoners, and a double train of wagons seven miles long south of Strasburg. The Union force, 50,000 strong, failed to trap Jackson and deprived McClellan of the 40,000 troops in McDowell's corps.

Skirmishes continued for ten days as Union columns continued to pursue Jackson. On two occasions they almost caught him. Jackson grew tired of being pursued. He put Ewell's division (6,500) in front of Frémont's stronger force (12,000) at Cross Keys and set his own division against two of Shields' brigades and elements of Frémont's force at Port Republic and defeated them both.

Stanton had seen enough of Jackson's tactics and withdrew Federal forces from the Valley. General Lee needed reinforcements on the Peninsula and summoned Jackson from the Shenandoah.

Jackson's Valley Campaign stands as one of the Civil War's outstanding examples of how a small force using extraordinary tactics could repeatedly defeat, or at the very least frustrate, a force twice its size. It provides an example of how a properly concentrated force with an exceptional commander could time and again outmaneuver a stronger force lacking a central commander. Banks, Frémont, and McDowell were not skillful commanders. None of them could manage large bodies of troops, and this accounts for their poor performance against Jackson's smaller division in the Valley.

THE PENINSULAR CAMPAIGN – PHASE ONE

On 17 March 1862 General McClellan began moving twelve divisions (112,000 troops) by transport to Fort Monroe, Virginia, where General Wool commanded another 12,000 men. The only Confederate troops in the area were Major General Benjamin Huger's division (9,000) at Norfolk and General Magruder's division (8,000) at Yorktown. The geography was such that the Peninsula was flanked on the north side by the York River and on the south by the James River. Huger and Magruder could not support each other because they were separated by the broad mouth of the James River.

On 4 April McClellan personally led the van of 58,000 men and 100 guns up the Peninsula and was abruptly checked at Magruder's defensive position across the Warwick River. After a two-day reconnaissance McClellan foolishly decided upon laying siege to a position he could have taken immediately by assault. This gave General Lee time to send reinforcements from Johnston's army, which increased the Yorktown line to 17,000 troops holding an eight-mile front. Lee also moved part of Johnston's command into defensive positions near Richmond behind the Chickahominy River. During the four-week siege of Yorktown, McClellan brought up his entire force. On 3 May he launched a massive assault, but Johnston, screened by Stuart's cavalry, had already deserted the fortifications and moved into new defensive works at Williamsburg. Federals stumbling through Yorktown's earthworks encountered a new weapon of war – land mines.

Brigadier General George Stoneman's Union cavalry, supported by two infantry divisions, pursued Johnston until being stopped by Longstreet's rear guard at Halfway House. Heavy rain and deep mud further delayed McClellan's advance. Brigadier General Joseph Hooker made an attempt to break the Confederate line at Fort Magruder but failed. McClellan brought more divisions forward. Once again the Confederates withdrew up the Peninsula during the night. Of 40,768 Federal troops engaged,

McClellan reported 2,239 casualties. Johnston reported Confederate strength at 31,823 and his losses at 1,603.

McClellan had been thoroughly bluffed, first by Magruder and then by Johnston, and these clear

Right: Union 1861 pattern 13-inch mortars in their firing positions outside Yorktown, Virginia, May 1862. McClellan spent the best part of a month preparing to besiege the town, then the defenders withdrew just before the bombardment could begin.

deficiencies spotlighted the first manifestations of "Little Mac's" inability to command a large army.

The Union advance triggered chain reactions. Johnston fell back to Richmond's defenses, and on 9 May, Huger abandoned Norfolk, destroyed the *Virginia*, and sent his division by rail to join Johnston. Union General Wool crossed Hampton Road, occupied Norfolk, and opened the James to Drewry's Bluff, seven miles south of Richmond. Because of Jackson's activities in the Valley,

Above: *The Confederate earthworks at Drewry's Bluff, Virginia dominated a bend in the James River, forming the last line of river defenses before Richmond. The Union fleet attacked Drewry's Bluff on May 15, but failed to force their way past the Confederate position.*

Washington would not release McDowell's corps from Fredericksburg. This forced McClellan to work north of the Chickahominy in the event that Lincoln and Stanton changed their minds and sent McDowell. Swamps bordered both banks of the Chickahominy, to the distinct disadvantage of whichever army attacked first. McClellan did not know the topography quite as well as Johnston, nor did he recognize that his left wing was in the air, but as the first two days of battle commenced, neither army fully appreciated the difficulties of the terrain.

Johnston believed he could turn McClellan's flank by attacking Major General Samuel P.

Heintzelman's III Corps on the Union left while Magruder and Major General Ambrose P. Hill made a feint on the Union right. Johnston also organized a simultaneous assault on the Union center and expected Longstreet's corps to swallow up Major General Erasmus D. Keyes IV Corps at Fair Oaks and Seven Pines. In what historian Douglas S. Freeman called "A Battle of Strange Errors," Longstreet made the first mistake by putting his division on the wrong road. He stumbled into Huger and Harvey Hill's divisions, which were on their way to turn Keyes' flank. The Confederate effort planned for dawn on 31 May to turn McClellan's left and destroy Keyes IV

Corps never got underway until 1:00 P.M. Keyes stopped Hill's attack because Huger's division failed to follow in support, and part of Longstreet's command arrived too late to decisively turn the tide. McClellan never took advantage of the Confederate army's blunders, and Johnston's well-conceived battle plan failed because of sloppy staff work and poor execution.

Johnston suffered a severe battlefield wound and was succeeded by Major General Gustavus W. Smith, who had been on the left wing of the Confederate army all day and unaware of the confusion on the right. Nonetheless, Smith ordered Longstreet to attack the same positions at dawn the next morning. Longstreet did not attack aggressively because he expected a counterattack. Fair Oaks and Seven Pines, separated from each other by about a mile, ended without clear resolution. The Confederates called Seven Pines a victory; McClellan touted Fair Oaks as a victory. The Confederates suffered 6,134 casualties; the Union 5,031 casualties. The two-day battle ranked as the bloodiest of the war. Jefferson Davis had seen enough. He was present at the battlefield and attended the wounded Johnston at the end of the day. Whether he made his decision known at that time is unknown, but on the afternoon of 1 June he

Above: *While the Confederate defenses at Drewry's Bluff covered the James River, the way past the fortification was also blocked by a string of blockships and underwater obstructions.*

Right: *By the end of May*
General McClellan's Army of the
Potomac was encamped before
Richmond, with half of the army
on either side of the swampy
Chickahominy River. Temporary
bridges such as this one were vital
to ensure some degree of
communication between the two
wings of the army.

named Robert E. Lee the new commander of the Army of Northern Virginia.

McClellan clamored for more troops, even though he had many more than Lee. On 8 June, after much debate, Stanton released Major General George A. McCall's division from McDowell's corps and followed it with orders exhorting McClellan to attack.

Learning that McDowell's force had been reduced, Lee expected no Federal threat from the north and conceived a plan for using Jackson's force in conjunction of those on the Confederate left to annihilate Major General Fitz-John Porter's V Corps, which dangled on the Union far right with few supports. (Fitz-John Porter's nemesis would come at 2nd Bull Run, when he would be cashiered for his apparent failure; he would only fully clear his name 23 years later.) The success of Lee's strategy depended upon the timely arrival of Jackson's division.

STUART'S RIDE

Twenty-nine-year-old Brigadier General James Ewell Brown (Jeb) Stuart, chief of cavalry, ran a loose outfit of high-spirited riders who adored him. His long reddish brown beard made him look older. He was renowned for his fierce recklessness and cavalier flamboyancy. He led his men on wild chases and loved attention. No brigade in the Confederate service enjoyed greater morale because Stuart was the epitome of the storybook cavalryman that every Virginian adored.

On 11 June Lee summoned Stuart to headquarters because he wanted the right flank and rear of McClellan's position on the Chickahominy reconnoitered. Lee was interested in the dispositions of General Porter's V Corps, which he planned to flank and rollup as soon as Jackson arrived from the Shenandoah.

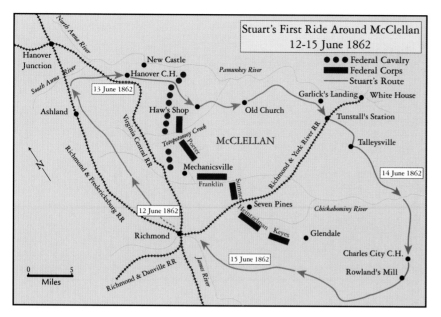

Stuart's First Ride Around McClellan
12-15 June 1862

● ● ● Federal Cavalry
▬ Federal Corps
— Stuart's Route

North Anna River
Hanover Junction
South Anna River
Ashland
Hanover C.H.
New Castle
13 June 1862
Pamunkey River
Haw's Shop
Old Church
Garlick's Landing
White House
Tunstall's Station
Talleysville
Totopotomoy Creek
McCLELLAN
Virginia Central RR
Richmond & York River RR
Mechanicsville
Franklin
Richmond & Fredericksburg RR
12 June 1862
Seven Pines
Chickahominy River
14 June 1862
Richmond
Heintzelman
Keyes
Glendale
15 June 1862
Charles City C.H.
Rowland's Mill
James River
Richmond & Danville RR
0 5 Miles

Above: J.E.B. Stuart's ride around McClellan's army began as a reconnaissance mission, designed to see how far north the Union right flank extended. The adventure proved humiliating to the Union, and served to boost Confederate morale in the weeks preceding the Seven Days campaign.

Right: Cavalry commander Brigadier-General James Ewell Brown Stuart (1833–64) was one of the most dashing figures in the Confederate army, and though he was criticised for his actions during the Gettysburg campaign, his performance during 1862 was exemplary.

At 2:00 A.M. on 12 June Stuart woke 1,200 handpicked troopers and in ten minutes had them mounted in their saddles. His force included two colonels, 26-year-old Fitzhugh Lee, a nephew of General Lee, and 25-year-old William H.F. "Rooney" Lee, the general's second son. No one, including the two colonels, knew Stuart's plans.

Stuart trotted north to deceive any spies. At the headwaters of the Chickahominy he turned abruptly east, rested until daylight, struck to the south, and swung behind Porter's corps. Early in the afternoon the column came face-to-face with a detachment from the 5th U.S. Cavalry. Rooney Lee peeled off the 9th Virginia Cavalry and in a wild saber-swinging scuffle chased the Federals down the road.

After raiding and burning a Federal camp at Old Church crossroads, Stuart had to decide whether to return to Richmond the way he had come or continue circling the Union army. He could not resist the temptation of taking the most dangerous route. Lieutenant John Esten Cooke, Stuart's brother-in-law, calculated their chances of survival at one in ten.

The long ride became a triumphal excursion that brought troopers back to their homesteads on the Peninsula. Women poured though doors to embrace husbands, sons, and sweethearts not seen since Virginia went to war. The troop lived off the generosity of relatives and friends but kept about the business of scouting McClellan's camps.

On 14 June Stuart knew Lee would be waiting and wondering where he was. Still 35 miles from Richmond, he found the Chickahominy flooded and too deep to ford. Scouts reported large columns of Federal cavalry searching the back roads. Another detachment discovered a large skiff anchored in the middle of the river where the banks were only forty feet apart. Using the skiff as a pontoon, men slung timbers across the river, and three hours later Stuart sent his entire troop across. On Sunday 15 June, having lost only one man, the jaded command trotted through the streets of Richmond with 165 prisoners.

Lee was not impressed by such recklessness, but Stuart's ride won the hearts of Virginians. The mission made Stuart famous and embarrassed McClellan, but "Little Mac" knew his dispositions had been scouted. He took prompt measures to change his deployments and disarranged Lee's plan of attack in the days to come.

PENINSULAR CAMPAIGN – THE SEVEN DAYS

On 15 June, after Stuart's swing around the Army of the Potomac, Lee and McClellan spent ten days adjusting their lines. McClellan transferred all his corps but Porter's south of the Chickahominy to move against Richmond. Lee had also rearranged his forces into new positions to attack McClellan. Before Lee could launch his offensive, McClellan decided to occupy a neglected stretch of boggy woodland for flank protection. He gave the assignment to Heintzelman's III Corps, and at 8:00 A.M. on 25 June three brigades from Hooker's division sallied forth to occupy the woods. Hooker, anticipating a

'The Seven Days' battles went by different names that are difficult to follow without clarification. They were called:

Oak Grove, 25 June, also Henrico; French's Field; King's School House; The Orchards.

Mechanicsville, 26 June, also Ellison's Mills; Beaver Dam Creek.

Gaines's Mill, 27-28 June, also First Cold Harbor; Chickahominy.

Garnet's and **Golding's Farm,** 27-28 June.

Savage's Station and **Allen's Farm,** 29 June, also Peach Orchard.

White Oak Swamp, 30 June, also Glendale; Charles City; New Market Cross Roads; Nelson's or Frayser's Farm; Turkey Bend.

Malvern Hill, 1 July, also Crew's Farm

On the morning of 26 June Lee sent 47,000 troops to Mechanicsville to destroy Porter's corps while holding the rest of McClellan's force in check. A.P Hill's division, followed by Longstreet and Harvey Hill's division, was to lead the frontal attack on Porter's right while Magruder and Huger's divisions occupied McClellan's force south of the Chickahominy. Stonewall Jackson's division, which was to have moved into position in Porter's rear, was to strike Porter's right flank.

After overwhelming Porter, Lee planned to move toward Cold Harbor, cut McClellan's line of communications to his base at White House, and deprive the Union army of the supplies needed to continue the campaign.

Right: The uniform and personal equipment of Brigadier-General J.E.B. Stuart, now on display in the Museum of the Confederacy, Richmond, Virginia. The artefacts shown here include his headquarters guidon, riding equipment, carbine, and his distinctive feathered hat.

limited engagement, struck Huger's division near Oak Grove. What started as a minor action drew reinforcements from both sides and intensified into an all day back-and-forth fight between infantry and artillery, thereby initiating the first of the Seven Days' battles. Confederates withdrew with their customary stubbornness to their main fieldworks, and as darkness enveloped the smoking landscape, the engagement ceased.

Though Lee had not anticipated McClellan's probe at Oak Grove, it did not change his mind about going on the offensive in the morning.

Lee had been watching Federal movements with interest. He could not understand why McClellan kept Porter's V Corps dangling on the far right and north of the Chickahominy after transferring the rest of the Union army across the river. Doing this deprived Porter of support.

Jackson, however, was not familiar with the terrain and never joined the action. A.P. Hill became impatient and attacked without authority. Hill's precipitous charge at Mechanicsville and Jackson's non-appearance cost the Confederates dearly. Lee's masterstroke collapsed, and Hill's division suffered excessive casualties.

The attack surprised McClellan, and he withdrew Porter's V Corps to Gaines' Mill. Lee pressed forward with Hill's division and at 2:00 P.M. on 27 June struck Porter's main defensive line at Boatswain's Swamp. Lee held the position waiting for Jackson to strike Porter's flank. Again confused by terrain, Jackson came up on Porter's center instead of his flank. An hour before dark Lee launched an attack

all along Porter's front and secured the battlefield's plateau, but the bloody fight cost Lee 8,750 killed and wounded, and Porter 6,837 casualties.

The intensity of the fighting worried McClellan, and he continued to withdraw toward the James. On 27-28 June Lee sent two brigades to test the strength on the Federal flank, one under Brigadier General George T. Anderson and the other under Brigadier General Robert Toombs. Anderson was immediately checked at Garnett's farm. Because of poor coordination, Toombs' attack on Golding's farm in the morning was also checked, but the two actions kept McClellan on the run.

During the night of 27 June McClellan made frantic dispositions to protect his withdrawal. At

Below: The confusing Seven Days Battles began with a vigorous but unsuccessful Confederate assault against the Union V Corps near Mechanicsville on June 26, then a second large-scale assault the following day at Gaine's Mill. This time the Confederates overran the Union position, precipitating a full-scale retreat toward the supply base at Harrison's Landing. Finally the threat to Richmond was repulsed.

first Lee could not believe that the Union army was actually retreating. The following day he issued orders for pursuit and developed hurried plans for encircling the enemy. He made a poor choice of commanders to spring the trap. He directed Magruder to attack part of Edwin V. Sumner's II Corps and part of William B. Franklin's VI Corps at Savage's Station.

Franklin was already withdrawing when Magruder struck Sumner's outposts at Allen's Farm. Magruder thought he was about to be attacked and stopped. When at 4:00 P.M. he discovered that Sumner and Franklin's forces were leaving the field, he attacked with two brigades instead of six. Darkness and a heavy thunderstorm interrupted the

engagement, and by the time Jackson arrived the following morning, the Federals had retired leaving tons of supplies behind.

On 30 June Jackson with Harvey Hill's division took charge of the chase and struck part of Franklin and Sumner's command at White Oak Swamp. Lee wanted to prevent McClellan from reaching Harrison's Landing on the James and sent Huger, Magruder, Longstreet, A. P. Hill, Ewell, and Holmes to cut off the Union retreat. McClellan was running too fast, but Jackson and Ewell almost got into the rear of Franklin, Porter, and Hooker. Poor staff work again prevented Lee from making a coordinated and decisive effort to cut off McClellan's retreat.

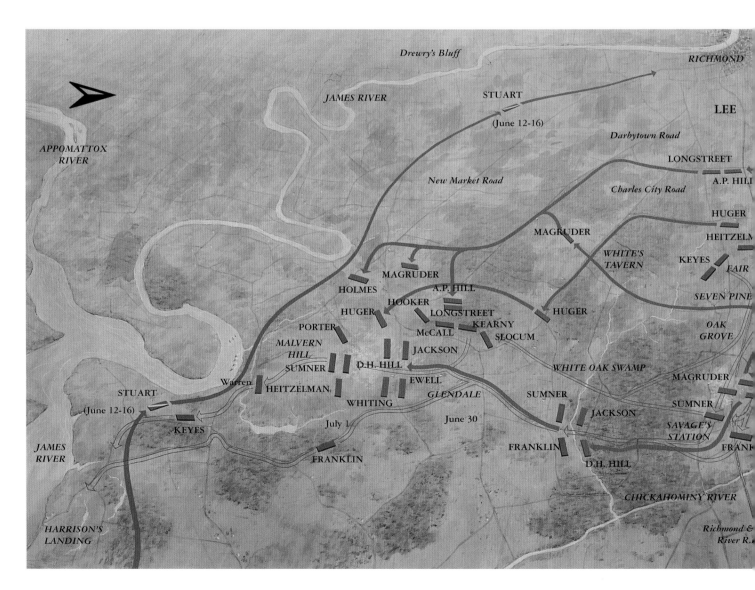

Left: *Captain Henry Benson's Battery M of the 2nd US Artillery Regiment formed part of the Artillery Reserve of the Union V Corps during the Seven Days Battles. The battery is near Fair Oaks, Virginia, June 1862.*

Below: *Union wounded at Savage's Station following the Gaine's Mill, June 27, 1862. The station was the scene of a hard-fought skirmish on June 29, and many were left behind.*

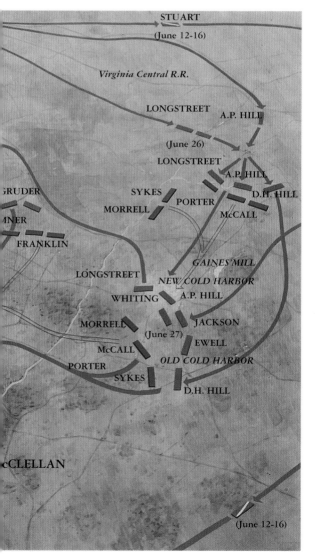

Seven Days	Engaged	Killed	Wounded	Missing
Union troops	100,000	1,734	1,011	6,075
Confederate troops	88,000	3,478	16,261	875

Above: 1,485 Confederates and 894 Union soldiers died at Gaine's Mill, but the slaughter was nothing compared to the battle fought less than a mile away at Cold Harbor two years later, when nearly 7,000 Union soldiers were killed or wounded in a single hour.

Confederates continued to lose the most men, but Lee's aggressiveness convinced McClellan that the Union army was greatly outnumbered.

On 1 July the last of the Seven Days' battles shaped beside the James River on Malvern Hill. Gunboats of the Union navy waited offshore to add their firepower to Colonel Henry Hunt's 250 guns, which covered all the approaches to the hill. McClellan had already prepared the position for defense. Lee had been forewarned that McClellan would make the hill impregnable, but after chasing the Union army across the Peninsula and losing so many opportunities to capture it, Lee decided on one

more assault. Once again, because of unfamiliarity with the ground, a swamp delayed Jackson, a guide put Magruder on the wrong road, and Lee lost time rearranging his divisions.

When Lee finally attacked, his Confederates were battered by Federal artillery and met on the hill by three corps of Federal infantry. Porter and Hunt knew they had won the initiative and urged a counterattack, but McClellan had lost all interest in fighting. He withdrew that night to his new base at Harrison's Landing and entrenched.

During the Seven Days' assault, Lee won the campaign without ever decisively winning a battle.

RICHMOND'S HOMEFRONT—1862

During the spring of 1862 Stonewall Jackson's success in the Shenandoah Valley brought new waves of recruitment activity to the streets of Richmond. Fife-and drum bands, mixed with black and white musicians, paraded down thoroughfares followed by officers in their natty gray uniforms and pretty women dressed in colorful hoop skirts. The celebration stopped in early June when the realities of war were literally brought home.

During late June, the first of more than 8,000 casualties began pouring into the city on wagons, carts, and railcars, some on litters and others afoot with bloody bandages wrapped around their heads. Sally Brock of Richmond reported, "Almost every house in the city was a private hospital, and almost every woman a nurse." For Richmond it was only the beginning. The town had no resources for such a sudden influx of misery. Hundreds of men died because they could not get their wounds cleaned and dressed. Union prisoners came into Richmond right along with

Above: The Seven Days Battles cost the Confederacy 20,164 men killed and wounded, while the Army of the Potomac suffered 16,849 casualties. This sketch shows wounded Confederate soldiers being brought to the field hospitals of Richmond during the last days of the campaign.

Confederate wounded. If they were badly injured, nurses patched them up before guards transported them to prison tents erected on nearby Belle Isle. Eventually the Union prisoners on the island numbered more than 10,000. They sapped the city's dwindling food supply, raising fears among townspeople of what a mass escape of prisoners might do to their fragile security.

Union officers imprisoned in tobacco warehouses fared somewhat better. When they received fresh clothing from home, they tore off their rags and threw them out the window. Slaves always knew when to be there. They took the rags home, washed them, mended them, and a few days later youngsters could be seen on Richmond's streets wearing faded and patched Union blue woolens.

As Lincoln put it at the end of the year: Fellow-citizens, we cannot escape history. We . . . will be remembered in spite of ourselves. No personal significance, or insignificance, can spare one or another of us." The citizens of Richmond were fast learning that they would not escape history.

Above: A Union battery of General Pope's Army of Virginia photographed while crossing a tributary of the Rappahannock River on August 9, 1862, the same day as the Battle of Cedar Mountain was fought some 25 miles away to the south-west. Jackson took full advantage of the dispersal of Pope's Army across Northern Virginia.

His losses were staggering (see page 93). McClellan prided himself on having saved his army, which Lincoln considered of little value if it did not fight. Lee lamented lost opportunities, remarking, "Under ordinary circumstances, the Federal Army should have been destroyed."

While McClellan dallied at Harrison's Landing, Lee left a few troops behind to watch the Federal force and took the Army of Northern Virginia north.

JACKSON AT CEDAR MOUNTAIN

General McClellan, neutered and dismayed in his defensive position at Harrison's Landing, begged for reinforcements to make another stab at Richmond. Lincoln no longer had confidence in his general, but he now had greater worries. With the Army of the

Potomac camped on the James River, Washington suddenly became exposed to attack if Lee turned his legions around and brought them north. The only Union forces standing between Richmond and Washington were three army corps commanded by McDowell, Banks, and Frémont: none had covered themselves in glory. Lincoln decided to pool the forces together under a strong commander and brought Major General John Pope from the West to head the new Army of Virginia.

On 14 July, the day Pope arrived at Sperryville to take command, he addressed officers and men and said, among other things:

"Let us understand each other. I have come to you from the West, where we have always seen the backs of our enemies . . . [and] I have come here to pursue the same system . . . I desire you to dismiss from your minds certain phrases, which I am sorry to find so much in vogue amongst you. I hear constantly of "taking strong positions and holding them," of "lines of retreat," and of "bases of supplies." Let us discard such ideas. The strongest position a soldier should desire to occupy is one from which he can most easily advance against the enemy."

Such bombastic braggadocio did not win the hearts or confidence of veterans. Instead of building morale, his words deflated it. Frémont refused to serve under Pope, and Lincoln replaced him with Franz Sigel, a well-traveled German with more pomp and ceremony than tactical experience.

Lincoln decided to temporarily leave McClellan's 90,000-man army at Harrison's Landing. If Pope's 50,000-man force succeeded in drawing the Army of Northern Virginia away from Richmond, then perhaps McClellan might capture the Confederate capital after all. Either way, Washington would be protected.

Lee, usually mild-mannered even toward his enemies, reacted to Pope's blustering by instantly

Below: Culpeper Courthouse in mid-August 1862. Confederate prisoners captured at the Battle of Cedar Mountain are pictured being held in the courthouse as the remains of Banks' defeated command prepare to evacuate the town and retreat north.

Cedar Mountain	Engaged	Killed	Wounded	Missing
Union troops	8,030	314	1,445	594
Confederate troops	16,868	231	1,107	0

disliking him. He kept Stuart busy watching the Army of Virginia's movements, and on 14 July when Pope moved toward Gordonsville, Lee believed he could seize the initiative because McClellan remained inactive. He gave the task to Jackson, who had proved that he could fight best when given an independent command.

Jackson asked for and received A.P. Hill's division, and on 7 August 12,000 men dressed in butternut moved by concealed roads toward Culpeper and slept on their arms. In the morning Brigadier General Beverly Robertson's Confederate cavalry drove off Federal scouts and screened Jackson's movements. Robertson reported that Pope's column stretched for twenty miles along the road from Sperryville. A brigade from Banks' II Corps led the march with other units following close behind.

On 9 August Jackson moved north, Ewell's division in the van, Brigadier General Charles Winder's division in the center, and Hill's division in the rear. The temperature hit 100 degrees, dust caked

Below: The aftermath of the Battle of Cedar Mountain. The dead horses and riders almost certainly belonged to George Bayard's Pennsylvanian Cavalry Brigade, which tried to cover the Union retreat during the closing stages of the battle.

parched throats, and men dropped from sunstroke. Winder became ill, took refuge in an ambulance, but stayed with his men. None of the division commanders knew Jackson's plans. Secretiveness had worked in the Valley, but now slowed things down.

At noon a courier from Early's brigade reported a strong enemy force approaching on the Culpeper road. Jackson moved quickly, placing Ewell in a favorable position on the western slope of Cedar Mountain. Early faced the center of the Federal line, and Winder placed his brigades on Early's left. Hill's Light Division remained in reserve, ready to support either front or flank. Jackson had gaps in his line, and no one knew what lay in the woods on the left.

Jackson did not expect much fight from Banks, with whom he had clashed in the Shenandoah. He sent Ewell and Winder forward and they brushed aside Banks' skirmishers. Winder, commanding the left, fell mortally wounded when struck by a Union shell. Minutes later Banks unleashed a massive assault on the Confederate left. Winder's division buckled, broke, and fell back. Jackson rode into the fight. He tried to raise his sword to rally the men, but because he never used it, the sword had rusted into the scabbard. He tried to shore up the left with the Stonewall Brigade, but even that vaunted unit became unhinged. Ewell's division on the right bent back but held. Hill began filling gaps, and in the twilight of early evening counterattacked. Banks' brigades withdrew grudgingly. Night fell, silencing artillery. Jackson held the field and claimed victory, but in truth he had never come so close to suffering a humiliating defeat.

SECOND BULL RUN

The dust of battle had barely settled over Cedar Mountain when General Lee learned that McClellan's

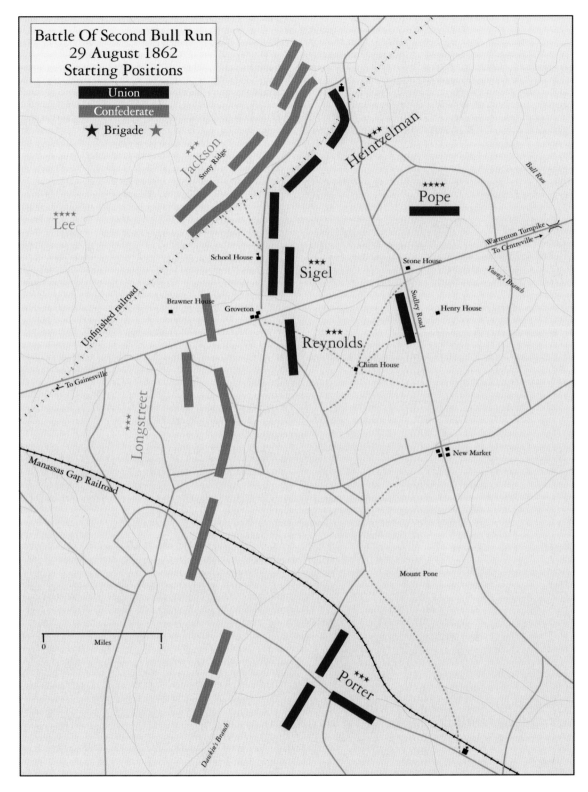

**Battle Of Second Bull Run
29 August 1862
Starting Positions**

Union
Confederate
★ Brigade ★

Jackson
Stony Ridge
Heintzelman
Lee
Pope
Bull Run
Warrenton Turnpike
To Centreville
School House
Sigel
Stone House
Young's Branch
Brawner House
Sudley Road
Henry House
Groveton
Unfinished railroad
To Gainesville
Reynolds
Chinn House
Longstreet
New Market
Manassas Gap Railroad
Mount Pone
Miles
0   1
Porter
Dawkin's Branch

Left: *The Battle of Second Manassas (Bull Run) began when Jackson placed his command across Pope's lines of communication near Manassas Junction. A two day battle ensued in which the Union Army of Virginia failed to dislodge Jackson from his strong defensive position, allowing Lee to fall upon the flank of the engaged Union army. For the second time a Union army was routed across Bull Run as it fled north.*

army was being withdrawn by water to reinforce Pope. Lee could not let that happen, so he grasped the opportunity to defeat Pope before the Union Army of Virginia could become any stronger. On 13 August Lee detached Longstreet's corps from Richmond's defensive perimeter and sent him with Major General Richard H. Anderson and Brigadier General John B. Hood's divisions to Gordonsville. Stuart's cavalry moved to Orange Court House to screen Longstreet's right. Longstreet reached

Above: Manassas Junction photographed after the withdrawal of General Johnston's Confederate army in March 1862. Union engineers had only just finished repairing the railroad and yards there when Jackson fell upon the town in August.

Right: Union railroad workers and army engineers repairing the Orange and Alexandria Railroad near Bristoe Station after Confederate cavalry tore up the tracks on August 22.

Gordonsville on 16 August, the same day that Jackson had secretly moved behind Clark's Mountain east of Orange Court House.

Lee followed a day later and joined Longstreet and Jackson, whose combined forces now contained 55,000 men. Pope, having been reinforced from the Army of the Potomac, now commanded 75,000. Jackson proposed using Clark's Mountain to shield a

movement that would turn Pope's right flank and cut off his line of retreat to Washington. Lee agreed but staff work delayed the attack. Meanwhile, Pope captured Jeb Stuart's adjutant and with him Lee's plan of attack. Pope adjusted his lines, sending Lee back to the drawing board. A few days later Fitzhugh Lee raided Pope's headquarters, captured the general's papers, and discovered that Federal reinforcements coming from the Peninsula could swell Pope's ranks to 130,000 men.

Lee chose to prepare a bold plan that military historians today still question. Though outnumbered by 20,000 men, Lee split his force, sending Jackson on a strategic envelopment to get astride Pope's communications, followed a day later by Longstreet and the rest of the army. Success depended upon speed and deception. Failure implied destruction of the Army of Northern Virginia, but doing nothing meant certain defeat. Lee, however, assessed the quality of leadership in Pope's command and decided that the benefits outweighed the risks. On 25 August

Left: *The bulk of the Union army marched past Sudley Church during their advance at the First Battle of Manassas, and the church lay on the left flank of Jackson's defensive line just over a year later during the Battle of Second Manassas.*

Below: *The stone bridge which took the Warrenton Pike over Bull Run Creek was destroyed after First Manassas, and a wooden structure built in its place. This bridge was subsequently destroyed after Second Manassas.*

Jackson, screened by Stuart's cavalry, marched from the Rappahannock with three days' rations and a small ammunition train. Twenty-six-miles down the road the command slept on their arms at Salem. He put the men on the road before daylight and that night, after marching another 36 miles, destroyed the Federal supply depot at Manassas.

Pope observed the Confederate movement of 25 August but mistakenly believed that Jackson was leading Lee's army back to the Shenandoah. Longstreet kept Pope guessing but on the 26th he disappeared. Hours later Pope learned that Jackson was in his rear and destroying the railroad and huge supply base at Manassas. Pope split his command putting McDowell and Sigel at Gainesville, Porter and Banks at Warrenton Junction, Heintzelman's III

Corps at Greenwich, and Major General Jesse L. Reno's division at Bristoe Station. This put a Federal force of 75,000 between Jackson (24,000) at Manassas and Longstreet (30,000), who was twenty miles west of Jackson. Pope missed a rare opportunity to defeat Longstreet and then Jackson; he simply could not find Longstreet.

Jackson, however, had enough strength to strike Pope's flank and hold it until Longstreet arrived. Sudley Mountain fitted his tactics best and he placed his force upon the ridge. On the evening of 27-28 August, and to confuse Pope, he sent A. P. Hill to Centreville and Ewell around the old Bull Run battlefield, who all returned and joined him that night on Sudley Mountain. The maneuver baffled Pope, who stopped looking for Longstreet and ordered his entire force to Manassas. Finding Jackson gone, Pope sent Franklin's Corps to Centreville and found no Confederates there. Brigadier Rufus King, while marching down the Warrentown pike, came under fire near Groveton. Jackson could have waited for Longstreet but he opened the engagement at Groveton to prevent Pope from moving his army into the strong fortifications at Centreville.

Pope remained confused and made the erroneous assumption that King had merely interrupted Jackson's efforts to escape to the Valley. He ordered all the units in the vicinity, some 62,000 strong, to converge on Groveton and destroy Jackson, who had more than 20,000 troops hunkered down behind trees, stumps, and rocks above the unfinished railroad cut that ran beneath Sudley Mountain.

2nd Bull Run	Engaged	Killed	Wounded	Missing
Union troops	75,696	1,724	8,372	5,958
Confederate troops	48,527	1,481	7,627	89

STRIKE UP THE BAND

Never had there been a better opportunity for Virginians to celebrate than after the Second Battle of Bull Run. The Union army had been forced from the Peninsula, shoved out of northern Virginia, and pushed back to the fortifications of Washington. Robert E. Lee listened to a band concert in camp and said, "I don't see how we could have an army without music."

Most Confederate bands had three of four musicians, usually German horn players and a drummer. When in camp they paraded around headquarters playing popular tunes. When in combat they played martial music. But when the musicians became hungry they drifted into prosperous-looking neighborhoods and played in exchange for food. Band members did not hesitate to step through unlocked doors, seat themselves around a piano, and play and sing until the room filled with people and supper was served.

Burke Davis wrote, "The 17th Virginia Infantry had Irish music from its fife-and-drum team, composed of a father and his son, the latter

Above: In the aftermath of the Second Manassas campaign the band of the 26th North Carolina Volunteer Regiment were able to equip themselves with instruments abandoned by the retreating Union army.

so small that his coattails dragged the ground behind, and his drum bumped in front."

Jeb Stuart, cavalry commander of the Army of Northern Virginia, carried his own ensemble wherever he went. He organized a country "jazz" band around a servant, "Mulatto Bob," who provided the tempo with bones. Sam Sweeney of Appomattox played first banjo. A team of fiddlers accompanied and troopers joined in dancing the jig. Stuart would often stop as he passed through a Virginia town, wake young ladies from their sleep, and serenade them through the night – even though he had important business elsewhere.

Music had a way of suspending the war. At nightfall, when Yankees and Rebels occupied trenches over a stretch of contested ground, bands dueled instead of artillery. The competition became so friendly that both sides sometimes shared musicians – a Confederate coronet player for a Union trumpeter. Before dawn the pair would re-cross the lines, put down their instruments, and pick up their muskets.

On 29 August Pope opened with piecemeal attacks that Jackson readily repulsed. At 11:00 A.M. Longstreet reached Groveton and filed into position on Jackson's right. Had Longstreet attacked instead of going into a defensive position, he might have destroyed the bulk of the Union army because a two-mile gap existed between Fitz-John Porter's corps and the Army of Virginia. Fitz-John Porter had been ordered to attack the flank and rear of Jackson's position, but could not execute the order because Longstreet's forces had come up and occupied the ground in front of him. Pope did not know that Longstreet had arrived, and when Jackson changed positions during the night, the Union commander believed Stonewall was preparing to retire and arranged a vigorous pursuit for the morning.

On 30 August, Lee let Pope commit his forces against Jackson on the left. He then enveloped the weakened Federal left with Longstreet's corps and attacked. Pope held onto Henry House Hill long enough to allow most of his troops to flee across the fords of Bull Run and into Centreville.

Lee remained on the offensive and on 1 September struck the west flank of Pope's position at

Below: The strategic importance of the Shenandoah Valley can be clearly seen in the Shenandoah and Blue Ridge Mountain ranges staking northwards to reach the Potomac River in the vicinity of Harpers Ferry. To the north lies Maryland.

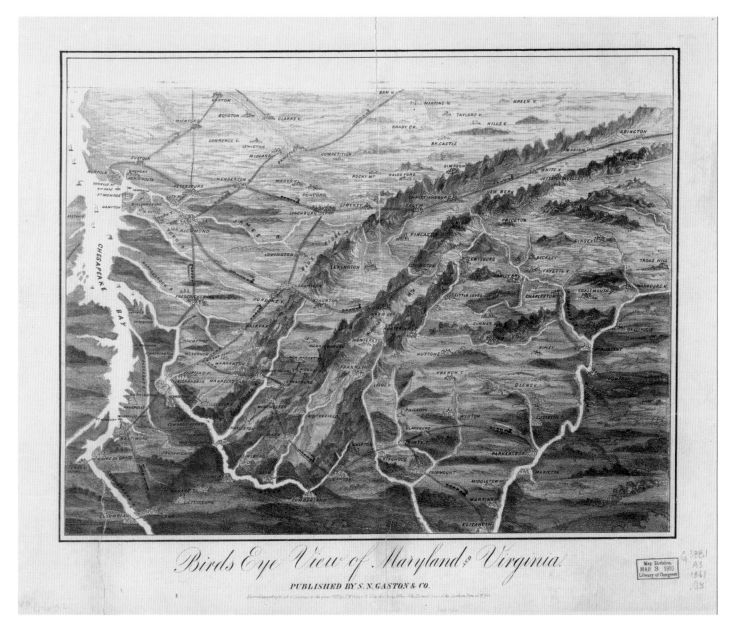

Birds Eye View of Maryland and Virginia.
PUBLISHED BY S. N. GASTON & CO.

Centreville. Near Chantilly, Jackson descended on two Federal divisions detached from Pope's main force and scattered them across the countryside. Pope had seen enough. He gathered the elements of his force and withdrew to the defenses of Washington. Blamed by Pope for the bitter loss at 2nd Bull Run Fitz-John Porter was relieved of his command and placed under arrest for disobedience of orders and misconduct in the face of the enemy, and court-martialed. His position was weakened by his friendship with the now-discredited McClellan. Found guilty in January 1863 he was cashiered. An inquiry conducted in 1878 found that Porter had been right in not committing his forces to an assault that Longstreet would in all probability have easily repulsed, and that his actions probably saved Pope's army from even worse defeat.

The unequal price paid in blood (page 102) attests to the superiority of Southern generalship.

ON TO MARYLAND

During late August and while resting at Chantilly, Lee had every reason to be content with what he had accomplished during the three months he commanded the Army of Northern Virginia. Anxious to keep the Federal invaders from the soil of Virginia, Lee wrote President Davis on 3 September suggesting that now was "the most propitious time since the commencement of the war for the Confederate army to enter Maryland." Lee knew the risks of taking his forces north, admitting, "The army is not properly equipped for an invasion of an enemy's country. It lacks much of the material of war, is feeble in transportation, the animals being much reduced; the men are poorly provided with clothes, and in thousands of instances are destitute of shoes. Still we cannot afford to be idle. . ."

Lee did not wait for an answer. Having been reinforced by two fresh divisions, a brigade of cavalry, and several batteries of artillery, he took the army to Leesburg and prepared to cross into Maryland. The army shed all superfluous wagons, gear, broken batteries, and worn horses. On 5 September, to the martial music of "Maryland, My Maryland" played by every band in the Army of Northern Virginia, men cheered and shouted as Stonewall Jackson led them across the shallow waters of the Potomac at Edward's Ferry. Lee marched to Frederick where he hoped to entice Marylanders to join the Confederate cause.

On 9 September, while resting at Frederick, Lee learned that General McClellan had returned to Washington, replaced Pope, and resumed command of the Army of the Potomac. He also learned that McClellan was cautiously pursuing him. Lee expected to have trouble getting back into Virginia by the same route so he chose another, the fertile valley of the Shenandoah. Once again Lee split his command and issued Special Order No. 191, sending six divisions under Jackson to rid the Harpers Ferry-Martinsburg area of some 12,000 Federals, and for Longstreet's four divisions to move toward the fords at Hagerstown. Four days later McClellan found a copy of Special Order No. 191 (opposite) and learned that Lee had divided his command. The story of the discovery is remarkable. XII Corps 1st division of General Alpheus Williams, was bivouacked about a mile southeast of Frederick, on a meadow occupied the day before by D.H. Hill's command. In the morning of 13 September, Private Barton W. Mitchell of the 27th Indiana, and Sergeant John M. Bloss, discovered an envelope containing three cigars wrapped in a piece of paper lying in the grass. The document turned out to be a copy of Lee's orders, addressed to Hill. The captured order gave McClellan advance notice of Lee's movements.

LEE'S LOST DISPATCH

Special Orders, No. 191
Hdqrs. Army of Northern Virginia
September 9, 1862

1. The citizens of Fredericktown being unwilling while overrun by members of this army, to open their stores, in order to give them confidence, and to secure to officers and men purchasing supplies for benefit of this command, all officers and men of this army are strictly prohibited from visiting Fredericktown except on business, in which cases they will bear evidence of this in writing from division commanders. The provost-marshal in Fredericktown will see that his guard rigidly enforces this order.

2. Major Taylor will proceed to Leesburg, Virginia, and arrange for transportation of the sick and those unable to walk to Winchester, securing the transportation of the country for this purpose. The route between this and Culpeper Court-House east of the mountains being unsafe, will no longer be traveled. Those on the way to this army already across the river will move up promptly; all others will proceed to Winchester collectively and under command of officers, at which point, being the general depot of this army, its movements will be known and instructions given by commanding officer regulating further movements.

3. The army will resume its march tomorrow, taking the Hagerstown road. General Jackson's command will form the advance, and, after passing Middletown, with such portion as he may select, take the route toward Sharpsburg, cross the Potomac at the most convenient point, and by Friday morning take possession of the Baltimore and Ohio Railroad, capture such of them as may be at Martinsburg, and intercept such as may attempt to escape from Harpers Ferry.

4. General Longstreet's command will pursue the same road as far as Boonsborough, where it will halt, with reserve, supply, and baggage trains of the army.

5. General McLaws, with his own division and that of General R. H. Anderson, will follow General Longstreet. On reaching Middletown will take the route to Harpers Ferry, and by Friday morning possess himself of the Maryland Heights and endeavor to capture the enemy at Harpers Ferry and vicinity.

6. General Walker, with his division, after accomplishing the object in which he is now engaged, will cross the Potomac at Cheek's Ford, ascend its right bank to Lovettsville, take possession of Loudoun Heights, if practicable, by Friday morning, Key's Ford on his left, and the road between the end of the mountain and the Potomac on his right. He will, as far as practicable, cooperate with General McLaws and Jackson, and intercept retreat of the enemy.

7. General D. H. Hill's division will form the rear guard of the army, pursuing the road taken by the main body. The reserve artillery, ordnance, and supply trains, &c., will precede General Hill.

8. General Stuart will detach a squadron of cavalry to accompany the commands of Generals Longstreet, Jackson, and McLaws, and, with the main body of the cavalry, will cover the route of the army, bringing up all stragglers that may have been left behind.

9. The commands of Generals Jackson, McLaws, and Walker, after accomplishing the objects for which they have been detached, will join the main body of the army at Boonsborough or Hagerstown.

10. Each regiment on the march will habitually carry its axes in the regimental ordnance-wagons, for use of the men at their encampments, to procure wood &c.

By command of General R. E. Lee
R. H. Chilton, Assistant Adjutant General

Above left: *The Battle Flag of the 7th Virginia Volunteer Regiment. The regiment formed part of Colonel James L. Kemper's Brigade, and fought at First Manassas, Fair Oaks, the Seven Days Battles, Second Manassas, Antietam, Fredericksburg, and Gettysburg.*

Right: *To protect the flank of Lee's army as it crossed the Potomac River into Maryland, Jackson led an attack on Harpers Ferry. Three Confederate columns converged on the town and surrounded it. The outnumbered Union garrison surrendered the following day.*

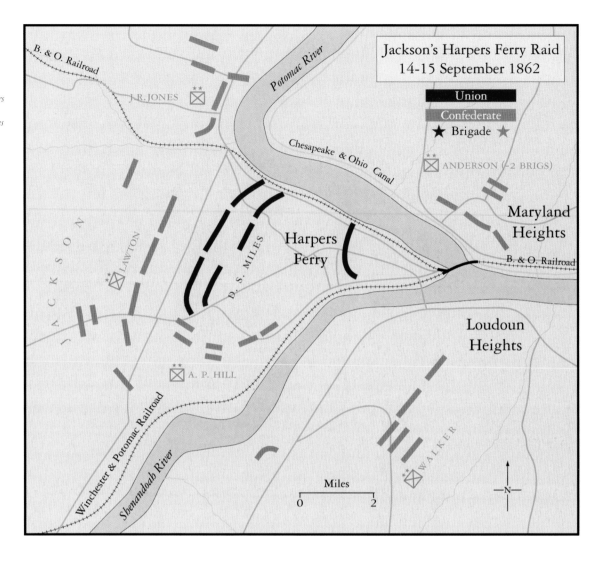

Holding the paper, McClellan exclaimed, "Here is a paper with which, if I cannot whip Bobby Lee, I will be willing to go home." By moving quickly McClellan now had the rare opportunity to crush Lee and bring a decisive end to the war. In the end and true to form, McClellan convinced himself there may be a trap and did not act decisively.

On the day McClellan discovered Lee's orders, Jackson's corps was already converging on Harpers Ferry. Stonewall split his command with the intention of bringing it together again later. By forced marches, Jackson's three divisions entered Martinsburg on 13 September and sent Brigadier General Julius White's Union garrison fleeing to Harpers Ferry, which is exactly where Jackson want-

ed them to go. On the same day, Major General Lafayette McLaws' Confederate division occupied Maryland Heights, directly across the Potomac from Harpers Ferry, and Brigadier General John G. Walker's division occupied Loudoun Heights, directly across the Shenandoah from Harpers Ferry. From both heights McLaws' and Walker's batteries looked down on Colonel Dixon S. Miles' Federal garrison that was scattered around the town.

On 14 September McClellan caught up with Lee in Maryland and fought two indecisive battles: one at Crampton's Gap and the other at South Mountain. The attacks, so unlike McClellan, surprised Lee until he learned that Little Mac had discovered his plans. On 15 August Lee's 19,000 troops began withdraw-

ing towards Sharpsburg for the purpose of crossing the Potomac and joining Jackson in Virginia. Jackson, however, had not yet captured Harpers Ferry. On the morning of 15 September, Jackson put his artillery into position and opened on Harpers Ferry. From Maryland Heights and Loudoun Heights, McLaws and Walker added their batteries to the shelling. Colonel Miles considered his position hopeless. He was killed waving a white flag while surrendering 12,000 infantry in the greatest Confederate haul of Union prisoners in the Civil War. The Confederates began rounding up 13,000 badly needed weapons and 73 cannon when Lee's courier arrived asking Jackson to hurry his command to Antietam Creek at Sharpsburg.

Around noon on the 15th a courier returned to Lee and reported Jackson's victory at Harpers Ferry. Had the intelligence arrived a day later, Lee would have been across the Potomac and into Virginia. Jackson's success, however, combined with McClellan's cautious nature, led Lee to stand and fight with his back to a river. Lee had only about 19,000 men on the field. If Jackson arrived, Lee would have 50,000.

Had McClellan attacked on the 16th, Lee's 19,000 could not have withstood the pressure. McClellan wasted a day closing up on the battlefield, deciding what to do, and getting 75,316 effectives into position. McClellan's final dispositions continue to puzzle historians to this day.

Above: *Maryland Heights, photographed in 1865 looking from Harpers Ferry across the river to the high ground on the northern bank. In 1862 McLaws' guns on Maryland Heights were able to enfilade the town.*

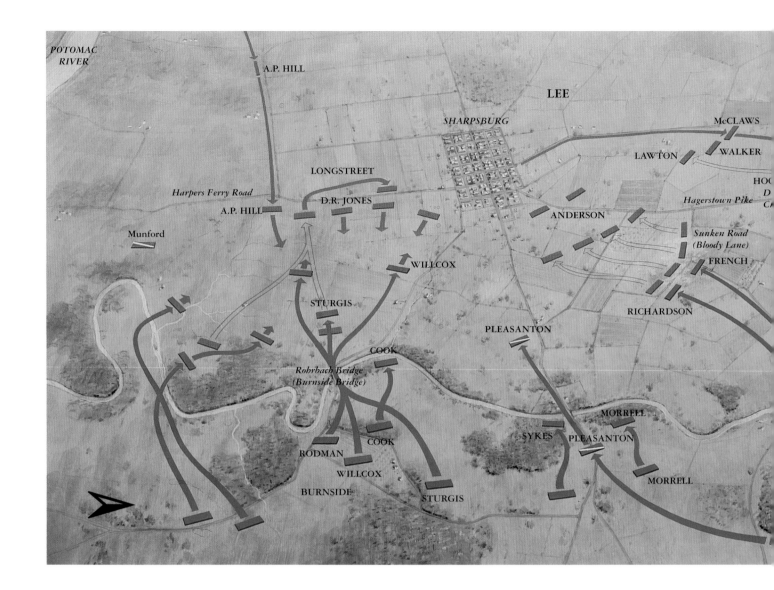

POTOMAC
RIVER

A.P. HILL

LEE

SHARPSBURG

McCLAWS

LAWTON

WALKER

LONGSTREET

HOO
D
CA

Harpers Ferry Road

D.R. JONES

Hagerstown Pike

A.P. HILL

ANDERSON

Munford

Sunken Road
(Bloody Lane)

WILLCOX

FRENCH

STURGIS

RICHARDSON

PLEASANTON

COOK

Rohrbach Bridge
(Burnside Bridge)

MORRELL

SYKES

PLEASANTON

RODMAN

COOK

WILLCOX

MORRELL

BURNSIDE

STURGIS

On 17 September McClellan launched a number of piecemeal attacks that allowed Lee to shift his small force from one side of the battlefield to the other. A. P. Hill's division did not arrive from Harpers Ferry until midafternoon and delivered a crushing counterattack. In "the bloodiest single day of the war," Lee stood his ground against the might of the Army of the Potomac, and as if to thumb his nose at McClellan, he remained in position the following day listening to arguments from Jackson and Longstreet against pressing a counterattack. Convinced that nothing could be gained by perpetuating a standoff, Lee withdrew that night leaving the field to McClellan.

Lincoln called the drawn battle a turning point and used it as the impetus for issuing the Emancipation Proclamation. The document changed the avowed purpose of the war from a political effort to preserve the Union to a struggle to abolish slavery. The proclamation reversed Europe's pro-southern stance to one of support for the Union and destroyed the Confederacy's last hope for foreign intervention.

PRELUDE TO FREDERICKSBURG

During early autumn Lee recuperated his bloodied army in the lower Shenandoah Valley, living partly off the land and partly off the provisions captured at

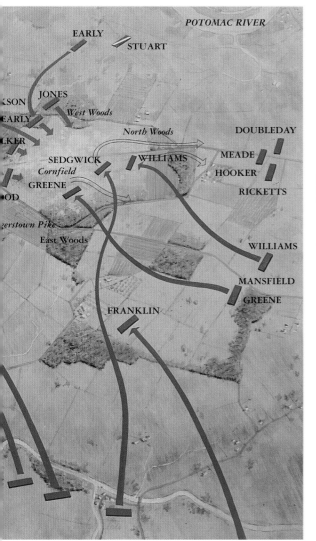

Antietam	Engaged	Killed	Wounded	Missing
Union troops	75,316	2,108	9,549	753
Confederate troops	51,844	2,700	9,024	2,000

Above: *A Confederate casualty at Antietam, his body lying next to the grave of a Union soldier. The side who held the ground enjoyed the privilege of burying its own dead first.*

Left: *On September 22 Lincoln visited the battlefield to confer with General McClellan (third from left). He then issued a preliminary Emancipation Proclamation, which took effect on New Year's Day 1863.*

Harpers Ferry. He watched McClellan because he expected Lincoln to insist upon another campaign into Virginia. He considered going back into Maryland to pounce on McClellan's flank, but the Army of Northern Virginia was in no shape for another major campaign. Instead, Lee settled for a cavalry raid into Pennsylvania to confuse McClellan and acquire fresh horses.

On 10 October Stuart departed from camp with 1,800 troopers and crossed the Potomac at Williamsport. The battalion trotted up the Cumberland Valley and on the following morning

Right: *In early November Lincoln removed McClellan from command. His replacement as head of the Army of the Potomac was Major-General Ambrose E. Burnside (1824-81), whose lack of ability would soon become all too apparent.*

entered Chambersburg, Pennsylvania. Stuart's officers circulated through town exchanging worthless Confederate currency for shoes, clothing, and fat horses. Stuart led his riders east, passed near the Antietam battlefield, circled around the rear of McClellan's camp, and at noon on the 12th crossed back into Virginia with fresh horses and fresh information on the Union army's dispositions. The bold maneuver so irritated Washington that Lincoln once again ordered McClellan to choose a line of attack and move against Lee in Virginia.

During Stuart's raid, Longstreet learned that he had been raised on 9 October to lieutenant general in command of the Army of Northern Virginia's I Corps. A day later Jackson received the same promotion, placing him in command of the II Corps. Lee now had the two finest generals in the Confederate army, a brilliant defensive militarist in Longstreet and a brilliant offensive militarist in Jackson.

McClellan did not want to take his army into the Shenandoah Valley, where "the strength of the hills" had always been a powerful ally for the Confederacy. He chose to draw Lee away from the Valley by crossing to the east of the Blue Ridge and investigating what military advantages might be obtained in the Piedmont region. On 23 October McClellan crossed the Potomac and marched slowly south. Detachments occupied the gaps of the Blue Ridge and made weak demonstrations toward the Shenandoah. The cautious advance fooled no one.

Lee concluded that McClellan was trying to barricade the Army of Northern Virginia behind the Blue Ridge while the Army of the Potomac attacked Richmond. He sent Longstreet's corps through Chester Gap, and on 6 November they reached Culpeper. A day later McClellan marched into Warrenton, ten miles to the northeast, after passing near the same roads Longstreet's corps had used the

day before. Jackson remained in the Shenandoah to protect the Confederate granary and to menace McClellan's right while waiting for Lee's call.

On 7 November the two wings of Lee's army stood 60 miles apart, but McClellan appeared to be unwilling to attack either of them. Lincoln had days before reached the nadir of his frustration with McClellan's hesitancy and replaced him with 38-year-old Major General Ambrose Burnside. Despite Burnside's undistinguished leadership on McClellan's left wing at Antietam, he had done well at First Bull Run and had led a successful operation against coastal installations in North Carolina. Burnside twice refused command of the Army of the Potomac, but on 7 November he accepted only on the urging of other generals who did not want the post given to Major General Joseph Hooker.

Burnside abandoned McClellan's good and detailed but unexecuted plan to strike the separated wings of Lee's army and defeat them both. Instead, he moved the Army of the Potomac east to attack Richmond by using the good roads emanating from Fredericksburg. Burnside, however, moved too slowly getting his forces into position, and this left him on the north side of the Rappahannock River opposite Fredericksburg. Burnside's movements telegraphed his intentions, so Lee pulled Jackson's corps out of the Shenandoah and posted him on Prospect Heights across the river where he could observe Burnside's left flank. Lee now had his entire army of 78,500 in position to confront a Federal force numbering 122,000. Then the wait began.

THE BATTLE OF FREDERICKSBURG

Burnside's plan depended on rapid movements against Longstreet before Jackson arrived and a Confederate line of defense could be established.

Burnside's plan also depended upon the timely receipt of pontoons to bridge the 400-foot river at Fredericksburg. When on 25 November the pontoons finally arrived, Lee had his army in position and Burnside had to modify his plans.

Whatever merit Burnside's strategy may have had in mid-November became utterly useless in December. His army was now spread across an eight-mile front with artillery positioned on both flanks. He divided the army into three "Grand Divisions" with Franklin commanding the "Left," Hooker the "Center," and Sumner the "Right." He hoped this would improve communications.

On 11 December Burnside's engineers began laying five pontoon bridges on the icy Rappahannock at three points across a six-mile front. Rather than maneuver, Burnside depended mostly upon frontal attacks, and his new orders were misleading, issued too late, sometimes difficult to comprehend, and often impossible to execute.

From Marye's Heights, Lee looked down upon Burnside's dispositions and moved troops into strong

Right: *A selection of field artillery projectiles, ranging on the left-hand page from the 20-pounder Parrot rifle shell (top left) to the 12-pounder solid shot fired from a 12-pounder "Napoleon" smoothbore. On the right-hand page the selection of shot includes a Confederate 10-pounder Parrot shell (top left) to the tiny 1-inch Williams solid bolt in the foreground.*

defensive positions designed to parry the logical points of attack.

When the battle opened on 13 December, Franklin's 50,000-man Left Grand Division crossed five miles below Fredericksburg. Jackson's 30,000-man corps waited across a 3,000-yard-wide sector with 14 guns posted on Prospect Hill, 21 guns on the left, and 12 guns behind the railroad track on the right. Stuart's dismounted cavalry deployed in an extended skirmish line on the far right with another 18 guns under the command of Major John Pelham.

Above: *Late on December 11, 1862, Burnside's army engineers completed building six pontoon bridges across the Rappahannock River, three opposite Fredericksburg, and the rest three miles downstream. The bulk of the Army of the Potomac was then able to cross the river.*

The one weak spot was in A. P. Hill's dispositions where a gap of 600 yards existed in a heavily wooded patch of swampy ground. Hill considered the dense, boggy ground impassable and left it undefended. The bad oversight gave Franklin's Grand Division a covered approach right to the heart of Jackson's position.

At 8:30, under the cover of morning fog, Franklin's Grand Division turned downriver on Old Richmond Road and formed line of battle. Confederates on the ridge could hear bands playing and the scuffling sounds of the Federal army in motion, but they could not see it.

At 10:00 A.M. the fog suddenly lifted, revealing a spectacular scene. Franklin's entire grand division was stretched in assault formation all the way back to the river. Longstreet, on the Confederate left, looked through his glass and said, "I could see almost every soldier Franklin had, and a splendid array it was. But off in the distance was Jackson's ragged infantry, and beyond that Stuart's battered cavalry, with their soiled hats and tallow butternut suits, a striking contrast to the handsomely equipped troops of the Federals."

Major General George G. Meade led Franklin's attack, and he pushed his men directly into the triangle of woods left unattended by Hill's division. Confederates were astounded to see Federals charging through woods declared impenetrable. Jackson made hurried adjustments to his line and initiated a series of desperate counterattacks. In frantic hand-to-hand fighting the Federals began to fall back. Jackson

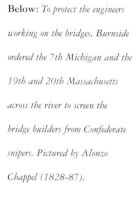

Below: To protect the engineers working on the bridges, Burnside ordered the 7th Michigan and the 19th and 20th Massachusetts across the river to screen the bridge builders from Confederate snipers. Pictured by Alonzo Chappel (1828-87).

Left: *Major John Pelham (1838-63), commanding "Stonewall" Jackson's Horse Artillery conducted a highly effective artillery barrage against the advancing Union troops on Burnside's left flank, and his guns held up the Union advance for two hours. In his report Lee commended "the gallant Pelham." The young Alabama-born officer was killed three months later during a skirmish at Kelly's Ford.*

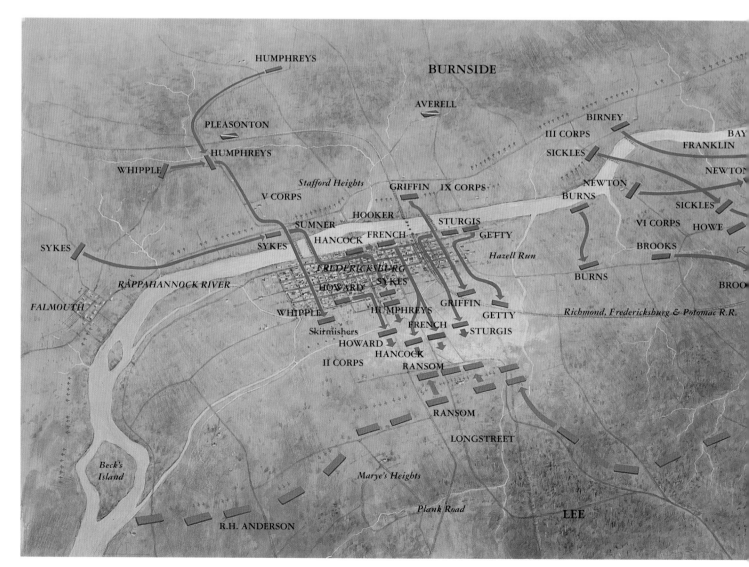

Bottom left: *The Battle of Fredericksburg involved two attacks against the Confederate positions on the heights west of the river. In the south Reynolds' I Corps attacked Jackson's Corps during the morning of December 13, but failed to breach his line. Shortly before noon French and Hancock's Divisions of Couch's II Corps were launched from Fredericksburg against Marye's Heights. When the assault failed a second attack was sent in, spearheaded by Howard's Division from II Corps, supported by Sturgis' Division from IX Corps. Finally as darkness fell Butterfield's V Corps were launched to help extricate the thousands of troops pinned down by Confederate fire in front of the Heights.*

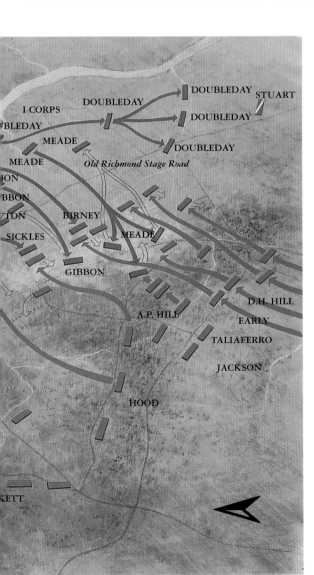

halted the pursuit at the railroad tracks because men were running out of ammunition and Federal artillery across the river had bracketed the position. Despite attacking vigorously up Prospect Hill, Franklin's grand division fell back and reformed in the rear. The repulse demoralized Franklin, and he fumed over Burnside's delay in getting the other two grand divisions off on time. For the remainder of the day Franklin became a spectator and did nothing to renew the attack on Jackson's position.

Sumner's grand division encountered unexpected problems at Fredericksburg. The attack on Marye's Heights was to have occurred in conjunction with Franklin's attack, but sharpshooters in Fredericksburg prevented Sumner's infantry from crossing the Rappahannock. In an ineffectual effort to drive the Confederates away, Sumner shelled the

Fredericksburg	Engaged	Killed	Wounded	Missing
Union troops	106,000	1,284	9,600	1,769
Confederate troops	72, 500	595	4,061	653

Longstreet had placed his men behind a stone wall that paralleled a sunken road. As Kimball's brigade began slipping up the muddy slope, a sheet of flame blossomed from the Confederate position, followed by one volley after another.

As more Federals filled the gaps, Confederate teams took turns mowing them down, one man firing while the other reloaded. The minié ball took a terrible toll. Within minutes, hundreds of Union dead lay piled up in the sunken road 40 yards from the wall. Yet more came, urged on by officers following orders, until nobody could get over the bodies of the dead and wounded clogging the battlefield.

Two Federal divisions, one under Brigadier General William H. French and the other under Major General Winfield S. Hancock, were decimated in the misdirected effort to take Longstreet's position by storm.

When Burnside suggested a bayonet charge, Major General Darius N. Couch looked out upon the battlefield and said, "It is only murder now." Couch tried to mount an attack on Longstreet's flank, but French and Hancock kept demanding reinforcements. Couch pressed a division forward. They tried to work around the battlefield dead but found the grass slippery with blood.

Brigade commanders finally ordered their men to lie down. Federal soldiers took refuge behind the mound of dead bodies. They shivered on the cold ground until sunset, and at nightfall those who could crept back to reserve positions in the rear. They knew Burnside had blundered and were filled with anger and discouragement. Only on 15 December did Burnside ask for a truce to retrieve the dead and wounded, who had by then spent two nights and days suffering in the field.

Historians have criticized Lee for not taking the offensive and destroying the rest of Burnside's force,

Above Following the failure of the attack on December 13, the Army of the Potomac could do little to harm the Confederates apart from bombarding their positions. This battery was hit by long-range Union fire from east of the Rappahannock River.

Far right: Sergeant Richard Kirkland of the 2nd South Carolina Regiment braved Union sniper fire to tend to the wounded lying in front of his position. For over an hour he brought water to the wounded Union soldiers, and was roundly cheered by both sides for his act of selfless humanity.

city. Infantry finally crossed in boats, drove off the grayclads, and engineers resumed work on laying the pontoon bridge. Sumner's and Hooker's divisions crossed the river and at 11:00 A.M. and massed at the base of Marye's Heights.

At noon Brigadier General Nathan Kimball's brigade led the first of several piecemeal frontal attacks against Longstreet's well-protected defenders. The Federals marched up the hill shoulder to shoulder, followed by one brigade after another in lines that reached back to the outskirts of Fredericksburg. Lieutenant William M. Owen of Lee's Washington Artillery recalled, "How beautifully they came on! Their bright bayonets glistening in the sunlight made the line look like a huge serpent of blue and steel. . . . We could see our shells bursting on their ranks, making great gaps. But on they came, as though they would go straight through and over us."

Below: *The farms and homesteads of Fredericksburg, like the Henry House at Gettysburg, were constructed from wood, offering little protection against Union fire. When the Union army evacuated the town on December 16 the townsfolk returned, only to find their houses badly damaged or destroyed, and the contents looted. Significant buildings have been restored since.*

but Lee did not fully appreciate the damage his men had done to the Union army. He expected to be attacked in the morning. The massive Federal artillery had not been touched and from the north side of the river dominated the battlefield.

Burnside did issue orders for resuming the attack on the 14th, but his generals talked him out of it. For the next two days Burnside ruminated over attacking or retreating, and on the night of 15 December pulled his entire command back across the cold river.

After the Battle of Fredericksburg, winter came quickly, and operations in Virginia ceased. During 1862 the Army of Northern Virginia had defeated four commanders of the Army of the Potomac – McDowell, McClellan (twice), Pope, and Burnside.

Union Brigadier General Gouverneur K. Warren of the V Corps, Army of the Potomac, summed up the situation by writing, "The army has become greatly disorganized . . . There is want of unity, accord and confidence in each other, in the general officers and in the Administration. The remedy must begin in Washington."

General Lee settled into winter quarters on Marye's Heights and waited for the next decision from Washington. His army was in rags, his men were tired, but they stood ready to follow wherever he led them.

TIMELINE – 1862

10 January: General Jackson occupies Romney in western Virginia.

27 January: President Lincoln orders General McClellan to commence operations against the Confederacy by 22 February.

24 February: General Nathaniel Banks seizes Harpers Ferry.

1 March: President Davis places Richmond under martial law.

4 March: General Lee is recalled to Richmond to serve as President Davis' military advisor.

6 March: The Confederate Congress authorizes the destruction of cotton and tobacco if the North advances into Virginia.

8 March: Lincoln approves McClellan's plan to attack Richmond by way of Virginia's Peninsula.

8-9 March: Battle between the *Virginia* and the *Monitor*.

9 March: General Johnston moves the Confederate army to the Rappahannock River.

17 March: General McClellan embarks for the Peninsular Campaign.

18 March: President Davis names Judah Benjamin Secretary of State.

23 March: Battle of Kernstown - prelude to the Valley Campaign.

5 April-3 May: Federal siege of Yorktown, Virginia.

16 April: Jefferson Davis authorizes the draft.

4-5 May: Battle of Williamsburg.

8 May-9 June: Jackson's Shenandoah Valley Campaign.

9 May: General McClellan's Peninsular Campaign begins.

31 May-1 June: Battles of Fair Oaks and Seven Pines.

12-15 June: General Stuart rides around the Army of the Potomac.

25 June-1 July: The Seven Days' battles.

9 August: Battle of Cedar Mountain.

28 August: Battle of Groveton.

29-30 August: Battle of Second Bull Run (Second Manassas).

5 September: The Army or Northern Virginia makes the crossing into Maryland.

13 September: McClellan discovers that Lee has divided his army.

14 September: Battle of Crampton's Gap, Maryland.

14 September: Battle of South Mountain, Maryland.

15 September: Jackson captures the garrison at Harpers Ferry.

17 September: Battle of Antietam (Sharpsburg).

9 October: Longstreet is promoted to lieutenant general and given command of the I Corps, Army of Northern Virginia.

10 October: Jackson is appointed lieutenant general and given command of the II Corps, Army of Northern Virginia.

13 December: The Army of Northern Virginia defeats the Army of the Potomac at Fredericksburg. 12,653 Union casualties: dead, wounded, missing.

Below: 1862 was the year when the realities of war hit home for both sides. Many glamorous but impractical items of clothing were abandoned in favor of more practical attire. This Union artilleryman's shako was reserved for ceremonial occasions far from the fighting, and serving gunners wore the less conspicuous kepi instead.

1863: GET THERE FIRST WITH THE MOST MEN

During that winter of 1862-63 the Army of Northern Virginia camped among the hills and the plantations of the lower Rappahannock. The men rested, cleaned their weapons, watched the Federals across the river, and waited for General Burnside to make another clumsy assault. Lee wrote his wife, "Our army was never in such good health and condition since I have been attached it. I believe they share with me my disappointment that the enemy did not renew the combat [at Fredericksburg]." Jeb Stuart made a reconnaissance around Burnside's right and rear and reported the Army of the Potomac in winter quarters along the line of the railway from Fredericksburg to Aquia Creek. Lee detached most of Longstreet's corps and sent it to Suffolk, south of the James, to winter where subsistence was more plentiful.

Smarting under his failure to move on Richmond by way of Fredericksburg, Burnside spent a month looking into opportunities to redeem himself. In mid-January a spell of good weather motivated him to haul his troops out of winter shelters and attack Lee's left. On 19 January, aided by Hooker and

> *"General Meade, I believe, is repairing the railroad, and I presume will come on again. If I could only get some shoes and clothes for the men I would save him the trouble.*
>
> *(ROBERT E. LEE TO HIS WIFE, 10 NOVEMBER 1863.)*

Franklin's corps, Burnside once again prepared to cross the Rappahannock at Fredericksburg and make a lunge toward Richmond. Thousands of Federals marched by the river in long columns. On 20 January snow fell, followed by 30 hours of drenching rain. Men slopped through knee-deep mud, caissons became mired above their wheels, mules sank to their bellies, and the Rappahannock overflowed its banks. Across the river Confederates erected huge signboards that read: "This way to Richmond." On 22 January Burnside called a halt and ordered the army back to winter quarters. Reporters recorded the episode as Burnside's "Mud March," and the label stuck like muck to the general's career.

Three days later Lincoln dismissed Burnside as commander of the Army of the Potomac and on 26 January replaced him with 48-year-old Major General Joseph Hooker. The new commander had a reputation for hard drinking and high living. Reporters noted that he had fought aggressively on the Peninsula and through a typographical error in a byline that should have read "Fighting – Joe Hooker" instead read "Fighting Joe Hooker."

Hooker hated the appellation, and said, "Don't call me 'Fighting Joe!'" The sobriquet always amused General Lee, who acceded to Hooker's request by laconically referring to him as "F.J."

Burnside's mud became Hooker's mud, but rainy weather soaked both sides of the Rappahannock. On 3 March Lee wrote his wife, "We are up to our eyes in mud now, and have but little comfort. F.J. Hooker looms up very large over the river. He has two balloons up in the day and one at night. I hope he is gratified at what he sees."

Lee did not remain completely immobile during the winter. Jeb Stuart's cavalry held the line of the Rappahannock from Falmouth to the Blue Ridge. He centered part of his command at Culpeper, near the Orange & Alexandria Railroad, and another brigade at Gordonsville, where he kept supplies. Several times during the winter Federal cavalry attempted to raid the area but Stuart's troopers always drove them back.

As spring approached, Stuart divided his time between watching Hooker's movements and conferring with Lee and Jackson on the approaching campaign season. Lee talked of moving into Pennsylvania, but first he would have to dispose of the Army of the Potomac, which during the winter and spring had grown to 134,000 officers and men. Compared with Lee's 61,000 veterans, Hooker's force was massive.

PRELUDE TO CHANCELLORSVILLE

Hooker designed an excellent plan for using his superior numbers to make a strategic envelopment of Lee's position on the old Fredericksburg battlefield. Out of sight of Confederate eyes, Joe Hooker planned to take a third of his army up the Rappahannock and to cross at Kelly's Ford in a

Left: The Confederates temporarily rebuilt the railway bridge across the Rappahannock River at Fredericksburg during mid-1863. The scars of battle can still be seen on the buildings.

RICHMOND—THE BREAD RIOT OF 1863

During the spring of 1863 the Confederate Congress passed legislation that taxed property, income, and profits. The most intrusive tax struck commodities, in particular corn, wheat, rice, cotton, oats, sugar, salt, potatoes, peas, beans, bacon, and other meats for the army. Farmers also suffered from "impressment" of crops, but the people who lived in the cities neither saw much food nor could afford the prices to buy it.

On 2 April a group of angry women in Richmond met at a Baptist church to hear Mary Jackson, a local huckster who one observer described as a "tall, daring, Amazonian-looking woman with a white feather erect from her hat" and a "six-shooter" in her hand. Miss Jackson convinced her listeners that they should demand food at fair prices or take it by force. The women, now highly aroused, stormed out of the church and inducted hundreds of supporters, including men, as they marched to Capitol Square. Mary Jackson stepped forward and presented her followers' grievances to Governor Letcher. He offered his sympathies but made no concessions. The crowd reacted furiously. They shouted, brandished knives and rolling pins, stormed the city's shopping district, smashed windows, rampaged through stores, and departed with bundles of food and clothing.

Davis ordered out a company of infantry armed with bayonets, and they began shoving the mob up Main Street. The women screamed and spit at the soldiers. When the turmoil reached the point of turning to bloodshed, Davis appeared. He mounted a wagon and ordered the mob to disperse. Women converged on the platform hissing and snarling. Davis shouted, "You say you are

hungry and have no money – here is all I have." He reached into his pockets and flung the contents at the crowd, shouting, "It is not much, but take it." Then he removed a watch from his vest, held it high for all to see, and said, "We do not desire to injure anyone, but this lawlessness must stop. I will give you five minutes to disperse. Otherwise you will be fired upon."

The crowd waited the full five minutes before backing away. They drifted sullenly from the square, disappeared among the byways of Main Street, and the "bread riot" faded to silent resentment.

Above: *A depiction of the bread riot, printed in Alexandria, Georgia, during the spring of 1863 shows how potentially serious the riot became by the time Confederate troops intervened.*

turning movement on Lee's left flank. Major General John Sedgwick's VI Corps, supported by the I and III Corps, would make a diversionary attack across the Potomac to hold Lee in place on the Fredericksburg line. The other third of the army would remain in reserve to reinforce both wings.

Longstreet and two of his divisions were on a foraging expedition, leaving Lee with barely enough men to defend against any one of Hooker's wings. When Stuart's scouts reported two Union corps screened by cavalry on the move near the upper fords, Lee concluded that Hooker would try to flank him. He also sensed that Sedgwick's corps, which was massing on Hooker's left flank, was there to threaten his fortified positions rather than attack them. In a bold move Lee split his force, leaving Early with 10,000 men in the Fredericksburg entrenchments to contain Sedgwick and marched the remainder of his force against Hooker's right wing.

Lee's unexpected countermovement distressed Hooker, and after crossing at Kelly's Ford on 29 April he called back the advance elements and organized a defensive line in the densely wooded and vastly confusing Virginia Wilderness. Hooker's mood, having changed from attack to defense, made strategic sense provided Lee actually intended to go on the offensive and attack using the few roads than traversed the woods. Lee, however, was not about to rush pell-mell into the Wilderness without first scouting the enemy's flanks.

Stuart's cavalry ranged unhindered through the Wilderness because Hooker, on 13 April, had sent Major General George Stoneman's cavalry corps on a useless mission to raid Lee's lines of communication. Stoneman did not cross the river until two weeks later – the same time Hooker crossed with three corps - because of flooding. Lee looked for opportunities and found one when Stuart reported Hooker's

right flank "in the air." Jackson responded and put his corps on back roads and made a forced march to Catherine Furnace. Lee said that the Federal right must be turned and told Jackson to figure out a way of doing it.

BATTLE OF CHANCELLORSVILLE

Jackson did not understand the confusing trails through the Wilderness any better than Hooker. He sent Major Jedediah Hotchkiss, his topographical engineer, to find roads that would take him around Hooker's position and to Wilderness Tavern. (Hotchkiss's mapping masterpiece, also prepared at

Below: *The Virginian General Jubal A. Early (1816-94), known as "Old Jube" served with distinction as a divisional commander during 1862 and 1863, and went on to command his own small army corps in the Shenandoah Valley in the following year.*

Above: *Wilderness Church, near Chancellorsville, the position occupied by General Howard's 11th Corps on the right of Hooker's line when Jackson fell upon the exposed Union right flank and rolled it up.*

the request of Jackson, would show all the offensive and defensive points of the Shenandoah Valley from the Potomac to Lexington.) Hotchkiss returned with a rough map he had sketched while talking with the owner of nearby Catherine Furnace. The route skirted the southern edge of the woods leaving only about two miles of exposed roads.

Wilderness Tavern lay beside the Plank Road and about 2,000 yards beyond Hooker's extreme right flank. Stuart had scouted the area and picked the spot for Jackson's flank attack. Lee split his force again, detached 26,000 men under Jackson, and retained 17,000 for holding attacks against Major General Daniel E. Sickles III Corps and Henry W. Slocum's XII Corps. Hooker had three additional corps spread out along roads connected with

Chancellorsville: Oliver H. Howard's XI Corps, Darius Couch's II Corps, and Meade's V Corps, which along with Slocum and Sickles' Corps numbered 75,000 men.

Jackson had the difficult task of moving his men 12 miles during daylight, crossing a two-mile section without woods while concealing his march, and arriving in the vicinity of Wilderness Tavern undetected. He rode near the head of the 10-mile-long column with a soiled oilcloth draped over his shoulders and a dirty cap pulled down over his eyes. From time to time he reined-up beside the road and as men passed would say, "Press forward! Close up that column! Press on! Press on!"

During the afternoon General Howard's Federal scouts observed part of Jackson's column passing up

the Orange Plank Road, but neither Howard nor Hooker considered the information accurate because in their opinion the woods were too thick to permit an attack. Other scouts went directly to Hooker's headquarters with the same information, only to be gruffly told that Lee was in full retreat.

At 4:00 P.M. the first elements of Jackson's corps moved onto the Plank Road and to their astonishment found no sign of Federal pickets. Two hours later Jackson had three divisions deployed in three lines perpendicular to the Plank Road and extending about a mile into the woods on either side with Robert Rodes' division in front, Raleigh Colston's division next, and A.P. Hill's division in the rear. With two hours of daylight left, Jackson turned to Rodes and asked, "Are you ready?" Rode replied,

"Yes." Jackson nodded and said, "Then press forward."

A mile down the Plank Road Rodes' skirmishers fired upon Federal pickets whose first indication of trouble was when they heard bugles blowing and the blood-curdling Rebel yell. Turning toward the sound, the Yanks observed deer, foxes, and rabbits running through their ranks, followed by thousands of Confederates in clothes that had been ripped to shreds during the lunge through underbrush. Rodes' division tore right through the dumbfounded pickets without bothering to fire a shot and fell upon four regiments guarding General Howard's flank. Two of the regiments fired a volley before joining the others in a footrace to the rear.

The Confederate attack struck the flank of every Federal brigade standing in the way and drove it

Above: Major-General Joseph Hooker established his headquarters at Chancellorsville House, and at one stage in the battle a Confederate shell struck one of the porch pillars close to where the Union commander was standing.

Below: The Battle of Chancellorsville was a huge gamble for Lee, who split his army in the face of a hesitant enemy, then launched Jackson in a flanking march around the Army of the Potomac to fall upon its exposed western flank. By the end of 1 May the Union line had been forced back into a salient, its head around Chancellorsville House, but the Army of Northern Virginia was unable to finish off the beaten enemy.

back upon the next in line. Howard stepped out of Dowdall's Tavern on the Plank Road when he heard firing to the west. He then jumped on his horse and trotted down the road to investigate. A thousand yards later he collided with his own panic-stricken corps, which fled past him and disappeared from sight. The Confederate tide, after sweeping over Howard's position, fell on the rear of Sickles' corps near Chancellorsville, forward elements of which had been battling Lee's smaller force at Catherine Furnace. Sickles refused to believe there could be Confederates in his rear and sent a cavalry regiment to investigate. The column rambled into Rodes' division and took heavy losses.

Hooker had been lounging in the Chancellor House with his aides and drinking brandy. Because of an atmospheric anomaly, he did not hear the clatter of musket fire emanating from Jackson's attack. Captain Harry Russell thought he heard shooting and went outside to investigate. In the fading evening light he trained his glass down the Plank Road, observed wagons, ambulances, and men streaming towards him in mass confusion, and shouted to Hooker, "My God! Here they come!" Hooker jumped on his horse, remembered that he had his old III Corps division in reserve, threw it into the breach on the Plank Road, and as darkness fell the Confederate attack lost momentum.

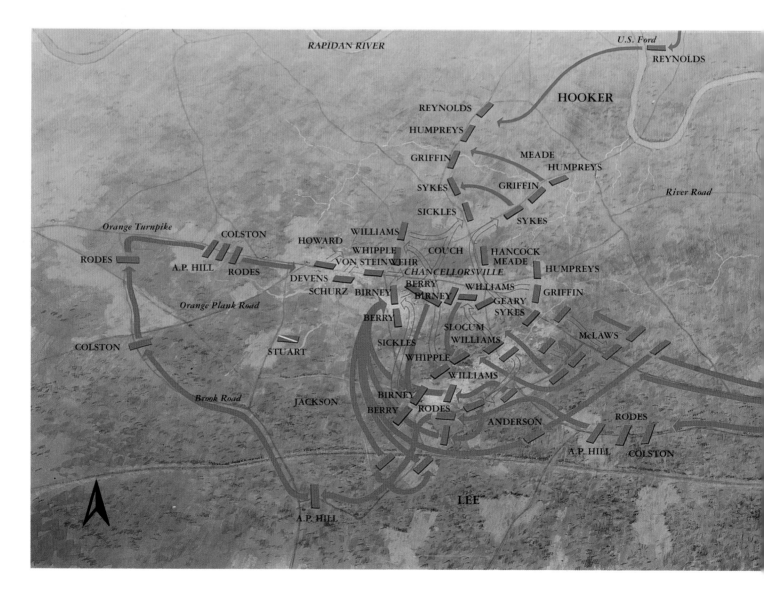

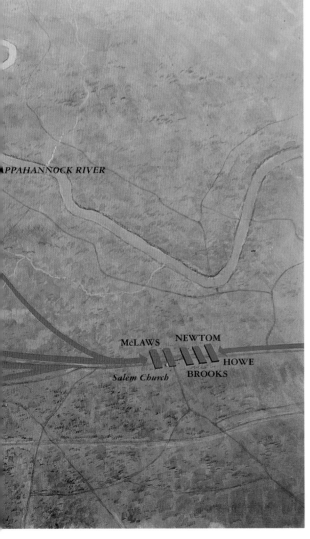

Jackson could not be content with an incomplete victory, so he brought A.P. Hill's division up from the rear and proposed a night attack. At 9:00 P.M. he rode ahead with Hill to scout the Plank Road. Having satisfied himself that if Hill's division moved quickly it could drive the Federals from their new defensive position, Jackson started back to order the attack. Nervous pickets from the 18th North Carolina mistook Jackson's party for Federal scouts and opened fire. Two bullets hit Jackson in the left arm, severing an artery, and another struck

Above left: *Major-General Ambrose P. Hill (1825-65) was one of Lee's most gifted divisional commanders, and after the wounding of Jackson he assumed command of III Corps.*

Left: *The dense woods made it difficult to bury the dead. This photograph was taken the following year.*

Chancellorsville	Engaged	Killed	Wounded	Missing
Union troops	133,868	1,575	9,594	5,676
Confederate troops	60,892	1,665	9,081	2,018

his right hand. Jackson hung onto his horse and returned to Hill's division, where a surgeon transferred the wounded general to a litter and took him to Wilderness Tavern. When told his arm had to be amputated, Jackson said, "Do for me whatever you think best." An hour later Jackson woke from the effects of chloroform and learned that A.P. Hill had also been wounded and turned his division over to Stuart. An aide came into the room and asked if there were any instructions for Stuart. Jackson, still under the influence of chloroform, said weakly, "Say to Stuart he must do what he thinks best."

On 3 May Hooker, now completely confused and suffering a concussion from a shell explosion, fell back to a secondary defensive position and quit the battle on the right. On the far left of the Union line, General Sedgwick finally got his wing in position and on 4 May struck Early's force southeast of Fredericksburg. After four bloody repulses, Sedgwick finally broke through Marye's Heights and began driving Early toward the Wilderness.

Lee left 25,000 men with Stuart to contain Hooker's 75,000 well-dug-in forces near Chancellorsville and took about 20,000 men in order to reinforce Early. Attacked on three sides, Sedgwick fell back across the Rappahannock at Scott's Ford. On 6 May Hooker pulled the entire army back across the Rappahannock and settled into his former impregnable position.

The Battle of Chancellorsville, by all accounts, became Lee's masterpiece – an almost perfect battle. But the victory came at great cost. Without Jackson the Army of Northern Virginia lost its greatest tactician and a man whose military instincts would be missed in the months to come.

CAVALRY CLASH AT BRANDY STATION

After the Battle of Chancellorsville, Lee observed Hooker's unwillingness to come out of his fortifications across the Rappahannock and fight. Having grown in numbers and tired of inactivity, Lee resurrected an old plan and decided upon a strategic movement down the Shenandoah Valley and into Pennsylvania to collect horses and grain during the harvest season. He instructed Stuart to screen the movements of the army and keep Federal cavalry away from the gaps in the Blue Ridge Mountains. On 5 June Lee's movements were in the early stages of organization when Stuart's cavalry blocked a reconnaissance in force from Major General Alfred Pleasanton's Federal cavalry at Franklin's Crossing on the Rappahannock.

Hooker became increasingly alarmed that Lee's army might be in motion. He directed Pleasanton to take an 11,000-man force of cavalry, two infantry brigades, and six light batteries to Culpeper and reconnoiter Lee's activities. Pleasanton departed from Falmouth on 8 June, never suspecting that only A.P. Hill's corps remained at Fredericksburg and the rest of Lee's army was concentrating at Culpeper.

Below: *Cavalry commander Major-General Alfred Pleasanton, at Warrenton, Virginia, photographed in September 1863. Though his tactics at Brandy Station have been criticized, the invincible aura that surrounded Jeb Stuart was distinctly tarnished by the cavalry battle.*

THE DEATH OF STONEWALL JACKSON

—THREE HEROES—

On 29 April when Jackson received a message from General Jubal Early that the Army of the Potomac was crossing the Rappahannock below Fredericksburg. Jackson kissed his five-month-old baby Julia goodbye and promised his wife Anna that he would return as soon as possible. The Jackson family had been living at the home of William Yerby, south of Fredericksburg, when Early's message arrived. Fearing the battle might reach Yerby's plantation, Jackson asked his chaplain, Reverend Beverly T. Lacy, to put his family on a train to Richmond.

On 3 May, after reaching the home of Governor Letcher, Anna learned that her husband had been severely wounded. She gathered up her belongings, little Julia, her servant Hettie, and on 7 May returned, to find her feverish husband lying in bed at Thomas Chandler's home.

For three days Anna sat by his side, read to him from the Bible, sang his favorite hymns, and when Jackson felt able, she brought Julia into the room and held her beside the bed.

Above: The three great Virginian heroes; Robert E. Lee, Thomas "Stonewall" Jackson and J.E.B. Stuart. After Jackson's death his considerable achievements were augmented by a romantic luster, making him one of the great unassailable heroes of the Confederate cause.

On 3:15 P.M. on Sunday, 10 May, Jackson became delirious from the effects of pneumonia. He barked orders at imaginary generals, and sometimes his dreams took him back to his beloved Shenandoah. Suddenly he opened his eyes, his face became cheerful, and he looked into the eyes of his wife and said, "Let us cross over the river, and rest under the shade of the trees." Then he died, and Anna embarked on more than a half century of widowhood.

A special car took the general to the Governor's Mansion where he lay in state. Anna purchased mourning clothes in Richmond's inflated economy, a crepe bonnet for $75 and a bombazine dress for $100. On 12 May Jackson's body was transferred to the Capitol and placed in a catafalque in the Confederate House of Representatives. Anna sat in a darkened room at the Governor's Mansion while 20,000 mourners paraded through the Capitol and paid their final respects in the same room where two years earlier the Virginia Convention had voted to go to war.

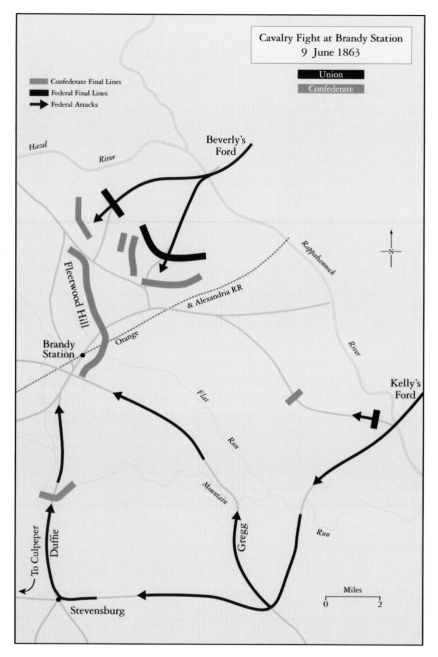

Cavalry Fight at Brandy Station
9 June 1863

Union
Confederate

Confederate Final Lines
Federal Final Lines
Federal Attacks

Hazel River

Beverly's Ford

Rappahannock

Fleetwood Hill

& Alexandria RR

Orange

Brandy Station

Kelly's Ford

Flat Run

Mountain Run

Gregg

Duffie

To Culpeper

Stevensburg

Miles
0   2

Above: The Battle of Brandy Station was the largest cavalry battle of the War, and demonstrated the growing professionalism and experience of the Union cavalry arm.

Pleasanton planned to cross the Rappahannock at dawn 9 June and attack Stuart's camp near Brandy Station in a pincer movement and then move in force down the road to Culpeper.

Screened by early morning mist, Brigadier General John Buford's cavalry division crossed at Beverly Ford and struck Brigadier General William "Grumble" Jones brigade on Stuart's left flank. At first, Buford's surprise attack rolled over Jones' position, but the Confederates regrouped and fiercely contested the ground as they withdrew toward Brandy Station.

Six miles downstream at Kelly's Ford cavalry divisions commanded by Brigadier General David M. Gregg and Colonel Alfred N.A. Duffié were to push aside pickets at the same hour and strike Stuart's right flank. Beverly Robertson's outposts covered the ford with Wade Hampton's cavalry posted nearby. At 4:00 A.M. Gregg pushed Robertson's pickets back from the ford, but Duffié arrived late and bungled the attack.

Stuart, from his headquarters on Fleetwood Hill, heard the uproar from Buford's attack on the left and promptly ordered a concentration of his scattered brigades. Hampton's Legion crossed from the right flank and joined Grumble Jones on the left, but they could not stop Buford's horsemen from storming up Fleetwood Hill.

The 12th Virginia Cavalry counterattacked down the hill just as more regiments from both sides clashed on the broad open field below Fleetwood

Hill. The brawl turned into a massive cavalry fight. Sabers flashed in the sunlight, pistols cracked, and shotguns boomed. Charge and countercharge soon covered the field with dust, and at times Stuart could see little of the action from the hill. He ordered up artillery, but gun crews had an almost impossible task differentiating between a butternut-clad Confederate trooper and a dust-covered Federal.

Confederate horsemen finally drove Buford's division off the field, only to be belatedly struck on the right by Gregg's division at Brandy Station. Hampton counterattacked and secured the heights on Fleetwood Hill. Five-and-a-half miles away Duffié collided with two Confederate regiments (500 troopers) and in a confusing fight gained the road but wasted the opportunity to get his division to Brandy Station in time to reinforce Gregg.

Pleasanton watched the action from the rear, and when he observed dust clouds rising above the road to Culpeper, he suspected that infantry were on the way and ordered a withdrawal. Though many have criticized Pleasanton for sloppy tactics, the Federal cavalry embarrassed Stuart. Some said the action at Brandy Station "made the Federal cavalry," which in earlier actions against Stuart had habitually been harshly punished. Stuart lost 523 and Pleasanton 936, but the deepest wound inflicted was surely to Stuart's reputation.

As the dust settled over Brandy Station, Lee departed for Pennsylvania with Ewell's II Corps, and Stuart made a personal commitment to use the campaign to revitalize his bruised reputation.

On to Winchester

On 10 June, after the action at Brandy Station, President Lincoln communicated with General Hooker regarding the Army of the Potomac's best strategy. Referring to Robert E. Lee, Lincoln said, "Fight him when the opportunity offers. If he stays where he is, fret him." Hooker had to first find Lee before he could "fret him."

Lee's army consisted of Stuart's cavalry corps of 6,000 men, the artillery corps under Pendleton with

Far left: *Colonel A.N. Duffié of the 1st Rhode Island Cavalry commanded one of the three Union cavalry columns to attack Stuart's force at Brandy Station, although his troops became lost, and played little part in the battle.*

Below: *Confederate cavalry accouterments. From left to right: Model 1859 Sharps carbine, Remington New Army revolver, Model 1840 cavalry saber, and McLellan saddle.*

RICHMOND 1863—SIN CITY OF THE SOUTH

In May 1863, while Richmond celebrated the Army of Northern Virginia's victory at Chancellorsville, the city's streets swarmed with prostitutes. They were everywhere. When the YMCA opened a hospital for the wounded, a shrewd madam opened a brothel across the street, posed half-dressed women in her windows, and wooed ambulatory convalescents into their bed-chambers.

Sidewalks became so congested with women of the street that newspapers complained of how decent people could no longer use the sidewalks. Confederate officers on leave took these painted women on their arm and escorted them into some of Richmond's finest restaurants and hotels, driving every lady away who wanted to protect her reputation.

Prostitutes quickly spawned a new epidemic of venereal disease, and soon gonorrhea and syphilis became all too common. If ejected from a bordello, infected prostitutes followed the army into the field. Some of them donned butternut uniforms, posed as men, and worked on until caught and banished. At times ten percent of a regiment could be infected by one of the two diseases. Surgeons sent the worst cases to hospitals in Richmond for treatment.

Slaves never entered the prostitution trade, but the sudden scourge of venereal disease struck their ranks with almost the same impact as it struck the population in general.

When General Hooker came to Virginia, he brought his own platoon of camp followers. Instead of calling them prostitutes, Federals called them "hookers." When the general abandoned

Chancellorsville, some of his "hookers" remained behind and drifted into Richmond.

There were surprisingly few recorded acts of sexual violence, probably because sex was so readily available. Richmond authorities hounded the provost marshal to clean up the city, but he could no more stop the "oldest profession on earth" from proliferating in the city than the armies could stop it in the field. The problem persisted until 1865 and sharply declined after the Confederate government evacuated Richmond.

Above: *While many decried the influence of so many troops and refugees on the morals of wartime Richmond, soaring inflation and food shortages meant that many Richmond households were forced to auction off their most prized positions, and young ladies of good families were forced to explore fresh avenues of fiscal support.*

200 guns, and a veteran infantry of about 60,000 men. Lee had divided the infantry into three corps. On 10 June, the day Lincoln offered his advice to Hooker, Longstreet's I Corps was at Culpeper, Ewell's II Corps was on the road to the Shenandoah Valley, and the newly formed but smaller III Corps under A.P. Hill was at Fredericksburg to restrain Hooker from rashly attempting another "on to Richmond" effort. By 12 June Ewell's corps with Lee had passed through Chester Gap to the west side of the Blue Ridge and was pressing down the Valley toward Winchester. Lee had left Stuart's cavalry behind with Longstreet and Hill, taking only Albert G. Jenkins, "Grumble" Jones, and John Imboden's cavalry brigades to provide scouts for Ewell's corps.

General Ewell had served under Jackson since 1862 and was well acquainted with the Valley.

During 2nd Bull Run he lost his leg during the battle at Groveton and now had to be helped onto his horse and strapped into the saddle to keep from falling. During his convalescence he had married the "widow Brown," and some said that she exerted more influence over him than General Lee. Douglas Freeman, who studied all of Lee's lieutenants, described Ewell as "bald, pop-eyed and long-beaked, with a piping voice that seems to fit his appearance as a strange unlovely bird . . . ." Under Jackson, who exercised the power of decision to near-perfection, Ewell had functioned well as a division commander. Whether he could shoulder the heavy burden as a corps commander under Lee, who issued discretionary orders, remained to be seen.

On 13 June Ewell jumped off to a good beginning. As the II Corps approached Winchester they

Right: *Captain Orson H. Hart, the Assistant Adjutant General (A.A.G.) of Major-General French's III Corps of the Army of the Potomac, photographed while the corps was in winter quarters near Brandy Station, Virginia.*

Fort. Ewell feared that Milroy would withdraw during the night and sent three brigades from Johnson's division around to the Martinsburg Pike to block the Federal escape route. At 9:00 P.M. Milroy faced encirclement. He decided to withdraw and began destroying his wagons and artillery. Four hours later the Federal retirement began along the route Ewell anticipated. At 3:30 A.M. Milroy clashed with two of Johnson's brigades four miles north of Winchester. A third brigade arrived on Milroy's right and tightened the noose. Milroy got away with a fragment of his command, leaving behind 95 killed, 348 wounded, and 4,000 captured or missing. Johnson drove the scattered Federals off the Martinsburg Pike and chased them and Milroy into Harpers Ferry, thereby opening for Ewell an uncontested straightaway into Maryland. At a cost of 47 killed, 219 wounded, and three missing, Ewell took possession of 23 cannon, 300 wagons, 300 horses, and tons of supplies.

Though Winchester represented a minor victory in a major campaign, Ewell exercised excellent tactical skills in his first engagement as a corps commander. He cleared the Martinsburg Pike of Federals and on 15 June opened the road for Jenkins' cavalry to sprint north.

Robert E. Rodes' division followed and that evening crossed the Potomac into Maryland. Jenkins did not waste time in Maryland. He led his brigade into Pennsylvania, captured Chambersburg, and during the next several days jogged through Carlisle and threatened Harrisburg, the state capital. A few days later Ewell followed. The Federal government panicked and called for another 100,000 troops to defend Pennsylvania.

On 15 June A.P. Hill advanced his corps to follow Ewell and the long Confederate column stretched from Culpeper, Virginia, to Chambersburg, Pennsylvania.

Above: Richard S. Ewell (1817-72), known affectionately as "Old Bald Head" by his men was a lieutenant of Jackson, fighting with him in the Shenandoah Valley and at Second Manassas. Ewell lost his left leg but returned to active service in time to lead II Corps at Winchester, Gettysburg, and the Wilderness.

brushed against skirmishers from Major General Robert H. Milroy's division. Ten thousand Federals held Winchester and occupied two strong forts: Flag Fort west of town and Star Fort north of the town. Together with two smaller earthworks, the forts overlooked the Martinsburg Pike and stood in Ewell's way.

On 14 June Ewell sent two brigades from Edward Johnson's division ahead to attract Milroy's attention while Jubal Early's division and artillery marched by way of a covered route to the west. The frontal attack drove the Federals back and into Flag

STUART MOVES NORTH

On 14 June, while Ewell fought Milroy at Winchester, Hill put the III Corps on the road. On 15 June, when the van of Ewell's corps crossed the Potomac into Maryland, General Longstreet followed with the I Corps. Both divisions marched along the same roads taken by Lee a few days before. Longstreet remained behind long enough to verify that Hooker had abandoned his position along the

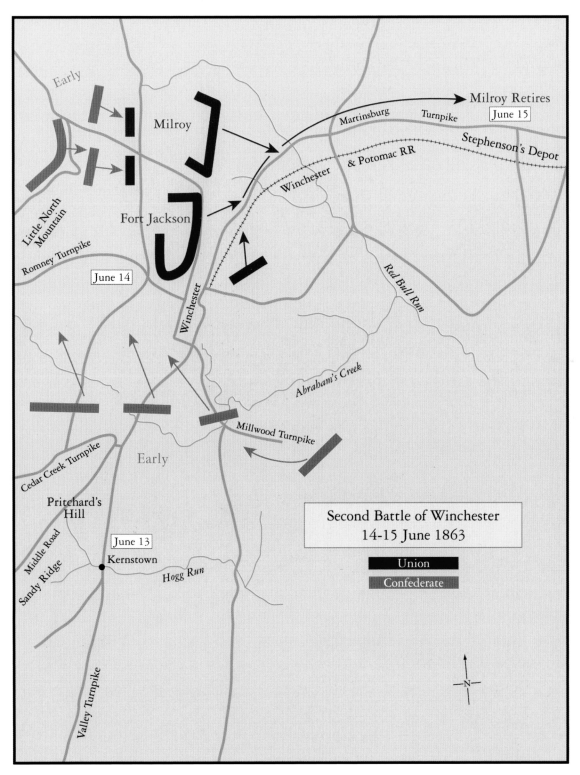

Early

Milroy

Little North Mountain

Fort Jackson

Romney Turnpike

June 14

Winchester

Martinsburg

Winchester & Potomac RR

Turnpike

Milroy Retires

June 15

Stephenson's Depot

Red Bull Run

Abraham's Creek

Millwood Turnpike

Early

Cedar Creek Turnpike

Pritchard's Hill

Middle Road

Sandy Ridge

June 13

Kernstown

Hogg Run

Valley Turnpike

Second Battle of Winchester
14–15 June 1863

Union
Confederate

—N—

Left: *The apogee of Ewell's career, the Battle of Second Winchester was described by Confederate artillery officer Major Robert Stiles as "one of the most perfect pieces of work the Army of Northern Virginia ever did."*

Rappahannock. Lee instructed Stuart to keep two brigades of cavalry along the eastern foot of the Blue Ridge but granted him broad discretion in the movements of the other three brigades so long as they "as speedily as possible" joined Ewell's advance in Pennsylvania.

On 22 June Lee dispatched a message to Stuart: "Do you know where Hooker is, and what he is doing? I fear he will steal a march on us and get across the Potomac before we are aware . . . Take position on Ewell's right, place yourself in communication with him, guard his flank, [and] keep him informed of the enemy's movements." Lee then instructed Ewell to move toward the Susquehanna River and, "if Harrisburg comes within your means, capture it." Lee thought he had everything timed almost to the day. In his view Ewell would be marching into Harrisburg and York about the same time

MOSBY'S RANGERS

Thirty-year-old John Singleton Mosby operated his own outfit of guerrillas in northern Virginia and took his band wherever he observed an opportunity to upset Federal operations. He was medium height, thin and wiry, and as fierce and reckless as a man can be during wartime. When the conflict began Mosby was practicing law in Bristol, Virginia. He joined "Grumble" Jones 1st Virginia Cavalry as a private and fought at 1st Bull Run. Jeb Stuart saw potential in Mosby and made him a scout. During the Peninsular campaign it was Mosby who served as Stuart's guide, and it was Mosby who convinced Stuart to ride around the Army of the Potomac. Mosby wanted his own independent command, and though Lee did not approve of such companies, Stuart did.

In late 1862 Mosby applied under the Partisan Ranger Law and in January 1863 obtained permission to form the Rangers. He moved into Middleburg in Loudoun County and began recruiting his company from volunteers, men on leave from regular army units, convalescents, and civilians who enjoyed adventure and excitement but were unwilling to join the army.

Most of the Rangers only met when Mosby summoned them through a grapevine of Paul Revere types. Some of the men lived at home, others boarded locally, and a few roamed about in small bands and lived off the country.

Above: *Virginian partisan leader John Singleton Mosby (1833-1916) was highly successful in disrupting Union supply routes and lines of communication in Northern Virginia during 1863-65. Although a regular officer, the enemy regarded him and his men as outlaws.*

Mosby became a specialist in guerrilla tactics and an expert in disguise, on occasion donning women's clothes. He made swift night attacks using small groups of Rangers to raid wagon trains and Federal outposts. He also tore down telegraph lines, barricaded railways, and caused turmoil in Federal camps. One night in March 1863 he made headlines by stealing into Fairfax Court House with 29 Rangers and capturing Brigadier General Edwin H. Stoughton from his bed. Mosby rolled back Stoughton's bedcovers and woke him by slapping his behind. Then he made off with the general, 32 Union troops, and 58 horses. Such derring do naturally fired the imagination of the populace.

On 10 June 1863 Mosby's outfit was reorganized as Company A, 43rd Battalion, Partisan Rangers, and mustered into the regular army. Mosby became a major and later a colonel. He eventually enlarged his battalion to four companies of 240 mounts, and in Virginia they became one of the most sought after guerrilla groups on the Union army's "most wanted" list. Captured Rangers were to be hung without trial, but Mosby's policy of retaliation in kind put an end to the practice.

In June 1863, as Stuart's cavalry began moving up the eastern side of the Blue Ridge to screen Lee's advance, Mosby's Rangers would be there to help.

that Stuart would be arriving from Virginia. After leaving Culpeper Stuart had been constantly engaged in skirmishes with Pleasanton's cavalry, which covered Hooker's route farther to the east.

This placed Stuart's cavalry and Pleasanton's cavalry in exactly the middle ground between the Confederate army and the Union army. Ever since Brandy Station the Federal cavalry had become annoyingly pugnacious. Both forces moving through Virginia's Piedmont at the same time caused a series of sharp engagements at Aldie, Middleburg, and at Upperville.

On 17 June each of three Confederate cavalry brigades covered a different gap in the Blue Ridge to screen Longstreet's advance. Fitz Lee's brigade, commanded by Thomas T. Munford, occupied a gap in the Bull Run Mountains at Aldie. At 4:30 P.M. Pleasanton arrived at the gap with Hugh Judson Kilpatrick's Union brigade from Gregg's division.

Kilpatrick scouts began driving back Confederate pickets when Thomas L. Rosser's 5th Virginia cavalry charged with sabers and drove the enemy back. A spirited series of inconclusive mounted and dismounted attacks followed that lasted until dusk.

While Munford was engaged at Aldie, Colonel Duffié's 1st Rhode Island moved through Thoroughfare Gap to Middleburg. Mosby reported Duffié's position to Stuart. A few hours later "Rooney" Lee's brigade, commanded by John R. Chambliss, and Beverly Robertson's brigade trapped Duffié in the gap and virtually destroyed the 1st Rhode Island Cavalry. Duffié escaped with only 31 men, though many more rejoined the division later.

On 19 April Pleasanton arrived at Middleburg two days late to help Duffié. Finding Stuart there, Gregg's division attacked through town with dismounted troops and artillery and drove Stuart into a defensive position a half-mile down the road. Stuart departed from Middletown, only to be driven unremittingly by Pleasanton toward Lee's columns in the Shenandoah. Stuart withdrew to Upperville and began gathering his strung out brigades for a major engagement.

Pleasanton brought Gregg's division and part of Buford's command to the Upperville area. Stuart collected Robertson, Hampton, Chambliss, and Jones' brigades. Kilpatrick charged but was repulsed. Gregg came up on Kilpatrick's left with cavalry supports and several pieces of artillery.

Kilpatrick charged again and this time struck Robertson's brigade as it was withdrawing through Upperville. Seeing Robertson in trouble, Hampton charged Gregg's division and thereby turned the cavalry battle into a standoff.

Stuart retired in good order to a defensive position in Ashby's Gap. Losses at Aldie, Middleburg, and Upperville cost Pleasanton 613 cavalry, Stuart 510, and took a terrible toll on horseflesh.

STUART'S TRAGIC DETOUR

On 23 June Jeb Stuart received Lee's last message urging a timely conjunction with Ewell in Pennsylvania so as to "guard his flank and keep him informed of the enemy's movements." The dispatch also suggested collecting "all the supplies you can for the use of the army" but placed the emphasis on a timely unification of forces with Ewell.

Since early June Stuart's brigades had been feeling the ill effects of constant combat with Federal cavalry. Stuart had gotten the job done, but no laurels had been won. So instead of joining Ewell by taking the shortest route along the eastern Blue Ridge, he chose a long and treacherous roundabout

Below: *So rash he was nicknamed "Kill Cavalry" by his own men, Brigadier-General H. Judson Kilpatrick (1836-81), fourth from left, commanded a division of Union cavalry during 1863. Kilpatrick and his staff posed for this group photograph in Stevensburg, Virginia near Brandy Station during the summer of 1863.*

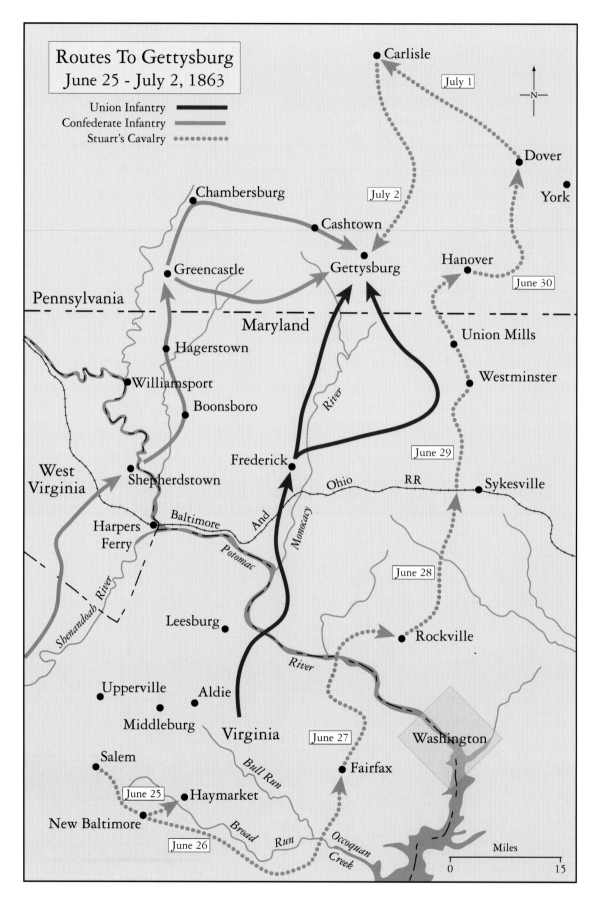

Right: *Lee's second invasion of the north was designed to bring the Army of the Potomac to a decisive battle, where the fate of the war could be decided. However, poor reconnaissance work by Stuart's cavalry meant that it was Meade and not Lee who would decide the time and place of the battle.*

Routes To Gettysburg
June 25 - July 2, 1863

Union Infantry
Confederate Infantry
Stuart's Cavalry

Carlisle

July 1

Dover

York

Chambersburg

July 2

Cashtown

Gettysburg

Hanover

Greencastle

June 30

Pennsylvania

Maryland

Hagerstown

Union Mills

Williamsport

Westminster

Boonsboro

River

Frederick

June 29

West Virginia

Shepherdstown

Ohio

RR

Sykesville

Baltimore

And

Monocacy

Harpers Ferry

Potomac

June 28

Shenandoah River

Leesburg

Rockville

River

Upperville

Aldie

Middleburg

Virginia

Washington

June 27

Salem

Fairfax

Bull Run

June 25

Haymarket

New Baltimore

Broad

Run

Occoquan

Creek

June 26

Miles

0   15

Left: *The 12-pounder "Napoleons" of Battery D, 2nd US Artillery photographed while in action near Fredericksburg, Virginia on June 19, 1863. Behind the gunners infantry from the "Vermont Brigade" of the Army of the Potomac's VI Corps can be seen drawn up in support of the batteries.*

Below: *A Union mule team crossing a stream, similar to those encountered by Stuart's cavalry near Rockland, Maryland during the Gettysburg campaign.*

route that would carry his command east of Hooker's army – an undertaking not unlike the ride around McClellan's army 12 months ago that had brought him instant fame.

On 25 June Stuart detached two brigades to keep watch on the Blue Ridge and at 1:00 A.M. rode east from Salem with 4,800 men from Hampton, Fitzhugh Lee, and "Rooney" Lee's brigades. They rode through the night and stopped to rest after encountering General Hancock's II Corps encamped east of the Bull Run Mountains and astride their route. On the 26th Stuart could have prudently retraced his steps but instead chose the more daring course. He detoured around Hancock's corps but that day covered only 23 miles. He also put two mountain ranges and the entire Federal army between himself and Lee's flank.

When Stuart moved out on the morning of the 27th, Ewell was already in Carlisle, Early's division had crossed South Mountain and was on the road to York, and both Lee and Hooker were across the

147

Potomac with their commands. Stuart had taken his-brigades into Federally-controlled Virginia and was more than 100 miles from Ewell. That afternoon Hampton's leading regiment spotted two cavalry companies from the 11th New York at Fairfax Courthouse and captured all but 18 of the men. During the evening Stuart's brigades crossed the Potomac at the mouth of Seneca Creek (Rowser's Ford), twelve miles from Washington, and was now at least a day behind schedule.

In the morning, as Stuart's jaded brigades reached Rockland, Maryland, scouts spied a long Federal supply train with brand new wagons, fat mules, and tons of provisions. Stuart recalled Lee's message, suggesting that he "collect all the supplies you can for the use of the army." Here before the

Confederate cavalry commander beckoned the opportunity for personal redemption.

Federal teamsters tried desperately to turn their mule-drawn wagons around and flee back to Washington, but Stuart's reinvigorated men, yelling as they charged, rode them down. The enormous haul consisted of 900 mules, 400 prisoners, and 125 wagons filled with provisions and fodder. When Stuart put the captured train on the road to Pennsylvania, it stretched for miles and slowed the daily pace down from 40 miles to 25.

On 29 June south of Westminster, Maryland, two small cavalry companies from the 1st Delaware charged Stuart's column. Confederate horsemen repulsed the Delaware boys, but the attack caused another delay and foreshadowed more trouble ahead.

Below: Devil's Den, Gettysburg. This body of a Confederate sharpshooter photographed amid the rocks was photographed by either Alexander Gardner or Timothy O'Sullivan shortly after the battle, although the image is usually and misleadingly attributed to the more famous Civil War photographer Mathew Brady.

At the outskirts of Hanover, Pennsylvania, the following morning, Stuart observed a body of Federal riders ahead and sent the 13th Virginia Cavalry to brush them aside. The Confederate pursuit carried into the streets of Hanover. Brigadier General Elon J. Farnsworth, commanding the 1st Brigade of Kilpatrick's division, rallied his men and mounted a spirited counterattack that routed the Virginians. Stuart would not have escaped capture or death had not his big mare, Virginia, leaped a deep 15-foot-wide ravine.

Stuart had intended to rendezvous with Ewell by going west, toward Gettysburg, and then north to Carlisle, but the engagement with Farnsworth forced him to change his plans. If he started west with the captured wagon train, he would be riding toward the enemy. If he abandoned the wagon train, his troopers would be able to cut their way through to Carlisle. But to save the wagon train he would have to go farther east, then north to York, and eventually to Carlisle. After bringing the captured train this far he could not turn it loose, so he chose the longer route and lost another critical day.

Nearing York late on 30 June, Stuart learned that Early's division had been there but left. He pushed on to Carlisle and on 1 July found the town in the hands of Pennsylvania militia. Stuart sent a note to Union General William F. Smith with surrender demands. Smith refused in salty language, so Stuart shelled the town and set fire to Carlisle's cavalry barracks. Instead of moving on, Stuart halted. Late that night a courier, one of eight sent by Lee to

Below: The Gettysburg home of John L Burns (1793-1872), a 70-year old veteran of the War of 1812 who fought alongside the Union army during the first day of the battle, using his old flintlock musket to fire on the advancing Confederates near McPherson's Farm.

Gettysburg	Engaged	Killed	Wounded	Missing
Union troops	88,289	3,155	14,529	5,365
Confederate troops	75,000	3,903	18,735	5,425

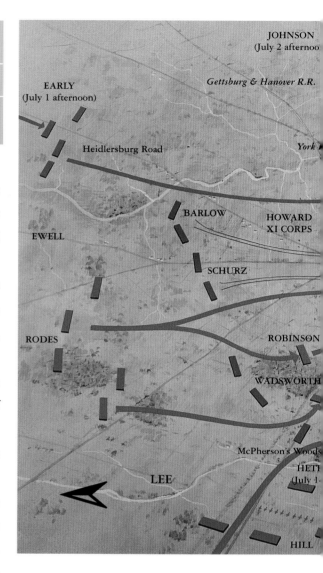

Far left: The Battle of Gettysburg (July 1-3, 1863) saw a series of Confederate attacks against Union positions, first on McPherson's Ridge, then on the Second Day against Culp's Hill, Cemetery Ridge, the Peach Orchard, and Devil's Den. On the Third Day Lee launched Pickett's charge against the center of the Union line on Cemetery Ridge.

find Stuart, rode up with news of fierce fighting at Gettysburg. At 1:00 A.M. on the morning of 2 July Stuart began another night march to answer the call of his beleaguered commander.

Major Henry McClellan, Stuart's adjutant, left a brief account of the meeting that afternoon between Lee, who reddened as his cavalry chief approached, and Stuart, who knew he was in trouble.

"I have not heard a word from you for days," Lee said accusingly, "and you are the eyes and ears of the army."

Stuart replied, "I have brought you 125 wagons and their teams, General."

"Yes," Lee agreed, "and they are an impediment to me now." Then Lee softened, and according to McClellen said, "Let me ask your help now. We will not discuss this matter further. Help me fight these people."

Stuart was willing but his men and horses were fatigued, still strung out over the countryside, and in no condition to join in an assault on the second day of the Battle of Gettysburg. Instead of praise, Stuart sustained another harsh blow to his ego.

GETTYSBURG —
HIGH TIDE FOR THE CONFEDERACY

When Hooker learned that Lee had crossed into Pennsylvania, he hurried his army north and by 28 June had it centered near Frederick, Maryland. He then ordered Slocum's XII Corps to Harpers Ferry to cut Lee's line of communications in the Shenandoah Valley, but Union General-in-Chief Henry W. Halleck countermanded the order. Hooker asked to be relieved, which came as good news to the administration, and Lincoln replaced him with 48-year-old Major General George G. Meade, commander of the V Corps. No general in the Army of the Potomac had particularly distinguished himself, but Meade was a Regular Army officer who had shown ability at Chancellorsville after Hooker suffered a concussion. Lincoln also took into account that Meade had been born in Spain, which would prevent him from becoming president should the general be fortunate enough to win the war.

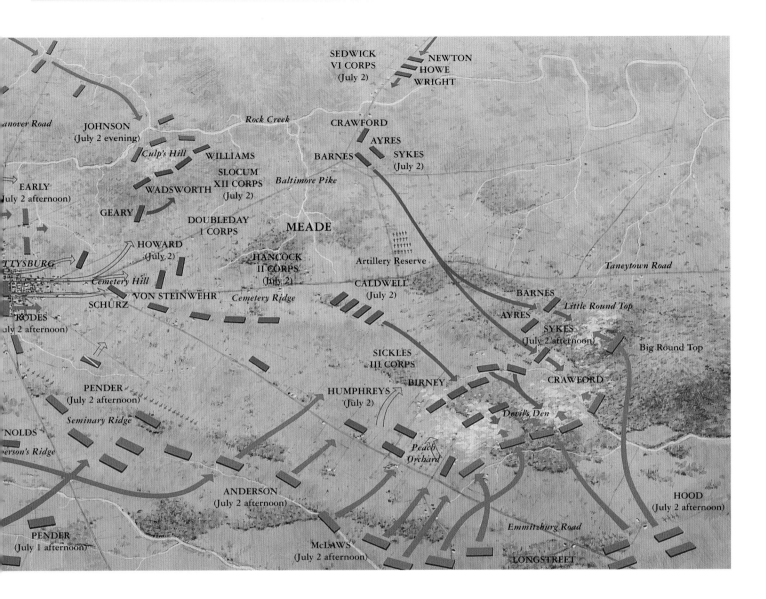

Also on 28 June Lee had not heard from Stuart, did not know the enemy situation, but nevertheless sent Ewell's Corps into Pennsylvania with orders to seize Harrisburg. Longstreet and Hill's corps moved into Pennsylvania but stayed in the neighborhood of Chambersburg and Waynesboro. That night Longstreet's mysterious agent, a man named Harrison, came to camp and reported the true position of Meade's army. Lee immediately took measures to reunify his army.

Meade worried about Lee's forces menacing Harrisburg. Like hooker, he wanted to strike Confederate communications in the Shenandoah and force a fight. Lee wanted to consolidate his forces by recalling Ewell's corps and joining it with Longstreet and Hill's corps near Cashtown.

On 1 July James J. Pettigrew's brigade from Henry Heth's division, while making a relaxed march towards Gettysburg to acquire shoes, unexpectedly collided with Buford's cavalry. By 10:30 A.M. what began as a skirmish with Buford's dismounted cavalry a mile-and-a-half from Gettysburg developed into a battle between two of Hill's divisions (Heth's and Pender's) and John F. Reynolds' I Corps. Hill's corps gained a clear advantage, and Reynolds lost his life trying to prevent the Confederates from overrunning his corps and securing a better defensive position.

Right: *General George Gordon Meade (1815-72), commander of the Union Army of the Potomac at the Battle of Gettysburg. Regarded as the army's only successful commander, he retained his command until the end of the war, although his achievements were overshadowed by his superior, General Grant, who accompanied the army during its campaigns in 1864-65.*

Oliver Howard's XI Corps arrived at 1:00 P.M. Two divisions took position on Reynolds' right flank just as Ewell's corps began arriving from Carlisle. Howard posted the third division in reserve on Cemetery Hill south of Gettysburg. Ewell struck Howard's two divisions and pushed them back onto Cemetery Hill, which worked against the Confederacy because the hill became the dominant defensive position on the battlefield.

Howard asked desperately for reinforcements from Slocum's XII Corps, five miles away, and from Sickles' III Corps, twelve miles away. When they arrived during late afternoon, both corps went directly to Cemetery Hill.

Lee came on the field and observed that Howard held Cemetery Hill and Abner Doubleday, now commanding Reynolds' I Corps, held Seminary Ridge. Lee wanted both the positions. He chased the I Corps off Seminary Ridge and expected Ewell to do the same at Cemetery Hill. Lee's instructions were discretionary, and Ewell chose to not make the attempt. The Confederacy won the first day's battle but failed to occupy the commanding position — Cemetery Hill.

Union General Hancock came on the field and recognized the strategic importance of Culp's Hill, which lay to the north and east of Cemetery Hill. He put troops on the hill and ordered them to hold it. He warned General Meade that Cemetery Hill could be turned and the Federal line of communications broken if Confederates took Culp's Hill. Meade spent the night of 1-2 July making strategic dispositions on Cemetery and Culp's Hill but failed to make adequate provisions for defending the Round Tops on the southern (left) flank.

Lee also wanted Culp's Hill and Cemetery Hill, but Ewell said they could not be taken and urged Longstreet to attack the Round Tops. Longstreet argued against any attack and urged Lee to take the defensive. Lee had won his battles by being aggressive and ordered Longstreet to attack the Round Tops in the morning.

At dawn, 2 July, Meade's army was arranged in a defensive fishhook with the shank on Cemetery Hill, the eye on the Round Tops, and the hook curving around the crown of Culp's Hill. Lee's lines stretched the full length of the fishhook. Meade's forces held the central position, enjoyed numerical superiority, and from a greater height could observe Confederate activity across a field of fire. Lee could not clearly see Meade's dispositions, and the absence of Stuart deprived him of finding weaknesses in the Union line.

Lee's orders for 2 July called for Longstreet to assault Little and Big Round Top with McLaws and Hood's divisions and roll up the Federal left on Cemetery Hill. The strategy made good sense because the Round Tops were weakly defended, though Lee did not know it. Lee also ordered Ewell and Hill to make secondary attacks to the north of Cemetery Hill and on Culp's Hill to keep Meade from sending reinforcements to the Round Tops.

Longstreet's tardy march to the Federal left consumed most of the afternoon. At 4:00 P.M. McLaws and Hood advanced toward the Round Tops but bumped into Sickles' III Corps, which without instructions from Meade had formed a salient by advancing to higher ground beside the Emmitsburg Road. Severe fighting erupted in the Peach Orchard, Wheatfield, Devil's Den, and spread to Little Round Top. The fierce battle caused Meade to shift troops from the right to the left to meet Confederate charges with Union counterattacks. Had Sickles not been in the wrong position, Longstreet's flanking movement may have worked because Meade had placed only skirmishers on Little Round Top.

A brigade of Federals arrived in time to repulse Hood's effort to take the Round Tops and secure the position. Having failed to penetrate Meade's left flank, Lee made twilight charges on Cemetery Hill and Culp's Hill, both of which Meade repulsed with heavy loss.

Two days of heavy fighting had bloodied both armies, but neither changed position. At first Meade could not decide whether to stay and fight, but his corps commanders urged him to do so. Lee unquestionably wanted to fight. Having unsuccessfully attacked Meade's flanks on 2 July, Lee resolved to attack his center the following day. Meade expected the center to be struck and made dispositions during

the night to strengthen it. Lee still believed his veterans were invincible and that Union morale was weak. Against objections from Longstreet, he assigned eleven brigades to a frontal assault on Cemetery Hill while Ewell continued to peck away at Culp's Hill. Lee chose Major General George E. Pickett's fresh division to lead the attack while Jeb Stuart's cavalry worked around the Union left flank and struck Meade's force from the rear.

At noon Ewell's seven-hour battle for Culp's Hill withered to a sputter and an hour of silence pervaded the battlefield. At 1:00 P.M. 140 Confederate cannon targeted Cemetery Hill. For two hours artillery pounded the heights, but the shells passed over the

Below: The uniform and personal belongings of Major-General George G. Meade. His wool frock coat shoulder strap insignia, slouch hat insignia, and epaulettes denote the rank of major-general. His Model 1839 topographical engineer's saber and scabbard were made by N.P. Ames, Springfield, Massachusetts.

crest and exploded in the rear. At 3:00 P.M. the guns fell silent and a short spell of ominous silence followed. Then human waves of 13,000 men dressed in butternut poured from the woods of Seminary Ridge. With clockwork precision they marched determinedly across open ground toward a clump of trees on the brow of Cemetery Hill. Artillery opened fire and southerners fell, leaving great gaps in their lines. But still they came, over the Emmitsburg Road, up the slope, and toward the trees. At 100 yards Federal infantry opened fire, and Pickett's charge stalled in a deadly fire of canister and minié balls. Lee watched through his glass as a handful of Confederates made a valiant attempt to reach the crest and then he saw

them fall. As the survivors streamed back to Seminary Ridge, tears welled in Lee's eyes, and he said, "It's all my fault. My fault."

Stuart's attack on the Federal rear also collapsed after three hours of disorganized fighting. The most crucial battle of the Civil War ended on the soil of Pennsylvania, and at a fearful cost. After the guns grew silent, Lee turned to an officer at his side and said, "We must now return to Virginia."

On the night of 3 July Lee gave Imboden's cavalry the task of rounding up the wounded and the army's supply wagons and conveying them back to Virginia. He kept the army on Seminary Ridge and cavalry on the flanks until 4:00 P.M. on 4 July, when Imboden's vulnerable wagon train started down the Chambersburg Pike. Then the skies opened. "The rain fell in a blinding sheet," Imboden recalled. ". . . the wounded men lying upon the naked boards of the wagon were drenched. Horses and mules were blinded and maddened by the wind and water."

On 4 July, as Lee prepared to retire from Pennsylvania, a saddened and disillusioned George Pickett paused to pen a letter to his young fiancée: "It is all over now. Many of us are prisoners, many are dead, many wounded, bleeding and dying. Your soldier lives and mourns and but for you, my darling, he would rather be back there with his dead, to sleep for all time in an unknown grave."

On 6 July, when Lee's advance guard reached Williamsport, the same storm that had drenched Imboden's ambulance train made the Potomac unfordable. Buford attacked but was repulsed by Imboden. The rest of Lee's army reached Hagerstown the following day and entrenched to wait for a new pontoon bridge. Meade could have attacked but decided against it. On the night of 13-14 July Lee took his army across the Potomac and started back to Virginia.

Right: Company of the 114th Pennsylvania Volunteer Regiment (Collis' Zouaves) photographed outside Petersburg, Virginia, 1864. This Zouave regiment, named and equiped in the style of French colonial troops, fought with distinction at Fredericksburg, Chancellorsville, and Gettysburg as part of the Army of the Potomac's III Corps.

The Confederate setback at Gettysburg changed the character of the war. The brilliant offenses of the past were gone for good. The Army of Northern Virginia lost some its finest line officers, and the dead and mortally wounded veterans could never be replaced. The Confederate tide that rose to new heights at Chancellorsville crested and ebbed at Gettysburg. Lee knew he could not win a war of attrition, but fight on he must.

A RESPITE FROM COMBAT

Wary of following Lee yet unable to resist demands from Washington to pursue and attack, Meade crossed the Potomac and nipped at the heels of the weakened Army of Northern Virginia. He followed the same route taken by McClellan the previous autumn, passing through the Piedmont and watching the passes of the Blue Ridge to guard against a surprise flank attack. While Meade concentrated on his front, Mosby's Rangers wreaked havoc on Union supply trains straggling in the rear.

On 24 July, conscious of Meade's timorous advance, Lee placed his army in front of Culpeper because he needed to cease military operations in Virginia and give his army time to recover. When Lee stopped, so did Meade.

Vicksburg had fallen on 4 July, which cut the Confederacy in two, opened the entire Mississippi to Federal gunboats, and throttled the flow of troops and supplies from the West. Only through the port of Wilmington, North Carolina, was there an opening to the outer world, and only through that port could supplies from abroad keep the Confederate army nourished.

In Richmond President Davis was besieged by calls for more men and more arms. With Rosecrans' army marching into eastern Tennessee, he could only

Above: *The Confederates were always unable to match the logistical superiority enjoyed by the Army of the Potomac. This supply wagon train attached to the Army of the Potomac's VI Corps was photographed near Brandy Station, Virginia during the late summer of 1863.*

shuttle troops by weakening one sector of the Confederacy to strengthen another. Lee fretted over mishandling the battle at Gettysburg, and on 8 August added to Davis' worries by offering to step aside. The general had not been well, manifesting early signs of heart failure. Davis replied, "I am truly sorry to know that you still feel the effects of the illness you suffered last spring . . . [but] to ask me to substitute you by someone in my judgment more fit to command, or who would possess more of the confidence of the army is to demand an impossibility."

A month passed and Lee moved across the Rapidan River to Orange Court House. Men began returning to duty from hospitals and by 10 August Lee's forces had grown to 58,600 men. On 9 September he detached Longstreet with two divisions (12,000 men) and sent them to Tennessee to reinforce General Braxton Bragg, who had been

pushed out of Chattanooga by Rosecrans' Army of the Cumberland.

On 13 September General Meade, with a two-to-one advantage in manpower, learned that Longstreet had been detached and advanced beyond the Rappahannock to discover what Lee was doing. Union scouts found Confederate forces entrenched in partially fortified positions in front of Orange Court House. Meade took a distant and considered look at Lee's preparations and withdrew to his camps at Culpeper. There he waited, hoping to lure Lee onto open ground.

THE BRISTOE CAMPAIGN

In early October Lee learned that the XI and XII Corps had been detached from Meade and sent to reinforce Rosecrans at Chattanooga. On 9 October he decided to cross the Rapidan and turn the Federal flank from the west, much like he had done at 2nd Bull Run, and then cut off the Union retreat. Meade detected the movement and during the night of 10 October retired across the Rappahannock.

Lee tried another flanking movement by way of Fauquier Springs, hoping to bring on an engagement on the plains of Fauquier, but Meade hastened to the south side of the Orange & Alexandria Railroad. The two armies then engaged in a race, at times in sight of each other from opposite sides of the railroad with Lee doing the chasing and Meade the running.

As Meade retreated through Brentsville, he detached Gouverneur Warren's II Corps at Bristoe Station to cover his withdrawal. Warren took a strong position behind the railroad embankment and waited. When Heth's brigades from A.P. Hill's corps rushed ahead to cut off Meade, Warren surprised them with a devastating fire from II Corps' artillery and three divisions of infantry. Instead of turning north to avoid the ambush, Heth's brigades wheeled around and charged Warren's strong position, never realizing that the Federals behind the embankment were the same veterans who had repulsed Pickett's charge at Gettysburg.

Hill lost 1,900 men, among them two generals and 31 officers. Lee was furious with Hill for attacking Warren's position, and equally irritated with Ewell for failing to close on Hill, thereby allowing

Below: *Correspondents from the New York Herald interview soldiers near Beolton, Virginia, August 1863. The press wagon accompanied the Army of the Potomac on campaign.*

Meade to reach the security of Centreville's fortifications. Once again Lee demonstrated his unremitting capacity for taking the offensive against enormous odds. It made him one of history's great commanders, but Longstreet was in Tennessee and Jackson was dead, and neither of them could be replaced.

At Bristoe Station, while Hill gathered the wounded and buried the dead, Lee wrote Davis: "Nothing prevented my continuing in his [Meade's] front but the destitute condition of the men, thousands of whom are barefooted, a great number partially shod, and nearly all without overcoats, blankets or warm clothing. I think the sublimest sight of the war was the cheerfulness and alacrity exhibited by this army in the pursuit of the enemy under all the trials and privations to which it was exposed."

MINE RUN CAMPAIGN

Nothing irritated Washington more than Meade's flight to Centreville, but in mid-October Lee had no alternative but to return to Culpeper. Meade picked up his army and slowly followed Lee back to the Rappahannock. After crossing the river Lee posted two of Early's regiments in entrenched positions on the north bank to guard a pontoon bridge. During a heavy late evening rain on 7 November, Meade rushed the Confederate position and captured both brigades. The disaster at the bridgehead broke up Lee's plans for wintering at Culpeper and forced him to move his army across the Rapidan and back to Orange Court House.

The winter quiet of Lee's camps was disturbed when on 26 November Meade, prodded by Washington to act, ordered the I and V Corps to cross the Rapidan at the Culpeper Mine Ford, the II Corps at Germanna Ford, and the III and VI Corps at the higher fords. Stuart's scouts reported the

movements and Bushrod Johnson's division repulsed the III Corps before it crossed the river.

Stuart continued to circulate through the area and discovered an excellent defensive position along

Mine Run, a few miles east of Lee's encampment. Meade sent Warren's II Corps to turn Lee's left and Sedgwick's VI Corps to attack Lee's right. On the frigid morning of 30 November Warren took 26,000 men to strike Lee's flank but was driven back by artillery and musketry. Sedgwick's attempt to turn Lee's left also failed. Meade decided the weather was too cold for operations and returned to the old

Below: Brigadier-General Robert O. Tyler (near Culpeper) commanded the Artillery Reserve during the Gettysburg campaign.

Brandy Station battlefield. For the remainder of the winter the two armies watched each other from across twenty miles of the Rapidan.

The Orange & Alexandria Railroad south of the Rapidan delivered supplies to the Confederates while the same rails north of the Rapidan delivered supplies to the Federals. And for three months the two armies rested, gathering strength for the inevitable spring campaign.

The Freezing Winter of 1863-1864

During what observers called the severest winter in many years, Lee's army contended with cold at times impossible to overcome. In Orange County, Virginia, the men constructed log cabins and slept without blankets on beds of straw. They had fuel, but rations were reduced to a quarter pound of pork and a scant portion of meal or flour per day, and sometimes even this was wanting. A depreciated currency in worthless paper dollars made buying the necessities of life impossible, even for officers of the highest grades. Corn meal sold for $50 a bushel; beans, $60; bacon $8 a pound and sugar $20 a pound.

Jedediah Hotchkiss, serving with Lee in Orange County, said, "The redeeming features of these days of gloom and suffering were the bright shining of the heroic virtues, not only of the men but of the women and children of the Confederacy, and the steadfast faithfulness of all the Negroes, most of them slaves, who, in quiet submission to home authority, cultivated the fields, and by the arts of handicraft helped to support the people of the Confederacy and their armies.

"Lee not only dwelt among his men, in simple fashion, but fared as they fared, saying, when luxuries were sent him, as they often were, and which he invariably sent to the sick and wounded in hospitals, 'I am content to share the rations of my men.'"

Among this hodgepodge of ragged tents and crude log cabins stood spacious hewn log chapels, for the small country churches could not hold so great a mass of soldiers on Sundays. Army chaplains and the ablest of local preachers shared the duty of serving the spiritual needs of Lee's veterans. Anybody looking across the Rapidan into the camps of the Federals would see the same. Yankee and Rebel, though they fought each other, nevertheless found solace in the same one God.

On 31 December 1863 the *Richmond Examiner* summed up a year of military setbacks on many fronts and wrote: "Today closes the gloomiest year of our struggle." No person living in Virginia could look ahead to 1864 with any rational hope for improvement.

Timeline – 1863

1 January: President Lincoln signs the Proclamation Emancipation.

20-22 January: Burnside's winter campaign ends in the "Mud March."

1 February: A Confederate dollar is worth 20 cents.

5 February: General Joseph Hooker becomes commander of the Army of the Potomac.

2 April: In Richmond, angry women storm the street in the "bread riot."

24 April: The Confederate government passes an 8% tax on agricultural products and 10% tax on profits made from food, clothing, and iron.

28 April: The Army of the Potomac crosses the Rappahannock for a spring offensive.

1-4 May: Hooker is defeated by Lee at Chancellorsville.

6 May: General A.P. Hill takes command of the II Corps, Army of Northern Virginia.

10 May: General Jackson dies of wounds received at Chancellorsville.

3 June: General Lee moves out of Fredericksburg and begins a month long campaign that brings his army to Gettysburg.

9 June: Confederates and Federals clash in the greatest cavalry battle of the war at Brandy Station.

10-12 June: The Army of Northern Virginia passes the Blue Ridge and moves into the Shenandoah Valley.

13-15 June: Second Battle of Winchester.

15 June: Longstreet departs from Culpeper for the Valley; Stuart screens his march.

17 June: Stuart clashes with General Pleasanton's Union cavalry at Aldie, Virginia.

19 June: Gregg's cavalry division repulses Stuart at Middleburg, Virginia.

20 June: President Lincoln proclaims West Virginia the 35th state of the Union.

21 June: Jeb Stuart skirmishes with Gregg's cavalry division at Upperville, Virginia.

25 June: Jeb Stuart breaks from his planned route to capture 125 Federal wagons and more than 400 prisoners.

28 June: Major General George G. Meade is given command of the Army of the Potomac.

30 June: Stuart and Kilpatrick clash at Hanover, Pennsylvania.

1-3 July: The Battle of Gettysburg. After the battle, Lee would look upon his shattered troops and lament, "Jackson is not here."

4-13 July: The Army of Northern Virginia retires from Pennsylvania.

9-22 October: Lee launches the Bristoe Campaign to trap the Army of the Potomac. A.P. Hill loses 1,900 men at Bristoe Station.

26 November-2 December: The Mine Run Campaign.

Above: *The Confederates had to use whatever resources they could to replace the war materials lost at Gettysburg. Of these two Virginia Manufactory 1st and 2nd Model flintlock pistols dating from the early 19th century, the 1st Model (top) was converted to percussion ignition as part of a drive to modernize obsolete weaponry.*

1864: GREEN SHOES FULL OF BONES

The long winter of 1863-64 passed quietly except for two mishandled attempts by Meade to penetrate Lee's defenses. On 6 February Meade sent a division across Morton's Ford on the Rapidan to test the winter temper of Lee's veterans. General Ewell met the attack with customary ferocity, kept the Yanks under fire all day, and by the next morning they were gone.

The next incursion occurred on 28 February when Union General Judson Kilpatrick and Colonel Ulric Dahlgren crossed Ely's Ford on the Rapidan with 3,585 handpicked cavalrymen, six guns, three wagons, and four ambulances for the ostensible purpose of releasing Federal prisoners held in Richmond. It would soon become clear (to the Confederates at least) that Dahlgren then separated from Kilpatrick to execute a more diabolical mission: that is, to burn Richmond and kill Jefferson Davis and his cabinet.

George Washington Custis Lee, the general's oldest son and aide to President Davis, rounded up the Local Defense Brigade of workers from the

> **"Lee's army will be your objective point. Wherever Lee goes, there will you go. . . Hammer continuously against the armed force of the enemy and his resources, until, by mere attrition, if nothing else, there will be nothing left him but submission."**
>
> **GENERAL GRANT TO GENERAL MEADE, 27 APRIL 1864**

armory, arsenal, Tredegar Iron Works, and other government departments and with 500 Confederate infantry and six guns blocked the main roads into Richmond. Kilpatrick reached the outskirts of Richmond on 1 March, found the defenses too strong, and withdrew. Dahlgren tried to work into Richmond by a different road but encountered stiff resistance from Lee's militia. The 5th and 9th Virginia Cavalry had been tracking Dahlgren's force for two days and finally trapped it near King and Queen Courthouse. In a brisk fight Dahlgren lost his life and the majority of his command surrendered. Kilpatrick's troopers fled east to the Union base at Yorktown. In Colonel Dahlgren's pocket were found papers exhorting his men, if not actually ordering them, to kill Jefferson Davis. The reaction in the South when the "orders" were publicised was outrage and dark plots to blow up the White House. Meade, Judson Kilpatrick, and even Lincoln himself were obliged to disavow any knowledge of the papers. Doubts as to the authenticity of the documents linger to this day.

Above: *A temporary prison camp was set up at Battle Plain Landing, Virginia to house Confederate prisoners captured during the Battle of Spotsylvania Courthouse. The majority of those pictured here were from Major-General Edward Johnson's Division, which was captured en masse at the "Mule Shoe" on May 12, 1864.*

Convinced that Meade could not lead the Army of the Potomac to victory, Lincoln called forty-two-year-old Ulysses S. Grant from the West and on 9 March promoted him to lieutenant general and General-in-Chief of the Armies of the United States. Grant had earned distinction by capturing Vicksburg on 4 July 1863 and for his recent victories in Tennessee. On 12 March he took charge of conducting the strategic direction of the war and instead of doing it from Washington chose to accompany Meade's Army of the Potomac into Virginia. Meade had not been idle during the wintering of his forces at Culpeper. His army had grown in efficiency and strength, and by the end of April numbered 122,000 men. One of Grant's officers referred to Meade's army as "the best clothed and best fed army that ever took the field." When Grant arrived at Culpeper in April, he came with a plan – to "hammer" Lee into submission, whatever it took, and "to fight Lee between the Rapidan and Richmond, if he will stand."

Against the massive blueclad army Lee's forces numbered about 62,000 men; 22,000 under Hill at Orange Court House; 17,000 under Ewell in Mountain Run Valley; 10,000 in Longstreet's two divisions at Gordonsville; 4,800 artillerymen manning 224 guns, and 8,300 cavalrymen in two divisions under Stuart.

THE WILDERNESS CAMPAIGN

On 2 May, with spring in full bloom, Lee took his binoculars and rode to the signal station atop Clark's Mountain. With him came General Longstreet, who had just returned from Tennessee, and other corps commanders to study the activity in Meade's Culpeper County camps. From the field outspread before him, and from preparations in the Federal camps Lee concluded that Meade's movement would be to the right and slightly west of the old Chancellorsville battlefield. He predicted that Meade would cross at Germanna or Ely's ford and told his officers to take up the line of march as soon

as the signal station waved instructions. On 3 May Stuart's scouts reported General Hancock's II Corps, Warren's V Corps, and Sedgwick's VI Corps assembling along the Rapidan. After confirming the next morning that Warren's corps was crossing at Germanna Ford and Hancock's corps was crossing at Ely's Ford, Lee put his army in motion. Ewell advanced along the Orange Turnpike to intercept Warren's Corps, and Hill advanced along the Orange Plank Road to intercept Hancock. Sedgwick's corps also crossed at Germanna Ford and followed behind Warren's force. Stuart was already at the front with his horse artillery and harassing the Federal advance.

Above: Both sides made use of rail guns during the war. This Union piece saw service during the Petersburg campaign.

Above: *The Army of the Potomac crossing the Rappahannock River at Ely's Ford immediately prior to the Battle of the Wilderness in early May 1864. Cavalry are fording the river in the foreground while infantry and artillery are shown crossing via the pontoon bridge in the distance.*

Far right: *The General-in-Chief of the Union Army, Ulysses S. Grant (1822-85) elected to accompany the Army of the Potomac during 1864, ensuring that Meade would not fall into the trap of his predecessors and retreat when pressed.*

Meade halted the night of 4 May to prepare for battle in the morning. From Hancock's camp on the old Chancellorsville battlefield south of Ely's Ford, Grant telegraphed a message to Washington: "The crossing of the Rapidan effected. Forty-eight hours now will demonstrate whether the enemy intends giving battle this side of Richmond." From Hancock's camp a good road led southward to Spotsylvania Court House, where better roads led directly into Richmond. Grant wanted those roads, but first of all he had to neutralize the Army of Northern Virginia.

On the morning of 5 May leading elements of Warren's V Corps struck Ewell's pickets on the Orange Turnpike. Meade ordered an immediate attack, but Warren waited too long. At 1:00 P.M. Ewell brought up heavy reinforcements and repulsed the attack. In an uncoordinated drive, Sedgwick attempted to turn Ewell's left flank, and in fighting that continued until nightfall failed to gain ground in the densely wooded Wilderness.

While Ewell battled on the north side of the Wilderness, Heth's division clashed with Hancock's corps on the Orange Plank Road.

The battle gathered momentum as Federal reinforcements arrived, but Heth's division fought from and in the woods until nightfall gave the exhausted Confederates a reprieve.

Grant was not satisfied and on 6 May ordered a 5:00 A.M. assault by Warren and Sedgwick against Ewell's corps while Hancock completed the destruction of Hill's corps. Meade threw Burnside's IX Corps into the gap between Warren and Hancock in an effort to strike the left flank of Hill. While the battle on the 5th had been concentrated near the roads, the battle of the 6th took place almost entirely in dense woods and underbrush.

Lee made his dispositions for the morning of the 6th without any particular plans other than to fight. Ewell thought he would surprise Warren and Sedgwick by striking them at 4:30 A.M. but was driven back because the Federals were about to launch their own offensive. Sedgwick and Warren battled Ewell's corps all day, and though the fight consisted of thrust and counterthrust, Ewell held the both the woods and the road. At 6:00 P.M. Ewell thought he had detected a weakness on Sedgwick's right flank and attacked. Sedgwick threw in reserves, and at nightfall the Confederates fell back to their original position.

At 5:00 A.M. on the other side of the battlefield, Hancock and part of Sedgwick's corps attacked Hill and drove the Confederates from the field. Burnside arrived late, and instead of rolling up the left flank of Hill's corps, ran into Ewell's reserve and was stopped. Under pressure from Hancock, Hill moved into the woods on his left as Longstreet's corps came up the road in reserve. Hill struck Burnside and abruptly stopped the Federal flank attack. Longstreet checked Hancock, whose divisions became too separated in the Wilderness to resume the offensive. Longstreet then moved four brigades against Hancock's right,

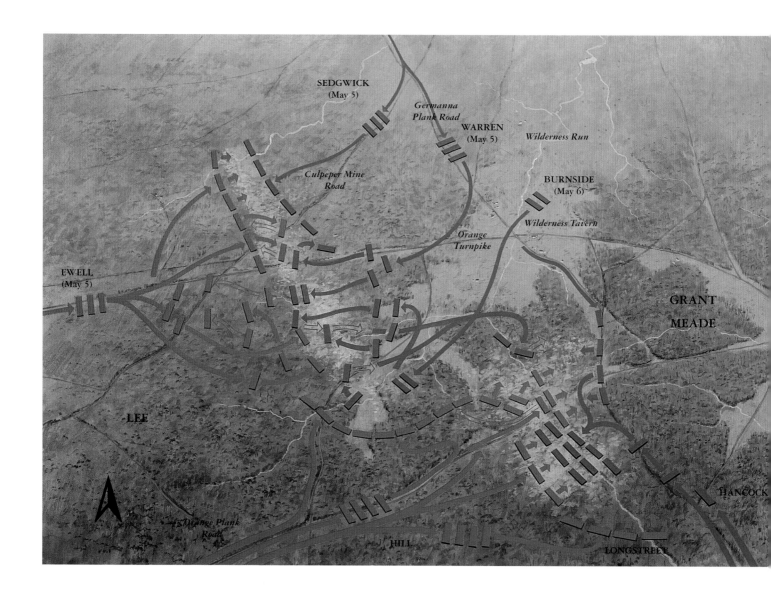

Above: *Battle of the Wilderness involved assault on Meade's army from the west along two axes. On the Orange Turnpike Ewell's Corps engaged Union V (Warren) and VI Corps (Sedgwick), while on the Orange Plank Road A.P. Hill engaged Hancock (II Corps). Fighting was fierce but inconclusive.*

CHANCELLORSVILLE

llery Reserve

The battle ended in a tactical stalemate with body counts reaching staggering proportions. The Army of the Potomac with 155,000 engaged suffered 17,500 casualties. The Army of Northern Virginia with 60,000 engaged lost 7,500. On 7 May Grant turned south, satisfied that he had won a strategic victory, but he still had many miles to go.

ORDEAL AT SPOTSYLVANIA COURT HOUSE

Lee anticipated Grant's next move and on 7 May began cutting a military road through the

Opposite, below: A supply train of the Army of the Potomac crossing the Shenandoah River near Front Royal, Virginia, 1864.

Below: The thickets which gave the Wilderness its name meant that fighting was largely confined to the Orange Turnpike and Orange Plank Road during the battle.

flanked the position, and drove the Federals from the south side of the Orange Plank Road and back to the Brock Road. At 4:00 P.M. Lee arrived on the field and launched a massive counterattack on Hancock's center. Union artillery joined the fight but by 5:00 P.M. the Confederate attack lost momentum and fell back. Longstreet suffered a serious wound from friendly fire during the battle and turned his corps over to Major General Richard H. Anderson. After losing Jackson, Lee could not afford to lose Longstreet.

On 7 May pillars of smoke and the repulsive stench of burning bodies filtered through the eerie calm over the Wilderness. Even the crows fell silent.

Below: *The Union purchased about 400,000 handguns during the War. Almost any handgun might have been taken to war by an enthusiastic volunteer in the early months, but on the field of battle most were Colts and Remingtons. From top to bottom: .44 caliber Allen & Wheelock Lipfire Army revolver; .36 Savage-North Navy revolver; socket bayonets, scabbards, and frog.*

Wilderness that would put his entire army by its right flank on the highway to Spotsylvania Court House. When Stuart reported Grant's wagons moving, and Ewell reported the Germanna road abandoned with Sedgwick's dead left unburied, Lee put Longstreet's corps on the route to Spotsylvania and that night issued orders for Hill and Ewell to follow.

Before daylight on 8 May Longstreet's corps, now under the command of Anderson, rested in a grove near Spotsylvania Court House, a tiny crossroads village southeast of the Wilderness. Warren's corps, having taken a shorter route, nonetheless arrived later and found Anderson and Fitz Lee's dis-

mounted cavalry blocking the roads to Richmond. This had not been Grant's plan. Grant wanted to interpose the Federal army between Lee's army and Richmond and force Lee to come out and fight. A day passed before Grant discovered to his dismay that Lee had stolen a march and moved Anderson, Hill, and Ewell's corps into an emergency line of crude and irregular defenses.

Lee rode along the line, found it weak in spots, and put men to work building a second line of stronger fieldworks in the rear. The new position featured a horseshoe salient around the crest of a spur between two branches of the Ni River. Anderson's

172

corps extended the line to the left, Ewell covered the "Mule Shoe" salient in the center, and Hill's corps extended the line to the right. Anderson's left flank rested on the Po River, and Hill's right flank rested on the Fredericksburg Road. Grant could not continue his march to Richmond without going through Spotsylvania, and there his advance stopped.

On 10 May, somewhat puzzled by the resourcefulness of Lee, Grant sent four corps (Hancock, Warren, Wright, and Burnside's) against the Confederate entrenchments. The Federals reeled back from a crippling fire. At 6:00 P.M. Colonel Emory Upton, massing 12 regiments on a narrow front, assaulted the "Mule Shoe" salient, breached the works, but could not expand the penetration.

Viewing the Mule Shoe as Lee's strategic defensive position, Grant decided to follow up on Upton's limited success and on 12 May threw Hancock's entire corps at the salient. On a wet and muddy morning, Hancock's brigades swarmed over the salient and into the trenches, capturing the bulk of Edward Johnson's division and the general himself. The battle in the salient at the "Bloody Angle" became one of "hand-to-hand encounters with clubbed rifles, bayonets, swords and pistols [where] officers of the opposing sides cut and slashed with

Below: *Imported handguns probably exceeded in number those manufactured by the Confederacy. While ammunition was sometimes a problem, imports were almost always of superior quality. From top to bottom: Le Mat First Model revolver; Columbus Fire Arms Manufacturing Company revolver; side knife and scabbard by W.J. McElroy; "Bowie" bayonet and scabbard by Boyle, Gamble and MacFee.*

their swords, and fired with their revolvers into the very face of each other."

Brigadier General John B. Gordon rode up, saw the Confederate line caving, and threw in three brigades from the left side of the salient. Lee rode up and Gordon asked, "What do you want me to do, general?" Lee said, "Counterattack!"

Gordon pulled in brigades from Rodes' division and at 5:30 ordered the charge. The relentless attack, accompanied by the bone-chilling Rebel yell, staggered Hancock's drive and pushed the Federals in disorder back to the toe of the Mule Shoe, where they took refuge in trenches captured the day before. After twenty hours of fighting, Lee pulled his men

Right: *A dead Confederate soldier from Richard Ewell's command lying in the area known as "the mule shoe" or "the bloody angle," a salient in the Confederate line near Spotsylvania against which Grant directed his attacks. Lee could ill afford the high level of casualties his army sustained during the Battle of Spotsylvania.*

out of the salient and put them into a new line of defensive works built across the base of the salient. Federals assaulted the new fortifications six days later and were repulsed.

On 19 May Lee's demonstrations against Grant's right resulted in more severe fighting. Two days later Grant withdrew, once more attempting to march around the Confederate right before being detected by Lee's scouts.

The Spotsylvania butcher's bill was high. In two days of fighting on 10 and 12 May, Lee lost 6,000 killed or wounded and another 4,000 captured. Grant's official toll was equally numbing with 10,920 killed, wounded, or captured. Lee could not afford the losses. Grant could. One Confederate, having survived the bloodshed at Spotsylvania, wrote of Grant, "We have met a man, this time, who either does not know when he is whipped, or who cares not if he loses his whole Army."

THE DEATH OF JEB STUART

On 9 May Major General Philip H. Sheridan, commanding Grant's cavalry corps, began moving around Lee's right flank at Spotsylvania. Grant's instructions were for Sheridan to get into the Confederate rear, break up Lee's communications at Beaver Dam Station, and make contact with General Butler's Army of the James at Bermuda Hundred.

Stuart was guarding Lee's ammunition train, and his scouting patrols were not strong enough to prevent Sheridan from passing on the right and gaining the highway to Richmond. Sheridan had been looking forward to a cavalry duel, so he purposely skirted Stuart's flank at a sedate walk, which also had the advantage of keeping his horses fresh.

When Confederate depot guards at Beaver Dam Station learned of Sheridan's approach, they burned 915,000 rations of meat and 504,000 rations of bread – enough to feed Lee's army for three weeks. Then they fled. George Armstrong Custer and Wesley Merritt's divisions are supposed to have finished the job, torching two locomotives and a large number of fully laden railway cars, including those holding most of Lee's medical supplies, but the

Right: *General Philip S. Sheridan (1831-88) commanded the cavalry of the Army of the Potomac during 1864 until he was given command of the Union Army of the Shenandoah in early August. His policy of destruction in the valley earned him a loathsome reputation in Virginia.*

evidence is not clear. Stuart reacted with alacrity. He divided his six brigades, leaving three with Lee. He put Lunsford Lomax and William C. Wickham's brigades under Fitz Lee and kept James B. Gordon's brigade of North Carolinians with himself. At nightfall the troop arrived a few miles up the North Anna River from Beaver Dam Station. They watched in rage as flames lit up the sky above the burning depot.

Stuart now had concerns for Richmond and on the morning of 10 May telegraphed Braxton Bragg, in command of the capital's defenses, to get ready for a fight. Then he detached Fitz Lee's two brigades and ordered them into Richmond to help Bragg block the Federal column from the front while he with Gordon's brigade harassed the enemy's rear. Stuart's horses had been overworked and underfed, and the Federal force outnumbered him by almost three-to-one, but he could not allow Sheridan to run unchallenged in Lee's rear.

After issuing his orders, Stuart made a short detour to visit his wife, Flora, and their two children at a plantation near Beaver Dam Station. As he rode into the yard, Flora rushed outside to greet him. He could not take time to dismount, but he leaned from the saddle and kissed her. For a few moments they talked, then he kissed her and the children again and said goodbye. An uncharacteristic pall hung over the typically ebullient Stuart as he departed from his wife. When he broke the silence and spoke, it was on a subject he seldom discussed—-death. He turned to Major Reid Venable, his friend and inspector general, and said that he did not expect to survive the war, nor did he wish to live in a defeated South.

At nightfall, 10 May, Stuart rejoined Fitz Lee's force at Hanover Junction and learned that Sheridan had camped ten miles away, only 20 miles from Richmond. Stuart wanted to move at once, but Lee coaxed him into first resting the horses and the exhausted command. Stuart, who was also fatigued, agreed, but he ordered saddles at 1:00 A.M. to steal a march on Sheridan.

In the early hours before dawn, Stuart sent Gordon's scouts ahead as the column gaited down the Telegraph Road. Two hours later scouts returned and reported seeing Sheridan's column moving on the Mountain Road. This put both cavalry columns on a collision course where the two roads met and merged to form the Brook Turnpike, a main artery running straight into the heart of Richmond. Less than a mile beyond the intersection stood an old abandoned and ramshackle stagecoach inn named Yellow Tavern.

At 8:00 A.M. Stuart rode into the yard well ahead of Sheridan's vanguard. He expected Bragg to join him during the morning and formed a thin defensive line across Mountain Road and Telegraph Road a few hundred yards above the intersection.

Bragg never came but Sheridan did. At 11:00 A.M. Colonel Thomas Devin's Union brigade struck Lomax's brigade on Stuart's left. For three hours the fight ebbed and flowed at the intersection. A cheering message from Bragg arrived promising to field about 4,000 convalescents and three brigades from Beauregard's force, which had been fighting General Benjamin Butler's army along the James River southeast of Richmond. With the promised reinforcements Bragg believed he could hold the capital and urged Stuart to hold the roads.

Stuart felt relieved and began organizing a counterattack, but at 4:00 P.M. Sheridan struck first. Federal horse artillery pounded Stuart's position, and soon elements from Wickham and Lomax's brigades began trickling to the rear. Stuart brought up his reserves—-only 80 men from the 1st Virginia—-and led them into the mêlée on the left, shouting, "Charge, Virginians, and save those brave

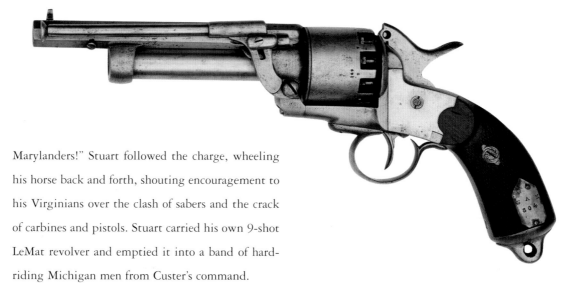

Right: *The French-designed Le Mat revolver was the favored sidearm of J.E.B. Stuart. The weapon combined a nine shot .44 caliber revolver with a small .65 caliber shotgun barrel, making it an extremely effective weapon at close quarters.*

Marylanders!" Stuart followed the charge, wheeling his horse back and forth, shouting encouragement to his Virginians over the clash of sabers and the crack of carbines and pistols. Stuart carried his own 9-shot LeMat revolver and emptied it into a band of hard-riding Michigan men from Custer's command.

The counterattack cleared the field of all but a few scattered patches of Federals who had lost their mounts. One 48-year-old private and former sharp-shooter named John A. Huff noticed a commanding figure with a red beard, plumed hat, and silk-lined

Right: *The death of General James E.B. "Jeb" Stuart (1833-64) was a grievous blow to the Confederate cause. The South was fast running out of gifted commanders.*

cape rallying his men from the saddle of an enormous horse. Huff raised his pistol, fired from 30 yards, and ran off the field. Stuart's chin dropped, his hat fell to the ground, and his hand clutched his right side. Blood oozed between his fingers. A trooper nearby asked Stuart if he was hit, and the general replied, "I am afraid I am."

Men from the 1st Virginia helped Stuart off his horse and escorted him to the rear. Fitz Lee rode through the flurry of battle and came up, lost for words. Stuart said, "Go ahead, Fitz, old fellow. I know you will do what is right," but the wounding of the Confederacy's most beloved cavalry chief took the fight out of the men.

Lee ordered that Stuart be put on an ambulance and taken to Richmond. With Federals swarming over the Brook Turnpike there was no direct route for Stuart's ambulance drivers, and he bounced on tortuous back roads for six hours. The ambulance carried him to the home of Dr. Charles Brewer, his brother-in-law, and there he suffered paroxysms of pain. He asked for his wife and children, and they began the arduous trip from Beaver Dam Station by carriage. During moments of lucidity he heard the heavy thump of cannon north of Richmond and knew that Bragg had placed artillery along the roads.

RICHMOND—PHOEBE YATES PEMBER AT CHIMBORAZO

Like thousands of women who had lost their husbands, 37-year-old Phoebe Yates Pember came to Richmond looking for employment. She became a matron at Chimborazo Hospital; a sprawling new institution perched on a high hill near the eastern boundary of the city. She worked for Dr. James B. McCaw, who Douglas Southall Freeman characterized as "one of the great men of the South." When Phoebe first arrived in 1862 the hospital had just opened, and every year thereafter continued to expand. During the war she became chief matron of Chimborazo's Hospital No. 2, which from its opening to the end of the war cared for 76,000 patients. Chimborazo was referred to as the biggest hospital on the continent and at its biggest with 8,000 beds, it probably was.

At first she encountered opposition. Despite the work of several thousand female nurses during the conflict (mostly in Union hospitals), and the postwar fame of such women as Clara Barton and Dorothea Dix, she was entering a world dominated by men. One of the ward surgeons, upon seeing her, said in unconcealed disgust, "One of *them* has come." Both sexes learned that this dynamic little woman could not be pushed around by anyone.

Though a refugee, nobody took the trouble of providing her with living quarters, so she stayed at the hospital until the secretary of war invited her into his home. Her consuming interest became the sick and wounded that filled her wards. The battles she fought and won were conducted for her patients. She would not tolerate red tape, or drunken doctors who killed their patients. When her patients made impossible demands, she tried to comfort them.

Above: *The Chimborazo Hospital was sited on a bluff on the eastern side of Richmond, Virginia, and had the capacity to treat up to 8,000 casualties at a time. The Confederates needed its facilities during 1864.*

One of Phoebe's more difficult hours occurred when a boy named Fisher, who had been convalescing from a hip wound, took his first steps and walked from one end of the ward to the other. He felt a sudden jab of pain and returned to his bed. Phoebe noticed a small stream of blood spurting from his wound.

A splintered bone had cut an artery. She stopped the flow with her finger and sent for the surgeon. The doctor said the severed artery could not be repaired.

The lad gave Phoebe his mother's address and asked, "How long can I live?"

She replied, "Only as long as I keep my finger on this artery."

A long silence followed, then the lad said, "You can let it go."

"But I could not," she wrote in her memoirs in later years. "Not if my own life trembled in the balance. Hot tears rushed to my eyes, a surging sound to my ears, and a deathly coldness to my lips. The pang of obeying him was spared me," she added, "and for the first and last time during the trials that surrounded me for four years, I fainted away."

He could not see the fight or know that Fitz Lee's cavalry and Bragg's infantry were attacking Sheridan's flanks and driving the Federal column back. Nor did he know on the morning of the 12th of the hellish struggle at what became known as Spotsylvania's Bloody Angle.

At 7:00 P.M. two clergymen entered Stuart's room. He said, "I am resigned if it be God's will, but I would like to see my wife." Thirty-eight minutes later Stuart died. Four hours later Flora and the children arrived.

That night a courier brought a message to Lee at Spotsylvania. He opened it, put it down, and for several minutes could not speak. He finally turned to his staff and said, "We have very bad news. General Stuart has been mortally wounded." Then he added, "I can scarcely think of him without weeping."

MANEUVERING WITH GRANT

On the night of 20 May, Hancock led Grant's third attempt to interpose between Lee and Richmond by moving to the eastward of Spotsylvania. Grant had lost 37,000 men, but he still had twice as many as Lee. When Grant brought up the subject of the quite horrendous casualties with Meade, George G coolly replied: "Well, general, we can't do these little tricks without losses."

Confederate scouts detected Hancock's movement and at 11:00 A.M. on 21 May Lee moved with Ewell's command toward the Telegraph Road. On the morning of the 22nd Anderson followed with the I Corps and Hill with the III Corps. The next day they joined Lee on the south bank of the North Anna River. The timely and well-executed movement placed the Army of Northern Virginia directly across the roads and railways serving Richmond. Major General John Breckinridge, after defeating Sigel in

Right: A Union pontoon bridge (known as "the Telegraph Road Bridge") under construction near Jericho Mills. In this photograph the 50th New York Engineers (attached to Warren's V Corps) have laid a canvas-covered roadway on top of their pontoon bridge.

the Shenandoah, arrived with a fresh division; General Pickett, having added new brigades to his division after Gettysburg, arrived at Hanover Station with another 9,000 men and Major General Robert F. Hoke's brigade from Petersburg.

Grant wanted to destroy Hanover Junction because it connected Richmond to the Shenandoah Valley, but Lee's presence on the North Anna River forced him to fight for it.

By moving south of the river, Lee occupied the best defensive position in the entire area. He put Ewell's corps on the right, Longstreet's corps in the center, and Hill's corps on the left. Along the north bank Grant moved into position from left to right with Hancock's II Corps opposite Chesterfield Ford, Burnside's IX Corps at Jericho Mills, followed by Warren's V Corps and Wright VI Corps. Lee waited for Grant to make the first move.

At Jericho Mills Warren's corps crossed first, pushed Hill's corps back, and dug in while Wright's corps came across. On 24 May Lee abandoned the temporary works at Chesterfield Ford, fell back to a stronger position, and allowed Hancock's II Corps to cross. Burnside remained in the meantime on the north bank.

Lee concentrated his force in strong breastworks south of the river, leaving the Federals scattered about and in a position where they would have to cross two rivers to reinforce each other. Grant admitted that he had worked himself into a stalemate and on 26 May began sliding east toward Cold Harbor.

ALMOST LIKE MURDER

As soon as Grant withdrew from the North Anna, Lee on 27 May ordered the II Corps, now under Early instead of Ewell, to move to the vital rail junction at Old Cold Harbor. Anderson's I Corps and Hill's III

Corps followed by way of the Telegraph Road. On the morning of 31 May New Cold Harbor, located a mile west of Old Cold Harbor, became the focal point of another furious battle when Grant ordered Sheridan to seize the village's intersecting crossroads. Sheridan encountered Fitz Lee's cavalry, drove the Confederates from the crossroads, and returned to camp. Grant ordered him to go back to Cold Harbor and hold it all costs.

When Lee learned that Sheridan held the crossroads, he ordered Anderson to retake the position. At dawn 1 June, Anderson attacked with two brigades, but Sheridan's troopers were armed with formidable Spencer repeating carbines and repulsed the Confederate assault.

Grant and Lee both recognized that Cold Harbor's crossroads provided the most direct route to Richmond. At noon Grant hurried Wright's VI Corps and Smith's XVIII Corps to relieve Sheridan and assault the Confederate line protecting Telegraph Road. Smith's arrival at the wrong position delayed the attack until late afternoon. At 5:00 P.M. six Federal divisions assailed Anderson's I Corps and Hoke's division. Struck by a brief and furious Union assault, Anderson mended a small break in the Confederate line with a vicious counterattack and the day ended in another impasse and with heavy casualties on both sides.

Grant labeled Wright's and Smith's repulse an unfortunate missed opportunity and ordered Hancock's II Corps into the line on the left for an early morning attack. In order to be in position by morning, Hancock had to march his corps around the Union line during the night. The first elements

of Hancock's corps did not reach the position until 6:30 A.M., 2 June, and because of the intensely hot weather and the exhausted condition of the men, Grant postponed the attack until the following day. By wasting another day Grant lost the best opportunity in his 30-day campaign to decisively win a battle and open a way to Richmond.

Lee took advantage of Grant's lost day and concentrated his entire army around New Cold Harbor. By late afternoon Lee's force covered a seven-mile front with the southern flank anchored on Grapevine Bridge. His brigade commanders spent the day combining the natural defensive features of the landscape with interlocked and overlapping fields of fire. By nightfall, 2 June, Lee had his army arranged behind well-made breastworks and in a virtually impregnable position.

Grant, however, would not be denied. At 4:30 A.M. on 3 June the Army of the Potomac advanced with 40,000 men in double lines across a six-mile front. Federal soldiers expected their lives were to be wasted and pinned their names to their blouses so they could be later identified. Concealed Confederates let the enemy advance and patiently held their fire. In perfect unison and at short range, Lee's infantry poked their rifles through loopholes and crevices cut into logs, took deliberate aim, and fired. A dense sheet of artillery and rifle fire erupted down a six-mile front, and when the smoke cleared piles of Federal soldiers lay dead and wounded the full length of the battlefield. Then the butchery began in earnest. One Confederate sergeant described Federals as falling "like rows of blocks or bricks pushed over by striking against one another."

Hancock's corps attacked the Confederate right and was hurled back by bullets and artillery. Wright and Smith's corps struck Lee's center, Warren and Burnside attacked Lee's left, and in ten minutes the front lines of Grant's assault collapsed in ruin. Two days later, during a truce to bury the Cold Harbor dead, a Confederate officer approached a Northern soldier and said, "It seemed almost like murder to fire upon you."

Furious, Grant ordered another attack. First Hancock refused, then Smith and Wright. After issuing three orders to renew the attack and being rebuffed by his corps commanders, Grant ordered the construction of regular approaches for the purpose of taking the Confederate position by siege. When Washington asked why, Grant argued the importance of preventing Lee from sending troops to the Shenandoah, where Union General Hunter was advancing on Staunton. The Shenandoah operation was part of Grant's original plan to use Hunter's army to advance on Charlottesville and Lynchburg and destroy the railroads and canals that were used to deliver provisions to Richmond and the Confederate commissary.

The two-day battle for Cold Harbor cost Grant 10,000 of his 110,000 men, 7,000 of which fell in the first ten minutes. During the next nine days he would lose 4,000 more while falling back to the

Below: The Confederate line at Cold Harbor stretched from the Totopotomy Creek in the north to here, close to the Chickahominy River to the south. Ignoring maneuver, Meade and Grant elected to launch a frontal attack against Lee's well-defended center.

James and another 3,000 because of sickness. Within the same timeframe Lee lost about 1,700 of his 58,000 effectives. At Cold Harbor Grant's war of attrition suffered a step backwards and marked the beginning of a new kind of warfare that would be fought around a vast network of trenches extending from Richmond to Petersburg.

THE VMI CADETS AT NEW MARKET

An important segment of General Grant's strategy for defeating the South involved Major General Franz Sigel's Shenandoah campaign in May 1864. Stonewall Jackson had beaten Sigel in the Shenandoah in 1862 and beaten him again in 1863 at Second Bull Run. With Jackson gone, Grant believed that Sigel understood the Valley well enough not to repeat the same mistakes and so provided him with 6,500 troops to secure the area.

In early May, with Lee's forces stretched thin at Spotsylvania, Sigel began moving up the Valley. Major General John C. Breckinridge scraped together all the local militia, none of whom he completely trusted to stand and fight, and on the evening of 10 May sent a messenger to the Virginia Military Institute asking if a company of cadets could be spared. The young men were enjoying a leisurely day off in recognition of the first anniversary of the death

Below: *At Cold Harbor over 10,000 Union soldiers were killed, wounded, or missing, 7,000 of whom fell in the second bloody assault. This photograph was taken over ten months later in April 1865, when burial parties were sent to inter the dead.*

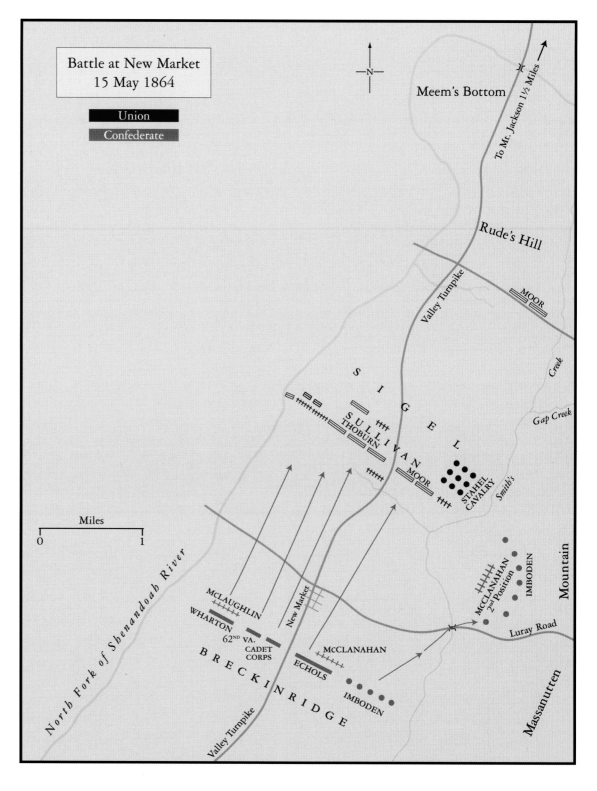

of the institute's foremost professor, Stonewall Jackson. They had just gone to bed when the rattling of drums called them to an emergency assembly on the parade ground. The cadets formed to learn that they were to march at dawn to Breckinridge's headquarters at Staunton, 32 miles to the north. For three years they had followed the war without ever becoming a part of it. "The air was rent with wild cheering," wrote cadet Corporal John S. Wise, "at the thought that our hour was at last come." In the morning 258 teenaged cadets picked up their knapsacks and Austrian-made rifles and began the hike to Staunton.

General Imboden's cavalry brigade of 1,500 horsemen had been pestering Sigel's deliberate advance and succeeded in slowing it down long enough for Breckinridge to collect about 5,000 men, including the cadets. On 14 May Sigel reached Mount Jackson, seven miles north of New Market, and would spend the day exchanging artillery fire with Imboden.

At daylight on 15 May Sigel marched south, crossed the north branch of the Shenandoah, halted a mile north of New Market, deployed his division and 28 cannon for battle, and waited for Breckinridge to take the initiative. Breckinridge deployed and waited for Sigel to strike. When nothing happened, Breckinridge studied Sigel's deployments and decided to go on the offensive.

After directing a furious cannonade at Sigel's lines, Breckinridge sent two infantry brigades, Imboden's dismounted cavalry, and the VMI cadets charging through New Market to the cheers of the townsfolk. Sigel immediately fell back to the eastern crest of a sloping hill. Seventeen Union guns opened and poured shells into the Confederate ranks. Following well behind the unsteady line came the cadets, nicknamed by the veterans "katydids." Sensing the battle had reached a critical stage Breckinridge turned to his adjutant and said, "Put the boys in, and God forgive me for the order."

Amid bursting shells and flashes of lightning from a drenching thunderstorm, the teenagers in their unsoiled gray uniforms filled a gap in the line and charged up the hill. Federal gunners unleashed double-shotted canister at the boys, but they refused to stop. A Federal officer remarked, "I think it would have been impossible to eject from six guns more

Left: *The German-born Major-General Franz Sigel (1824-1902) commanded the Union Army of the Shenandoah in early 1864, and soon after was removed from command for his lack of aggression.*

missiles than these boys faced in their wild charge." Losing 20 percent of their numbers, the cadets, now shoeless from crossing a muddy rain-soaked gully, reached their objective, a rail fence north of an orchard. They filled the Confederate gap, knelt behind the rails, raised their dripping rifles, and fired into the Federal line. The 26th Virginia came up on the left of the cadets, who had been stubbornly holding their sector against a fierce frontal fire.

Nobody could remember if an order had been given to charge, but the whole Confederate line, including the cadets, rose up and knocked aside two Federal regiments. The cadets kept going and captured the first Federal gun. Sigel tried to hold his men together but could not. Breckinridge tried to take Sigel's entire division, but Imboden could not get across swollen Smith's Creek in time to destroy the bridge to Mount Jackson.

During the Battle of New Market Sigel lost 831 and Breckinridge 577, including 10 VMI cadets

Above: *The headquarters of Major-General Benjamin Butler's Army of the James at Bermuda Hundred, Virginia, 1864. Following the failure of his attack in May 1864, his troops were virtually imprisoned in a loop of the James and Appomattox Rivers.*

killed and 47 wounded. After the battle Breckinridge pulled his command together and said, "Well done, Virginians." His eyes passed over the cadets and he said, "Well done, men." Then the cadets fell out. One wrote later, "He turned and rode away, taking with him the heart of every one of us."

Four days later General Grant relieved Sigel from command of the Valley and replaced him with Major General David Hunter, a man fixated on revenge.

CORKING BUTLER'S BOTTLE

On 9 April, when Grant took command of the Union army, his strategy to squeeze Virginia into submission included the capture of Richmond by the 39,000-man Army of the James. Grant may have achieved his goal had he not given command of the army to

former Massachusetts politician Major General Benjamin F. Butler, a conniver more adept at manipulating the law than managing military campaigns.

Grant's instructions were clear and simple. Butler was to take his army up the James River on transports and debark them at Bermuda Hundred, a peninsula in the river about 15 miles south of Richmond. Once ashore, Butler was to march ten miles west to the Richmond and Petersburg Railroad, tear up the track, cut the capital's communications, and attack Richmond to the north or Petersburg to the south.

On 5 March, when Butler began landing at Bermuda Hundred, there were only 2,000 Confederate troops at Petersburg. He wasted five days plodding across a narrow peninsula flanked on one side by the James River and the other side by the

Appomattox River. General Beauregard commanded the Petersburg area, but he was too sick to respond to the emergency and turned the command temporarily over to General Pickett.

On 7 March Pickett arrived at Swift Creek, Virginia, with 3,500 men and occupied a string of old earthworks. Butler gave Pickett more breathing space by stopping to construct a three-mile-long line of entrenchments across the peninsula's neck.

He advanced skirmishes to test the Confederate position, but Pickett's defenders repulsed the weak attempt. Another Federal detachment reached the railroad, destroyed tracks, cut telegraph lines, and having accomplished their mission returned to Bermuda Hundred.

Butler wasted another day before deciding on 9 May to move against the thin Confederate line protecting Petersburg. To reach Petersburg involved

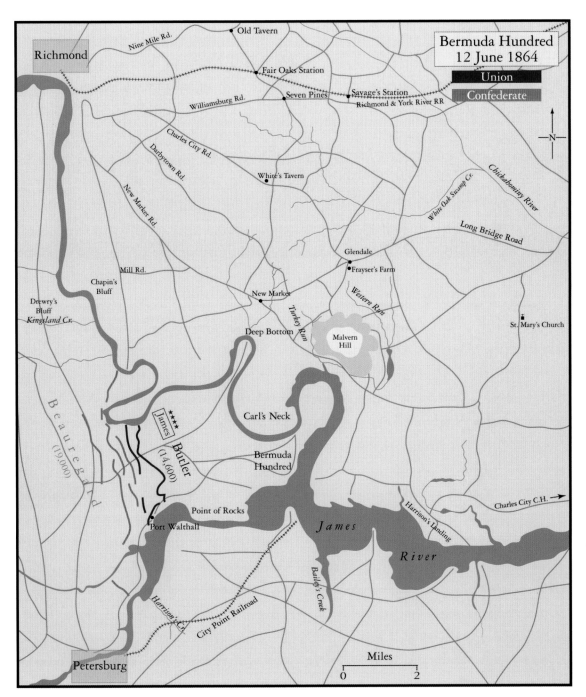

Left: The Bermuda Hundred campaign involved a spirited plan to cross the James then cut the rail link between Richmond and the rest of the South. Instead General Butler received ridicule for building defensive works across the peninsula that bottled-up his own army.

191

Above: *The area to the west of Petersburg down the Appomattox River was too swampy to permit large-scale military operations. Therefore Lee was confident that his position at Petersburg was unlikely to be outflanked.*

crossing Swift Creek, across which lay Bushrod Johnson's drastically diluted Confederate division and Pickett's men. Johnson initiated the engagement by sending one brigade on a reconnaissance in force. It butted against Butler's trench line and returned. Butler misinterpreted the Confederate withdrawal as weakness and ordered a strong demonstration during the afternoon, but the Federals were again stopped at Swift Creek. Butler's two corps commanders, William F. Smith and Quincy A. Gillmore, suggested moving around Johnson's position by erecting a pontoon bridge, but Butler vetoed a plan that might have resulted in the capture of Petersburg. Instead, Butler withdrew from Swift Creek and settled into his defensive works across Bermuda Neck.

During Butler's back and forth shuffling at Bermuda Hundred, Beauregard recovered from his illness and pooled together 20,000 Confederate troops. He hoped to find a way to lure Butler's 39,000-man army onto open ground. When scouts reported the possibility that Butler would move on Richmond, Beauregard sent seven brigades under General Hoke to Drewry's Bluff, where strong Confederate works overlooked the James River five miles south of the capital.

On 12 May Butler left two infantry divisions and his cavalry behind and started toward Richmond with 15,000 infantry from Gillmore's X and Smith's XVIII Corps.

On the morning of the 13th Butler drove Hoke's elements from the outer works into the main fortifications at Drewry's Bluff. Butler spent the next two days trying to decide whether to go on the offensive or retrench.

Beauregard made his mind up for him. Arriving at Drewry's Bluff on 14 May with more troops from Richmond, he organized them into three divisions, and went on the offensive. At 4:45 A.M. on 16 May, Major General Robert Ransom's four brigades struck Smith's right flank and routed the Federals. General Hoke, delayed by heavy fog, attacked Gillmore's lines. Major General William H.C. Whiting with two brigades never got into Butler's rear and missed an opportunity, partially hindered by a thunderstorm, to surround Butler's entire force.

The Army of the James fell back in confusion to their defensive position across Bermuda Neck, which was shaped like the spout of a bottle. Beauregard followed aggressively, threw defensive works opposite Butler's line, and "corked" Bermuda Hundred until Meade's army arrived in mid-June and liberated Butler from his own earthworks.

DEPREDATIONS IN THE VALLEY

Sixty-two-year-old Major General David Hunter hated slavery, hated Southerners even though he came from a prominent Virginia family, and hated anyone who disagreed with him. He grumbled about everything and everyone to the extent that Lincoln once warned him, "You are adopting the best possible way to ruin yourself." By putting Hunter in charge of the Department of West Virginia, Grant gave the general an opportunity to vent his venom on those he hated most, along with an opportunity to ruin himself.

On 26 May Grant ordered Hunter's 8,500-man force to move against the Virginia Central rail centers at Charlottesville and Lynchburg. Despite words of caution from Grant about safeguarding private property and avoiding "indiscriminate marauding," Hunter was already creating havoc in the Valley by burning homes, barns, and outbuildings. After Mosby's Ranger's struck one of his wagon trains and ran off with another, Hunter ordered the area where the raids occurred to be torched to the ground.

Hunter's march up the Shenandoah Valley took time because of his frequent stops to destroy property. On 8 June Brigadier General George Crook joined Hunter with another 10,000 men and commenced tearing up 50 miles of Virginia Central track while Hunter's firebrands torched the depot, factories, and mills at Staunton.

On 10 June elements of Hunter's army entered and plundered Lexington. They looted Washington College, ransacked and burned the Virginia Military Institute, and set fire to the home of Virginia governor John Letcher.

When Lee learned of the despoliation, he detached Jubal Early's II Corps at Cold Harbor and sent it to Lynchburg. He ordered Early to stop Hunter and then, by swift marches down the Valley, cross the Potomac and, if possible, menace Washington, D.C.

Below: Confederate trenches outside Petersburg, Virginia, late 1864. Lack of numbers made it necessary for the Confederates to dig extensive earthworks to make the most of the limited manpower they had left.

RICHMOND'S LIFELINES—THE RAILROADS

General Grant's spring offensive included an all-out attack on Virginia's railroads, and in particular those that nourished Richmond and Lee's Army of Northern Virginia. Four major railroads fed the capital: the Richmond, Fredericksburg & Potomac that connected with two links running north from Wilmington, North Carolina; the Virginia Central that stretched into and looped around the upper Shenandoah Valley; the Richmond & Danville that connected Petersburg with the Carolinas; and the South Side Railroad that connected with the Orange & Alexandria and the Virginia & Tennessee at Lynchburg. A number of small short lines like the Weldon Railroad also served Petersburg from North Carolina. Grant's spring campaign put part of the Richmond, Fredericksburg & Potomac out of business north of the capital, but the line still operated to the south. Butler was to have destroyed the Richmond and Petersburg spur that connected Wilmington to Richmond but failed. General Sigel was to have destroyed the Virginia Central at Staunton, but also failed. When Grant demoted Sigel, destroying the Virginia Central became General Hunter's first responsibility.

All the lines feeding Richmond were 4 foot 8 $\frac{1}{2}$-inch gauge track. Two of the major lines, the Richmond & Danville and the South Side were 5-foot gauge tracks, which meant that cars had to be unloaded at Petersburg before the freight could be forwarded to Richmond, causing enormous delays.

Every effort to destroy Virginia's railroads had been frustrated by Lee, but on 7 June, when Grant decided to move his army from Cold Harbor to the James, he detached 6,000 cavalry under General

Sheridan and ordered him to join forces with General Hunter and destroy the Virginia Central. While Hunter's troops marched at a leisurely pace towards Staunton and Sheridan towards Gordonsville, Wade Hampton moved west with 5,000 Confederate cavalry to intercept Sheridan.

On 11 June, Hampton caught up with Sheridan two miles northeast of Trevilian Station, a freight and water stop on the Virginia Central. Each committed one division to a dismounted fight that took place in dense woods and underbrush. Late in the morning Sheridan committed a second division that struck Hampton frontally and pushed him back. In stifling heat Hampton counterattacked and assailed Brigadier George Armstrong Custer's Michigan brigade from three sides. Custer escaped but with heavy losses. Both sides retired to recover from fatigue and cool down the horses. Early on 12 June Sheridan made another attempt at destroying the railroad, but Hampton counterattacked and nearly broke the entire Union line. The Virginia Central survived.

Above: *The bridge carrying the Richmond & Fredericksburg Railroad over the North Anna River north of Hanover Junction, Virginia, photographed after its destruction by Lee's retreating army.*

On 13 June, while Hunter was still ravaging Lexington, Early marched to Charlottesville and communicated with Breckinridge at Lynchburg. Breckinridge's force consisted of two understrength brigades, and Early urged him to hold the town until he arrived.

During the afternoon of 17 June the vanguard of Early's corps disembarked from trains at Lynchburg and filed into defensive positions. Hunter's force was already on the northern outskirts of town and pushing toward the rail junction.

Hunter stopped during the afternoon and wasted the day preparing for the next morning's assault. During the night the rest of Early's corps arrived, and by daylight, 18 June, the extended Confederate line bristled with another 8,000 rifled muskets. Hunter made several probes, each of which Early's corps quickly and bloodily repulsed. On the night of 18-19 June Hunter initiated one of the fastest retrograde movements of the war.

What Early observed as he moved down the Shenandoah Valley in pursuit of Hunter made him furious. "Houses had been burned, and helpless women and children left without shelter," he recalled. "The country had been stripped of provisions and many families left without a morsel to eat. Furniture and bedding had been cut to pieces, and old men and women and children robbed of all the clothing they had except that on their backs." Hunter must have sensed Early's anger. He fled beyond the Alleghenies of West Virginia and took his command completely out of the war. A month passed before Grant or Halleck knew where he went, leaving Early with complete control of the Valley and an uncontested road to the Potomac.

STALEMATE AT PETERSBURG

On 15 June, because General Butler had failed to turn Lee's flank at Petersburg and became bottled-up

Far left: *The South Carolinian cavalry commander Major-General Wade Hampton (1818-1902) commanded Lee's cavalry after the death of J.E.B. Stuart.*

Left: *The staunch abolitionist Major-General David Hunter (1803-88) campaigned in the Shenandoah valley during the summer of 1864, beginning the policy of wanton destruction which Sheridan would adopt with equal zeal.*

with his army at Bermuda Hundred, Grant directed General Hancock's II Corps and Burnside's IX Corps to capture Petersburg, but if the city could not be captured, to take a defensive position until more troops arrived. On the morning of 16 June Burnside's corps began deploying on Hancock's left. Beauregard responded by bringing Bushrod Johnson's Confederate division back from Bermuda Hundred and placing it opposite Burnside on the Confederate right. To avoid being squeezed between Butler's army and Meade's army, Beauregard then abandoned Bermuda Hundred and brought the balance of his force to Petersburg.

Lee became irritated when he learned that Beauregard had withdrawn from Bermuda Hundred and sent Pickett and Major General Charles W. Field's divisions to keep Butler penned up. Lee had not yet received conclusive evidence that Grant's

main force was attacking Petersburg south of the James and no longer menacing Richmond north of the James. Had Beauregard not withdrawn to Petersburg, Brigadier General Henry A. Wise, Virginia's former governor, would have had only 2,200 men – one understrength brigade and local militia – to man the trenches.

Grant had stolen a march on Lee and on the afternoon of 16 June ordered a general assault on the Petersburg works with Hancock's II Corps, Burnside's IX Corps, and William Smith's XVIII Corps. When Hancock and Burnside advanced, Beauregard faced three army corps with only 5,400 men. Smith helped Beauregard by dallying in the rear, his attack coming late and overcautiously. He captured a few outer redans but squandered an opportunity that might have shortened or rendered unnecessary Grant's ten-month siege of Petersburg.

Right: *In late June and early July General Jubal Early led his small 15,000-strong Army of the Valley in a raid across the Potomac which threatened Washington D.C. itself. Union reinforcements saved the Union capital from assault.*

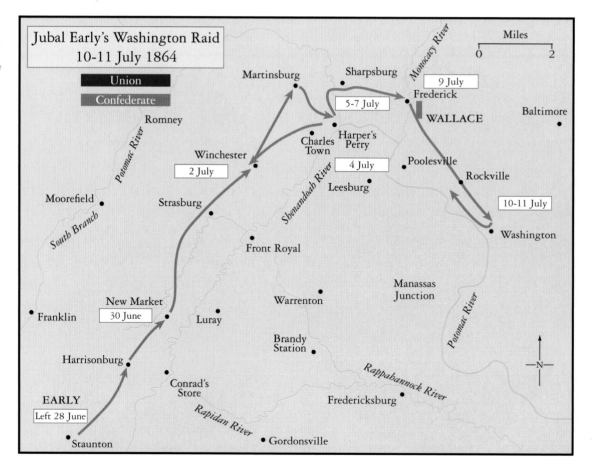

EARLY'S WASHINGTON RAID

Above: A house near Fort Stephens photographed soon after Early's army withdrew. The roof shows traces of the damage inflicted on the dwelling by Confederate fire.

On 23 June Jubal Early's 14,000 ill-clad and barefoot Confederates began marching down the Valley pike towards the Potomac. To improve communications he divided his command into two corps of two divisions each, the first corps under Rodes and the second corps under Breckinridge. Lee expected Early's raid to draw forces away from Grant, so Early set about the task of attracting Grant's attention. He sent one corps against Sigel's force at Harpers Ferry, which fled, and took the other corps across the Potomac and into Pennsylvania.

Passing through Hagerstown on 6 July, Confederate cavalry under Brigadier General John McCausland exacted a ransom of $20,000 in exchange for not burning the town. On 9 July Early added another $200,000 to the coffers by demanding the same terms at Frederick, Maryland.

Until 5 July Grant and Halleck had ignored Early's raid as nuisance activity, but on that day they began funneling 5,000 infantry to Major General Lew Wallace's Union brigades near Frederick. Four days later Early collided with Wallace's force at the Monocacy River and in a fierce fight that cost the Federals 1,880 men drove Wallace back to Baltimore. The fight, however, cost Early one crucial day.

Though exhausted from fighting in the torrid heat and dust, Early began the march to Washington and at noon 11 July had reached the capital's outskirts. Refugees fleeing ahead of Early's advance entered the Federal capital with horror stories of atrocities and greatly exaggerated accounts of the size of Early's army. Frenzied officials began searching hospitals and convalescent wards in order to press the walking wounded into defensive duties. Halleck's generals assembled about 10,000 troops to man the city's 900 cannon and mortars. Fifteen hundred dismounted cavalry arrived from the Army of the Potomac. Another 15,000 men were on the way from the VI Corps and the XIX Corps.

Observing that the Washington works were being reinforced, Early spent the afternoon of 11 July reconnoitering for soft spots and ordered an assault in the morning. During the evening he learned that Wright's VI Corps had arrived and postponed the attack. On the morning of the 12th he sent a body of skirmishers against Fort Stevens, which he thought to be feebly manned, but later decided he lacked the strength for a successful assault. Precious hours slipped away. Early had arrived one day late. One bedraggled Confederate soldier said, "We haven't taken Washington, but we scared Abe Lincoln like hell!"

Above and right: Gabions were a useful form of improvised field defense. When filled with earth these wicker cylinders could be used as an improvised breastwork, serving until more substantial defenses could be created. The gabion section (above) forms part of a reconstruction of the Petersburg defenses in 1864.

Warren's V Corps arrived on the morning of the 17th, took position on the Federal left, captured more redans in the outer works, but also failed to breach the Confederate line. Grant's assaults were costly in Federal dead and wounded, but Beauregard's small force could no longer hold the string of redans in the outer defenses and withdrew to the strong inner trenches.

Grant moved his base to City Point on the James River, and Lee moved the Army of Northern Virginia into what became a 40-mile-long line of trenches that extended from Cold Harbor, through the outskirts of Richmond, and to Hatcher's Run south of Petersburg. Lee left Early's corps in the Shenandoah Valley, pulled every other available regiment into the long defensive line, and eventually assembled 54,000 men. Grant's supplies reached him by way of the James at City Point, five miles below Bermuda Hundred. Lee's supplies came by way of four railroads connected to Petersburg.

Left: *City Point, Virginia became Grant's headquarters, and the main supply base of the Army of the Potomac during the Siege of Petersburg.*

Above: *A supposedly bomb-proof stable used to shelter the horses of the Army of the Potomac's cavalry close outside the Confederate lines at Petersburg during 1864.*

There had been six railroads serving Petersburg, but the first Federal assault cut the tracks serving the city from City Point and Norfolk. For the following ten months Grant would try to capture or destroy the other four railroads.

On 16 June, and for the next three days, Grant threw one corps after another at the Confederate entrenchments, only to be decisively repulsed each time with heavy loss. None of the attacks were well organized or effectively coordinated. One Union regiment lost 632 of 900 men engaged in 30 just minutes. The Union losses for the 15–19 June assaults totaled 11,386 men either killed, wounded, missing, or captured. After the heavy fighting ended on the night of 18 June, Grant abandoned his attempts to take Petersburg by frontal attacks.

Beauregard probably rendered the Confederacy his greatest service at Petersburg. He had skillfully shifted his thin ranks to the poorly coordinated points of Union attack at a time when Lee had been deceived by Grant's movement to new positions south of the James.

THE CRATER

On 19 June Lieutenant Colonel Henry Pleasants of the 48th Pennsylvania proposed digging a mineshaft from the Union line to the Confederate line and blowing up a salient occupied by 23-year-old Lieutenant Colonel William J. Pegram's battery. General Meade opposed the effort and Grant remained skeptical, but Colonel Pleasants said his Pennsylvania coalminers could dig it and blow a hole in the Confederate line large enough for the Union army to funnel through and capture Petersburg.

General Burnside needed to do something spectacular to compensate for his usual bungling and persuaded Grant to approve the scheme.

On 25 June Pleasants' coalminers began digging a shaft that began a hundred feet behind the Union lines, extended across a 350-foot battlefield, and passed beneath Confederate chevaux-de-frise and advanced rifle pits until it reached Pegram's redan. The 586-foot shaft was five feet high, 4.5 feet wide at the bottom and two feet at the top, and at the end had two lateral 38-foot galleries that ran like a crossed T directly underneath the Confederate

Below: On 30 July a mine was exploded beneath Pegram's Salient in the Confederate defenses outside Petersburg. Burnside ordered a massed assault, but the attackers found themselves trapped inside the huge crater created by the explosion, where they were cut down in their thousands. Burnside was duly relieved of his command after the débâcle.

Right and below right: *The canal at Dutch Gap was cut across a bend in the north bank of the James River in an attempt to outflank Confederate river defenses. The Confederates redeployed their batteries and so the engineering feat proved of little operational value. Freedmen were paid to do the work.*

trenches. After four weeks of digging the miners began packing 320 kegs (8,000 pounds) of black powder into the galleries, laid a fuse, and tamped dirt into part of the main tunnel to keep the explosion from blowing out the shaft. On 29 July Pleasants completed the technical side of the operation and turned the assault over to Burnside.

Confederates knew full well a mining operation was in progress because they could hear it from under their trench. Beauregard ordered countermining

SLAVE LABOR

During the conflict some 3,500,000 slaves contributed their labor to the war effort in the South. In 1863 the Confederate Congress authorized widespread impressments of slaves and provided compensation to their masters, often three times as much as the $11-a-month paid to privates in the infantry. Some slaves worked on plantations; others spent long months of hard labor building earthworks and trenches.

Slaves eventually dug 40 miles of trenches, rifle pits, redans, and bombproofs along the Petersburg-Richmond line. Ten to fifteen feet of earth could stop a heavy artillery shell. Two feet of earth would stop a bullet.

Connected trench lines usually consisted of two or three rows linked together by zigzags to the rear. Some lines led through covered ways protected by logs and earth, and some were wide enough to allow wagon trains to pass. Scattered along the line were forts with burrow-like dugouts that served as bomb-proofs. Each section of trench also contained traverses, which protected the rifleman from enfilading fire. Some trenches were so deep that the man doing the digging had to transfer a bucket of rocks and dirt to a second man stationed near the top. To repel assaults, slaves cut logs, sharpened the ends to a point, and embedded them in the ground facing the enemy. Setting the logs could not always be done during the day, and slaves risked their lives to do it at night.

They also cut and strung chevaux-de-frise and arranged it in endless rows 50 to 100 yards in front of the trenches. The apparatus consisted of 10 to 12-foot logs 8 to 10 inches in diameter with ends sharpened to a point and laid together in upright Xs along a common spine.

The Federals also used black labor but paid for it. During the summer of 1864 General Butler, after his entrapment on Bermuda Hundred, thought he might take Richmond by building a canal at Dutch Gap to bypass Trent Reach, where Confederate batteries and obstructions in the James kept Federal gunboats from reaching Richmond. Engineers, helped by black refugees, completed the 174-yard neck on 30 December. The canal only went into service in April 1865.

Above: *Fort Sedgwick, a major bastion in the Union lines outside Petersburg was constructed using paid slave labor. The redoubt would later be dubbed "Fort Hell" by the soldiers who defended it.*

operations but never found the shaft. He placed heavy mortars around the threatened area.

On 29 July, the day before the scheduled detonation, Meade ordered Burnside to substitute Brigadier General Edward Ferrero's division of black troops, which had been trained for the assault, with a division of white troops. Instead of choosing his best division, Burnside allowed his commanders to draw straws. Brigadier General James H. Ledlie, the most incompetent of the trio, drew the short straw and was assigned to lead the attack.

At 3:30 A.M. on 30 July the Pennsylvanians lit the fuse, but nothing happened. Miners crawled into the shaft, spliced the fuse at the break, and lit it

Left: Gracie's Salient, a protruding section of the Confederate lines outside Petersburg close to the Union stronghold of Fort Steadman. It was named after Colonel Albert Gracie, the commander of an Alabama brigade.

Below: A bomb-proof field kitchen and store tents, Petersburg, Virginia, 1864.

Right: *A 145-foot high union signal tower located near Peebles Farm near Petersburg, 1865. It gave Grant's men a clear view of Petersburg and its approaches.*

again. At 4:45, in a horrible pre-echo of an event 53 years later at the Messines Ridge, four tons of powder lifted Pegram's salient and nine companies of the 19th and 22nd South Carolina into the air. The blast created a crater in the Confederate line 170 feet long, from 60 to 80 feet wide, and 30 feet deep. Surviving Confederates on both sides of the crater fled in fear.

Ledlie remained in a bombproof drinking liquor while his division charged. He did not see them plunge into the crater instead of going around it. When Burnside observed that Ledlie's men were making no progress, he sent in the other two divisions. Confederates led by Major General William Mahone regrouped and counterattacked. Artillery and mortars hammered the Federal troops thrashing about in the bottom of the crater. By 8:00 Mahone's division had sealed the breach in the Confederate line. Burnside then decided to throw in Ferrero's black division, but it was too late. There were reports that when the blacks rushed the crater, Mahone's men seemed to take extra pleasure in shooting them, even after they surrendered.

The unique opportunity to breach the Confederate line ended in catastrophe. Burnside lost 3,798 men in what Grant described as a "stupendous failure." He later added, "Such opportunity for carrying fortifications I have never seen, and do not expect again to have."

FLANKING MINUET AT PEEBLE'S FARM

On 30 September, while Ben Butler's Army of the James made a move toward Richmond, Meade sent part of the Army of the Potomac to the far right of Lee's lines southwest of Petersburg in an effort to penetrate the Confederate flank. On the one hand, Grant suspected that Lee had already weakened his southern flank by rushing reinforcements to oppose Butler. On the other hand, Grant believed that a timely attack on Lee's flank might prevent him from doing so. Regardless of what Lee did, Grant deduced that either Butler or Meade would benefit by an attack on Lee's right flank.

In the morning Warren moved two divisions of the V corps toward Poplar Springs Church, followed by two divisions of Major General John G. Parke's IX Corps and Gregg's cavalry on the left. In the assault across Peeble's farm, Warren's leading division under Brigadier General Charles Griffin captured a Confederate redan, the supporting line of trenches, and about 100 prisoners. Brigadier General Robert B. Potter's division from Parke's corps, while moving around Griffin's left, collided with two Confederate infantry divisions (Wilcox and Heth's) that were advancing to recapture the lost redan. Potter expected to be supported by Griffin, but when no supports arrived, Potter attempted to go on the defensive. Before he could organize his lines, Wilcox and Heth's infantry attacked and drove the Federals back. Griffin finally arrived from the other side of Peeble's farm and with Potter checked the Confederates. Both Federal divisions disengaged but held their positions on Peeble's farm.

During 1 October Warren and Parke consolidated their gains, reinforced Peeble's farm, and started entrenchments along the Squirrel Level Road. This secured the Federal left flank and permanently gained ground for Grant.

On 2 October Heth and Wilcox made one more effort to oust the Federals but were repulsed. At a cost of 3,000 casualties, the Federals succeeded in extending their entrenchments and connecting them to works at Hatcher's Run and Globe Tavern, but Lee's lower flank still remained secure. The clash at Peeble's farm typified one of many efforts by Grant to penetrate the Petersburg entrenchments, capture the railroads feeding into the city, and drive Lee's army out of the trenches.

SHERIDAN VERSUS EARLY

Having resigned himself to months of siege at Petersburg, Grant detached Major General Philip Sheridan from the Army of the Potomac and on 6 August put him in charge of the Middle Military Division in the Shenandoah. Grant wanted Early's army eliminated, and Sheridan had demonstrated that he could function as an infantry commander as well as a cavalry commander. Sheridan spent six weeks reorganizing his forces and maneuvering

Above: Sheridan's Army of the Shenandoah moving south through the valley in pursuit of Early. Sheridan's men destroyed everything of worth to the Confederates as they advanced.

Below: A courier reporting to Sheridan during his Valley campaign of 1864.

northeast of Winchester to strike Early's force from the Martinsburg Pike while 33,600 infantry crossed directly east of Winchester. Early had only 11,150 infantry and artillery and about 1,000 cavalry to meet the two-pronged attack. Had Sheridan's infantry moved in unison and with urgency, Early's forces would have been separated and surrounded.

They did not and Early regrouped, charged General Emory's XIX Corps, routed it, and rolled back Wright's VI Corps. Sheridan counterattacked with a reserve division and saved the army from further damage. At 3:00 P.M., as the Confederate attack against Emory and Wright petered out, George Crook's VIII Corps and two Union cavalry divisions struck Early's left flank. The small Confederate force could not stand against the Union onslaught and as darkness fell retired to an old trench-line prepared at Fishers Hill, 21 miles south of Winchester and a mile beyond Strasburg.

In the Third Battle of Winchester, Sheridan lost 5,018 killed, wounded, and missing: Early lost 3,921. But Early also lost Robert Rodes, one of the finest division commanders in the Confederate army, and Fitz Lee, who suffered a bullet wound in his thigh. Neither man could be adequately replaced.

Early decided to make a stand at Fishers Hill, a high and steep bluff flanked by Massanutten Mountain on the east and Little North Mountain on the west. It was also the only fortified position from which Early had any prospects of preventing Sheridan's army from overrunning the upper Shenandoah. If adequately manned, the position was virtually impregnable, but Early had only 9,000 troops and not enough men to effectively protect his flanks. He could find no practical use for his cavalry, so he dismounted General Lomax's demoralized troopers and put them on the vulnerable left where Fishers Hill sloped into a valley before rising onto

against Early before launching a campaign that would continue into 1865.

On 16 September Sheridan learned from Rebecca West, a Quaker schoolteacher and Union spy in Winchester, that Early had returned Kershaw's division to Longstreet. Early had misinterpreted Sheridan's inactivity as timidity and weakened his force by detaching Kershaw and leaving his other elements somewhat scattered. On 19 September Sheridan sent 6,400 cavalry across Opequon Creek

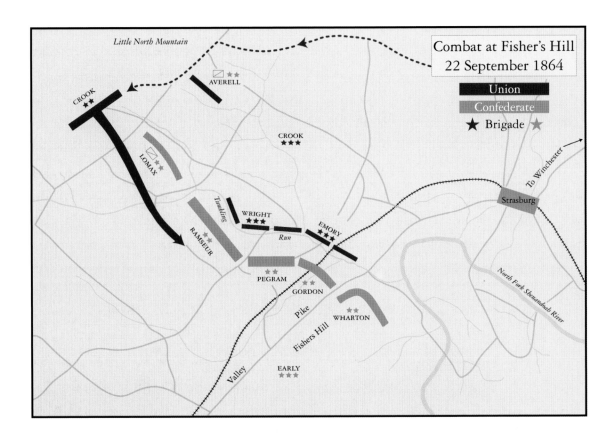

Little North Mountain. Though small in number, Early's men felt secure and apparently welcomed another Federal attack.

Late on the 20th Sheridan began assembling his command a few miles from Fishers Hill. He had been there before and experienced the difficulties of a frontal attack, but this time he had enough men to do whatever he wanted. Crook suggested using his corps in a flank attack while Wright and Emory assaulted Early's front. Sheridan approved the plan, and as a secondary measure sent two divisions of Major General Alfred T.A. Torbert's cavalry around Fishers Hill to block Early's escape route.

From the heights, Early's infantry watched for two days as Wright and Emory maneuvered. Without scouts patrolling the lower regions, nobody observed Crook's concealed movement around Little North Mountain that put part of the VIII Corps on the Confederate flank and rear. At 4:00 P.M., 22 September, Crook's two divisions charged down the

mountain's boulder-strewn slopes and smashed into Lomax's left flank. The startled dismounted cavalry fled into Major General Stephen D. Ramseur's infantry lines. Ramseur tried to turn his flank to parry Crook's attack, only to be struck in front by Wright and Emory's corps storming up the hillside. Though his lines had been broken on the front, flank, and rear, Early rallied the men until dark and barely escaped total destruction by retreating into the Blue Ridge Mountains with about 8,000 men.

Sheridan believed Early had been permanently neutralized and on 6 October began withdrawing his force down the Valley. On the 16th he departed for a Washington conference but left a strong force at Cedar Creek near Middletown. Following victory at Fishers Hill, his cavalry laid the upper Valley to waste. Barns burned from Staunton to Strasburg in what became known as "Red October." Such atrocities put fight back into stubborn warriors like Jubal Early. (Though Confederates in the Virginia conflict

Above: The Union victory at the Battle at Fisher's Hill was won as a result of a flanking march by Crook's Corps, which fell upon Early's flanks. Outmaneuvered, Early's army broke and ran.

at this time were not without stain. Following a failed attempt by Union Brigadier-General Burbridge to destroy the saltworks at Saltville, Smyth County down in the south-west on October 2, Confederate soldiers were said to have murdered a number of wounded and captured black soldiers.)

After reorganizing in the Blue Ridge, Early obtained reinforcements, bringing his corps back to 18,410 effectives. He wanted to find a way to strike back at the 31,000 Federals who had defeated him at Fishers Hill and torched the Valley.

General Gordon scouted the Federal position with Major Jedediah Hotchkiss and devised a plan of attack that appealed to Early's aggressive nature. Being outnumbered nearly two to one seemed not to bother Early in the least.

On the night of 18–19 October, Ramseur, Pegram, and Gordon's divisions moved into position to strike the rear of Crook's corps. Kershaw and Wharton division's moved to the left to support the attack. Before daybreak all five divisions charged through thick fog, struck the sleeping Federal

Right: *Confederate artillery artefacts. As in other branches, much of the equipment was captured, such as the Model 1851 Colt Navy revolver and model 1833 Union Foot Artillery short sword pictured. Artefacts include trouswrs, forage caps, and short-style jackets. The shells are, from left to right, 6 lb spherical solid shot, 20 lb Parrott shells, and a 50 lb shell produced by the Confederate ordnance factory at Dahlgren, Virginia.*

camps, and sent two of Sheridan's three corps reeling in confusion across the barren fields around Middletown.

General Wright, in command during Sheridan's absence, held the VI Corps together and with Federal cavalry began building pockets of resistance. By 10:00 A.M. he had reformed enough units to stop the Confederate onslaught. Early's force invited its own destruction by not pressing the attack, but the half-starved grayclads could not resist tarrying in deserted Federal camps to eat and rest.

Sheridan, having returned to Winchester, heard the distant rumble of artillery emanating from the direction of Middletown. Sensing trouble, he jumped on his horse, galloped 14 miles, and at 10:30 found Wright forming a strong defensive position north of the town.

Sheridan told Wright that he intended to take the offensive and rode along the front inspiring his men to prepare for launching a counterattack. Early was also trying to form a line, expecting to follow up his victory with a thorough thrashing of Sheridan's

forces, but his men seemed to be content with their morning's work and the majority had lost most of their fighting zeal.

At 4:00 P.M. Sheridan advanced his lines, breached Early's left, and sent the Confederates reeling back to Fishers Hill with heavy losses. Early withdrew to New Market and spent the rest of the year in virtual idleness. He was deeply perplexed by the defeat. Though Sheridan's force lost 5,665 men and the South only 2,910, the Federal assault had erupted so suddenly that Early lost most of his artillery, all his ammunition wagons, and much of his baggage and forage.

On 8 November Lincoln won reelection, which guaranteed that the war would continue until either the South surrendered or the people starved. The Union army enjoyed the advantage of manpower, weaponry, warm clothing, plenty of food, success on every front, and complete control of the seas. The Confederate soldier had only cold and hunger, siege life in the trenches, undernourishment, and no winter clothing. Yet one Southern soldier wrote home

that his buddies "cooked, ate and slept, played cards, checkers, cribbage and chess, laughed, talked, jested, and joked . . . and were not altogether unhappy."

Such cheerfulness could not last. On the last Thursday of November, which Lincoln proclaimed Thanksgiving Day, the Federal army opposite Petersburg numbered 120,000 men. Lee's Army of Northern Virginia numbered 57,000.

In recognition of the new Union holiday, Lee agreed to a day of ceasefire. Yankees and Rebels came out of their trenches and shook hands with each other. As evening fell Confederates returned to their earthworks with the full conviction that the war could not last much longer.

Yet despite the inequality of the armies, there was still more blood to be spilt.

TIMELINE: 1864

18 January: All white males between 18 and 45 are conscripted into the Confederate army.

17 February: The Confederate Congress suspends the writ of habeas corpus.

28 February-3 March: Kilpatrick-Dahlgren raid on Richmond to free Union prisoners.

9 March: Ulysses S. Grant is named lieutenant general and general-in-chief of the Union army.

8 April: The U.S. Senate passes the Thirteenth Amendment, which abolishes slavery in the United States.

9 April: General Grant issues marching orders for General Sigel to capture the Shenandoah Valley, General Butler to capture Richmond, and General Meade to advance against Lee.

27 April: General Grant's spring offensive in Virginia is announced.

4-7 May: The Battle of the Wilderness.

5 May: General Butler lands 39,000 Federal troops at Bermuda Hundred, Virginia.

7-19 May: Spotsylvania Court House Campaign.

12 May: General Stuart dies of mortal wounds received 11 May at Yellow Tavern, Virginia.

15 May: Union General Sigel is defeated at the Battle of New Market.

16 May: Battle of Drewry's Bluff (Bermuda Hundred).

23-26 May: Battle of North Anna River.

1-3 June: Battle of Cold Harbor.

10 June: The Confederate Congress extends the limits of conscription age to men between 17 and 50.

11 June: Union General David Hunter burns the Virginia Military Institute.

15 June: The 10-month-long Petersburg Campaign begins.

17-18 June: General Jubal Early's Washington Raid begins with the repulse of Union General David Hunter at Lynchburg, Virginia.

23 June-12 July: General Early's Washington Raid.

30 July: The Federal repulse following the mine assault at Petersburg.

30-31 July: General Early burns Chambersburg, Pennsylvania.

7 August: An 8-month Shenandoah Valley campaign begins between General Early and Union General Sheridan.

22 August: Early's defeat during the Battle of Fishers Hill.

2 September: Lee suggests that white laborers in the army be replaced by black slaves to free greater numbers of whites for service in the army.

16 September: Generals Hampton and Rosser seize 2,500 head of Federal cattle from Union yards at Coggins' Point, Virginia.

30 September-2 October: Battle of Peeble's Farm.

8 November: President Lincoln defeats George B. McClellan in the Union election for president.

Below: *A Confederate leather cartridge box and carrying strap, worn by a soldier to hold his issue of ammunition for his rifled-musket. It could hold approximately 40 cartridges.*

1865
DIED OF A THEORY

Above inset: *Forage cap of Captain G. Gaston Otey, Co. A, 13th Battalion, Virginia.*

Far right: *Grand review of the armies of Grant and Sherman at Washington, on 23 and 24 May 1865; looking up Pennsylvania Avenue from the Treasury Buildings. To triumph in a civil war is a terrible thing; nevertheless, the North was triumphant and acted accordingly.*

Right: *A Confederate artilleryman's haversack (top). a wooden canteen, and an officer's haversack. Most of these were empty of provisions at the beginning of 1865.*

As the New Year approached, General Grant recalled Wright's VI Corps from the lower Shenandoah Valley. General Lee responded by removing most of Early's brigades from the upper Valley and moving them into Richmond's defenses. "From this time forward," Grant reported, "the operations in front of Petersburg and Richmond, until the spring campaign of 1865, [will be] confined to the defense

"Go to your homes and resume your occupations. Obey the laws and become as good citizens as you were soldiers."

GENERAL LEE'S PARTING WORDS TO THE ARMY OF NORTHERN VIRGINIA AT APPOMATTOX COURTHOUSE, 9 APRIL 1865.

and extension of our lines and to offensive movements for crippling the enemy's lines of communication." It still rankled Grant that Sheridan's 56,000-man army had not been able to put the Virginia Central Railroad out of action at Staunton, Charlottesville, and Gordonsville, and that the Virginia & Tennessee Railroad still operated unimpeded out of Lynchburg.

For the Confederate soldier, however, the war had dismally changed for the worse. The life-sustaining food boxes from home stopped, not because the railroads ceased to operate but because there was no food. When news came on New Year's Day that the women of Richmond were preparing a grand banquet of beef, venison, and pork for the men in the trenches, Lee's army put their skimpy rations aside and waited all day for the promised meal. Much of it did not arrive until the following morning. When the culinary labors of Richmond's women reached the trenches, each man received two small slices of bread with a thin piece of ham. They washed the sandwich down with a cup of icy water from the bucket in the rear of the earthworks. Nobody whined about the frugal repast. One salty corporal lit his

Right: *13-inch "Dictator"
mortar at Petersburg. Front and
right is Brigadier-General H.J.
Hunt, Chief of the Artillery, an
old friend of Confederate General
Braxton Bragg. Bragg had
written to Hunt three years
earlier: "We have been united in
our views on almost all subjects,
public and private . . . here we
are, face to face, with arms in
our hands . . . How strange."*

pipe and said, "God bless our noble women. It was all they could do; it was all they had."

During the first two months of 1865, fighting was sporadic and rare at Petersburg, but the fire of Grant's artillery and mortar batteries never stopped. Dr. Henry Alexander White recalled those months, writing: "Winter poured down its snows and its sleet upon Lee's shelterless men in the trenches. Some of them burrowed into the earth. Most of them shivered over the feeble fires kept burning along the lines. Scanty and thin were the garments of these heroes. Most of them were clad in mere rags. Gaunt famine oppressed them every hour." But, he added, "The frozen fingers of Lee's army of sharpshooters clutched the musket barrel with an aim so steady that Grant's men scarcely ever lifted their heads above their bomb proofs."

It became a well-established fact that while the half-starved, ragged Confederate infantrymen enjoyed none of the comforts of the Union soldier, most kept their weapon cleaned and oiled, always loaded, and knew how to use it.

GENERAL-IN-CHIEF OF THE ARMIES

President Davis did not relinquish control willingly. He never agreed with the five men he appointed as secretary of war, and he became critical of the men he chose to lead the Confederate forces. The only army that functioned with Davis' full support was Lee's Army of Northern Virginia. (There are identifiable, biographical reasons for Davis' reluctance to trust others in military strategy: Davis the West Point graduate, Indian fighter, wounded hero of the Mexican war, and perhaps more significantly, son of a daring infantry officer of the Revolutionary War and younger brother of three heroes of the War of 1812.) On 16 January the Confederate Senate,

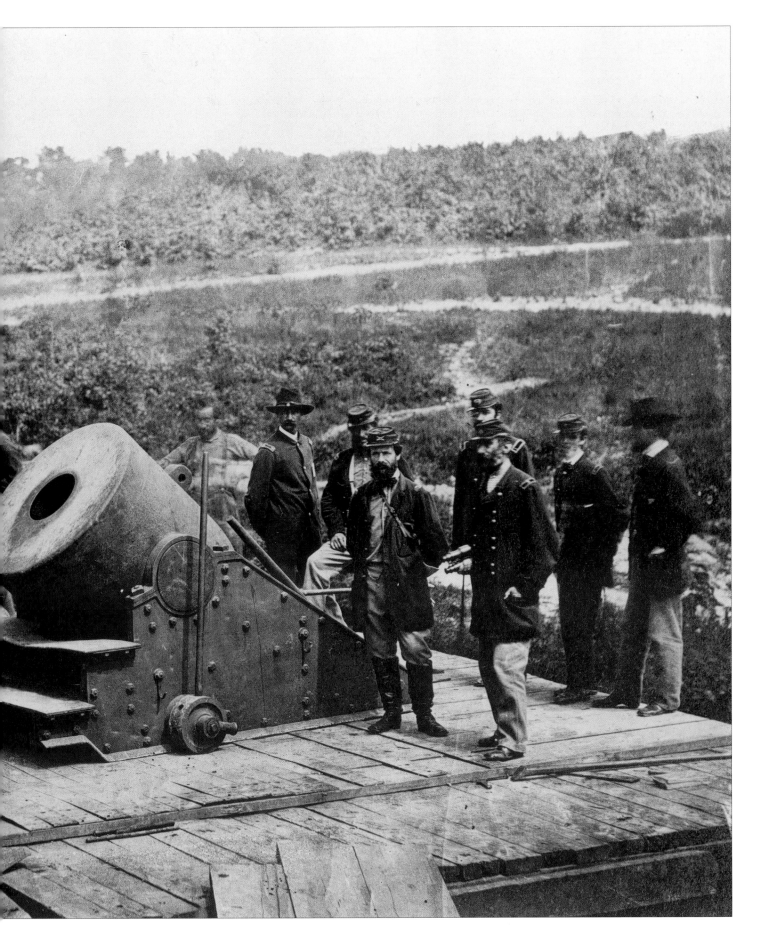

back in command of the Army of Tennessee. He also concurred with the Confederate Congress that James Seddon should be removed as secretary of war and replaced by Major General John C. Breckinridge, an experienced commander and former vice president of the United States. Davis complied with all the se requests and more and purchased a small amount of

Above: *The remains of Fort Sedgwick, or Fort Hell. Fifteen Confederates had been killed here on November 5 1864, and 35 wounded, in the most serious attack; which seems a tiny number in view of the damage. But that was just one day.*

having grown weary of Davis' control of military matters, passed a resolution urging the president to appoint Lee as general-in-chief. Davis was already becoming unpopular with the public and needed something to revitalize his image. Though still unenthusiastic about putting anyone in charge of the military other than himself, Davis nonetheless mustered enough equanimity to convince Lee that he was sincere in offering the appointment. On 19 January Lee accepted the post, but it took another 22 days for Congress to approve it. Lee's promotion to general-in-chief came three years too late.

Lee initiated many changes. He asked the president to pardon all deserters who reported back to their commands within 30 days. He put General Joseph Johnston, another casualty of Davis' disdain, political capital, but the changes came too late to compensate for years of blunders, or to help Lee.

The president also attempted to open peace talks with Lincoln's administration, an effort strongly supported by Lee. Davis appointed a committee of three led by Vice President Alexander Stephens, with whom he also differed on matters of policy. Lincoln considered the meeting important and on 3 February attended it himself. Stephens wanted an armistice first with discussions regarding reunion postponed. Lincoln insisted upon recognition of Federal authority as the first step toward peace. He also wanted Stephens to understand that the Federal government was in the process of obtaining ratification of the

Left: *The Stars and Stripes flies beside this Petersburg redoubt. Notwithstanding the obvious psychological importance of heavy artillery, something approaching 90% of wounds inflicted during the War came from bullets, not shell and shot.*

13th Amendment abolishing slavery. Davis still demanded independence, so the three-hour peace conference ended without positive results.

On 21 February Lee became involved when General Longstreet and Major General Edward O.C. Ord met under a flag of truce and decided that perhaps the generals could stop fighting by mutual agreement and let the politicians resolve their differences by negotiation. Lee obtained Davis' approval and communicated with Grant, suggesting that they meet to discuss arrangements for peace. Grant forwarded the communication to Stanton asking for

Right: A justifiably famous and often-reproduced picture of Union troops outside Petersburg. Nothing posed here, no burnished buttons and swords, just wariness and weariness. Each of these men probably knew that the War was won: survival then must have come to the fore in everyone's thinking.

direction. Lincoln replied to Grant through Stanton, writing: "You are not to decide, discuss, or confer upon any political question. Such questions the President holds in his own hands . . . Meantime you are to press to the utmost your military advantages." The war would be fought to a military conclusion.

HATCHER'S RUN: BEGINNING OF THE END

On 27 October 1864 Grant made an unsuccessful incursion at Hatcher's Run but was repulsed. Since then, the Federals made no determined effort to breach the Petersburg defenses for three months, and

the dreariness of trench warfare dominated the landscape between the two armies.

The area around Hatcher's Run appealed to Grant. The stream crossed under the Boydton Plank Road, which Lee used to bring wagon trains into Petersburg. At Hatcher's Run the Confederate entrenchments were irregular and with undefended gaps. Grant felt that if he could extend the Federal line south and west, he could shut down the Boydton Road and the South Side Railroad and drive the Army of Northern Virginia out of the trenches.

On 5 February Grant committed 35,000 troops to the operation. In sleet and ice Brigadier General Henry E. Davies' 2nd Cavalry Division spearheaded the march, followed by Major General Andrew A. Humphreys' II Corps and Warren's V Corps. The troopers passed through Reams' Station south of Hatcher's Run, occupied Dinwiddie Court House, destroyed a few Confederate wagon trains moving along Boydton Plank Road, capturing a handful of prisoners. Davies returned with his division to report no Confederate infantry south of Hatcher's Run.

Below: A group of freedmen photographed in Richmond in 1865. If the War had continued, these men might have fought in the C.S.A. in exchange for their freedom, had Lee's suggestion been taken up. From a distance in time, the suggestion looks like an extraordinary piece of casuistry.

Humphreys' corps moved promptly toward Hatcher's Run where the Vaughn Road crossed the stream and deployed in front of freshly dug Confederate trenches. Warren moved the V Corps two miles farther to the south and paused at Monk's Neck. Both corps contained inexperienced and fatigued draftees and bounty men unaccustomed to winter operations. Confederate elements of A.P. Hill and John B. Gordon's corps responded swiftly and tried a few tentative sorties against the Federal position. Late in the afternoon Mahone's division launched a counterattack against Humphreys' position but was repulsed by numbers.

On 6 February Warren sent a reconnaissance in force toward Dabney's Mills to test the possibility of working around or through the Confederate far right flank. As a countermeasure, Gordon sent John Pegram's veteran division to plug gaps. Instead of plugging gaps, Pegram slashed into the Federal line and lost his life in a fruitless effort, falling at the head of the division. (The Virginian aristocrat Pegram was admired for his piety, gallantry, and comportment; but his tactical record was abysmal. When compared with the actions of Confederate leaders such as Stonewall Jackson, James Longstreet, and Jeb Stuart, his failures hint that Lee was not untainted by the desire to promote on social rather than military grounds, despite his reputation for ridding his army of mediocre commanders.)

Pegram's fierce attack produced a temporary benefit. Humphreys and Warren abandoned the Boydton Plank Road, moved back to Vaughn Road, and fortified the area where the road crossed Hatcher's Run.

The effort cost Grant more than 2,300 casualties, but it forced Lee to extend his already perilously thin lines and put Grant in an excellent position to launch his spring offensive.

A DESPERATE STRATEGY

Lee warned Secretary of War Breckinridge that Grant's shift of forces to the south foreshadowed ominous difficulties as spring approached. He reminded Breckinridge that men were starving and deserting, and unless something could be done immediately to reinforce and feed the army, "you must not be surprised if calamity befalls us."

The situation at Hatcher's Run and the urgent need to bolster Lee's army with more recruits revived the question of employing slaves as soldiers. While the Confederate Congress held secret sessions on the issue, Lee on 18 February added his comments by writing, "I think the measure not only expedient, but necessary. In my opinion, the Negroes under proper circumstances will make efficient soldiers [and] I think those who are employed should be freed. It would neither be just nor wise, in my opinion, to require them to serve as slaves." Four weeks passed before President Davis signed a bill containing Lee's advice. Northern newspapers warned the public to expect a mass influx of Southern blacks attempting to escape military service. The South never had time to implement the legislation, and no slave was ever inducted into the Confederate army.

The enemy's actions at Hatcher's Run, though temporarily in abeyance, also induced Lee to consider his broader options as general-in-chief. General William T. Sherman's Union army had burned a swath across Georgia and was driving General Johnston's Army of the Tennessee back to Charlotte, North Carolina. General Early still had a small command in the Shenandoah. Pooling all the Confederate forces together seemed to Lee to be the likeliest way to survive. On 19 February he wrote Breckinridge, "It is necessary to bring out all our strength, and, I fear, to unite our armies, as separately they do not

Above: Confederate prisoner Lieutenant Washington, his slave, and Captain Custer: another photo opposrtunity for the publicity-hungry young cavalryman.

seem to be able to make head[way] against the enemy. Provisions must be accumulated in Virginia, and every man in the States must be brought off. I fear it may be necessary to abandon all our cities, and preparations must be made for this contingency." Two days later Lee made it clear that abandoning cities included Richmond.

Lee's warnings had barely registered in Richmond when on 2 March Union General George Custer's cavalry of 4,840 troopers struck Early's diminished command at Waynesboro, Virginia. Custer captured 1,600 ragged Confederates, all their guns, and all their supplies. Only Early, two of his generals, and 20 others escaped. Custer's destruction of Early's command brought Lee to Richmond for a

conference with Davis. It was decided that Lee should march his army to Danville, join it together with General Johnston's 18,000-man army, and give battle in North Carolina against General Sherman's 90,000-man army before Grant could intercede with reinforcements from the Army of the Potomac. Before agreeing to the plan, Davis wanted assurance that his government would be able to escape from Richmond. Lee proposed to check Grant's efforts to extend the Union left toward the South Side Railroad, which connected Petersburg with the Richmond & Danville. This required a desperate assault on Union fortifications near Grant's line by the Appomattox River and almost directly in front of the Crater.

Left: *Custer wears the insignia of a Major-General, as from April 15, 1865. Custer had been in action since 1st Manassas (1st Bull Run) and served with distinction throughout the War.*

Davis approved the plan, hoping that just one more offensive effort might perhaps retard Grant's spring campaign.

FIASCO AT FORT STEDMAN

On 25 March Lee placed the remnant of the II Corps, elements from the other two corps, and a division of cavalry under the command of General Gordon. The force numbered slightly less than half of Lee's effectives. Lee allowed Gordon to decide where to launch the assault and Gordon picked Fort Stedman, mainly for the simple reason that it was only 150 yards from the Confederate lines. Gordon believed that if the Union works could be penetrated and opened at Stedman, a follow-up attack on City Point would break Union communications, force Grant to shorten his lines, and enable some of Lee's troops to shift into North Carolina to help Johnston's beleaguered army.

At 4:00 A.M., 25 March, Gordon made a fine beginning. The Confederates seized Fort Stedman, three supporting batteries, and the adjacent field-works at a time when Grant and Meade happened to be elsewhere. Gordon expected to find a number of supporting works in the rear of the fort. He planned

to occupy and use them to widen the gap and enfilade the Federal rear, but none were there. This created consternation because the gap was not wide enough to enable the cavalry to pass unmolested, and Fort Stedman, without support on the flanks, could not indefinitely withstand counterattacks. Instead of returning to the safety of the Confederate works, Gordon tried to capture Federal forts on his right and left but failed. At daylight those same forts opened and raked Gordon's position.

At 7:30 two Federal infantry divisions supported by artillery began converging on Fort Stedman. Thirty minutes later Lee ordered a withdrawal.

Hundreds of Gordon's men were caught in the open and chose to surrender rather than step into a murderous crossfire. Meade arrived on the field and sent more units against the Confederate position. Gordon ordered a general retreat and the remainder of his force dashed across a "no man's land" and into the Confederate line.

Lee never had time to count his losses, but that morning the toll was between 4,000 and 5,000 veterans. The bloody fiasco on Fort Stedman marked Lee's last offensive of the war, and on the following day he advised President Davis that Richmond would have to be evacuated.

Below: April 5, 1865, Petersburg; just four days to the surrender at Appomattox Courthouse.

A. P. Hill held the line in front of Grant's force, and on 29 March Lee transferred Pickett's 10,000 infantry and cavalry from the left to Hill's threatened position on the right. Lee could see most of what was occurring on his front. At 5:00 A.M., 29 March, a

Above: *Major-General Charles H.T. Collis (left) in front of Petersburg. Collis's wife, Septima Maria, wrote* A Woman's War Record, *a fascinating document packed with telling details. "We overtook a negro soldier very badly wounded in the arm, but marching proudly erect to City Point, still carrying his gun, cartridge-box, and haversack. Mr. Collis told him to throw these encumbrances away, but he refused, and then upon being ordered to do so, begged most earnestly to be permitted to retain them, because, as he expressed it, 'I don't want de fellows at de hospital to mistake me for a teamster.'"*

FLANKING PETERSBURG

Grant had been developing a strategy for his spring campaign, but the bungled Confederate assault on Fort Stedman encouraged him to move immediately. Convinced that Lee planned to join forces with Johnston, Grant did not want to prolong the war by letting this happen. He knew the Confederate line must be broken and the Richmond & Danville Railroad destroyed before Lee used it to move troops.

On the night of 27 March, Grant moved three infantry divisions and a cavalry division from the right and by the morning of the 29th had them in position near Hatcher's Run. Sheridan's cavalry, joined by the II Corps and the V Corps, moved into the same area (Globe Tavern) that night. By the morning of 30 March Grant had an unbroken line from the Appomattox River to Dinwiddie Courthouse. He also had in his immediate command 124,700 men, including 13,000 cavalry. Lee's force numbered about 45,000 men, 5,000 of which were Fitz Lee's cavalry mounted on equine skeletons.

division of Warren's V Corps drove skirmishers from the crossing at Rowanty Creek and forced them back upon Quaker Road and Gravelly Run. Lee took personal command of three brigades and with help from Bushrod Johnson pushed Warren's corps back across Gravelly Run, but the Federals captured the Boydton Road – Lee's supply route – and entrenched.

At the same hour, Sheridan moved against the Confederate flank to turn Lee out of the Petersburg trenches, but Pickett's infantry blocked the effort,

Left: Rodman on the inner lines of the Confederate defenses at Petersburg. By 1865 the Union army had an overwhelming superiority in heavy artillery.

Above: *For the Confederate soldier, the phrase "regulation issue" had little relevance. The official color was supposed to be "cadet gray" but uniforms distributed by the Richmond government varied from an almost Union dark blue to browns and butternuts. The infantry accouterments pictured here include a 1st Sergeant's frock coat and trousers, a linen havelock, a Fayetteville rifle and Model 1860 Colt Army revolver.*

forcing Sheridan back to Dinwiddie Courthouse. Pickett attempted to pursue the advantage but encountered thousands of Federal infantry in Sheridan's rear and withdrew.

Lee evaluated his precariously thin lines and feared that Grant's next flank attack would succeed, so he detached 19,000 infantry and cavalry – almost half his force – and sent them westward under General Pickett to Five Forks. Lee told Pickett "at all hazards" to hold Five Forks, which to a small degree protected the South Side Railroad. Without the railroad, Lee could not transport his army to Danville or to North Carolina. Grant clearly understood the importance of denying the use of the railroad to Lee, and as Confederates moved west, a new battle began to take shape.

COLLISION AT FIVE FORKS

On 29 March, with rain drenching already muddy fields, Grant sensed an opportunity to use his cavalry despite the weather. He spoke with Sheridan and told him to forget the railroad, push around the enemy, get on his right rear, and, if possible, occupy Five Forks. Grant promised to move up the infantry, but he had no definite plan of action. He simply said, "I feel now like ending the matter, if it is possible to do so."

On the 30th the rain continued to pour, and Grant canceled the operation. The decision made Sheridan furious. He plodded along seven miles of muddy roads to meet with Grant and argue for reviving the attack. Before going to headquarters he

stirred up support of the original plan with a group of the general's staff officers. He took some of them into Grant's office and said, "I can drive the whole cavalry force of the enemy with ease." All he requested was enough infantry to roll up the Confederate flank. "I tell you," Sheridan said, "I'm ready to strike out tomorrow and go to smashing things!" Grant could not say no.

Lee had a clear idea of what to expect when he sent Pickett's force to Five Forks. On 1 April, as soon as the rain stopped, Lee knew that Pickett's 19,000 infantry and cavalry would have to face 50,000 Federals. Pickett put Rooney Lee's cavalry division on the western flank, five infantry brigades (Ransom, Wallace, Steuart, Mayo, and Corse's) in the center at Five Forks, and tried to cover the eastern flank by turning part of Corse's brigade on the left at an angle and posting Munford's cavalry over a two-mile front to watch the eastern flank and rear. The infantry brigades dug shallow trenches beside the White Oak Road, but Pickett's position created a three-mile gap between Five Forks and Lee's right flank on the Petersburg line. Pickett had no means for covering the gap other than a weak cavalry force under the command of Brigadier General William P. Roberts and a few dismounted cavalry. Lee had given Pickett a near-impossible task when he told him to hold Five Forks "at all hazards."

During three days of heavy rain Rooney Lee had been skirmishing with elements of Sheridan's cavalry and Warren's V Corps. When the weather cleared on 1 April, two divisions of Sheridan's cavalry under Wesley Merritt struck Pickett's right flank and drove the skirmishers back to the entrenchments. Because of wooded terrain, part of Merritt's cavalry dismounted to fight on foot while another brigade swept around the front of the Confederate position and struck Roberts' troop east of Five Forks. Sheridan waited impatiently for Warren's corps to form and circle behind Pickett's weak eastern flank while Merritt's dismounted cavalry kept Confederate infantry busy in the front.

Right: It was the failure of Lee's cavalry at Five Forks above all that made the Confederate overall position untenable. The last link to Petersburg, the South Side Railroad, was lost. Because of faulty reconnaissance by Sheridan's staff, when Warren's columns reached the White Oak Road and began to wheel as ordered, they found the Confederate flank was still at least 800 yards away. The error eventually made no difference and one of Warren's divisions swung north to attack from the rear.

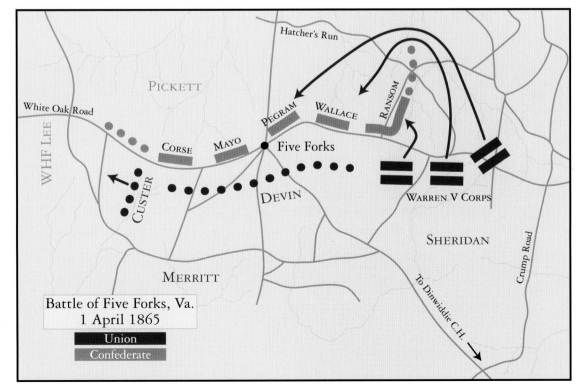

Battle of Five Forks, Va.
1 April 1865
Union
Confederate

At 4:00 P.M. Warren's delayed attack got underway. The flank attack landed in the air because Pickett had no force guarding his east flank except skirmishers and a few cavalry. Warren turned his corps westward and Brigadier General Romeyn B. Ayres' division, operating on Warren's left, ran into heavy volleys of enfilading fire from Corse's brigade.

Because the thrust of Warren's attack had struck 800 yards too far east, Sheridan reacted with exasperation and superseded Warren. He reformed Ayres' division and sent Warren's other two divisions in a sweeping movement around Ayres and into Pickett's rear. Ayres struck the Confederate flank while the other two divisions struck the rear. The sudden and unexpected assault threw the entire Confederate line into chaos. Pickett had been in the right rear and away from the fight enjoying a shad bake when the Federal assault exploded. He galloped through a shower of bullets to direct the defense but actually understood very little of what was happening. By the time he arrived at Five Forks, two of his brigades had been shattered and the other three were reeling from the Federal attack on the left and rear.

General Devins' cavalry, which had been fighting partially dismounted along the Confederate front, jumped on their horses, stormed over the works, seized cannon, and captured more than 1,000 prisoners.

Though Sheridan had removed Warren from overall command, the V Corps took 3,244 prisoners and the Federal cavalry captured 2,000 more. The action severed the remnant of Pickett's command from Lee's main army, turned the Confederate right flank, and captured the South Side Railroad. Grant finally had his opportunity and in the morning launched a massive assault that would end eight days later near a small country village named Appomattox Court House.

THE LAST RETREAT

On 2 April, from the fortifications at Richmond to the bloody fields at Five Forks, Confederates spilled out of their earthworks and headed for Amelia Court House, where the Confederate commissary promised there would be food and supplies. Two days later, as Lee's scattered elements converged on Amelia, they found nothing and therefore wasted a day collecting

Left: *An 1886 lithograph of the Battle of Five Forks, depicting "the charge of General Sheridan." While Sheridan did personally direct the attack, this is a fanciful interpretation of events.*

subsistence from the countryside. "The delay was fatal," wrote Lee, "and could not be retrieved."

That day General Grant, accompanied by the II and VI Corps, reached the Richmond & Danville Railroad at Jetersville, a few miles beyond Amelia, and placed a superior force across Lee's line of retreat. The IX Corps, following the South Side Railroad, occupied Burkeville, shutting down another leg of the Richmond & Danville. The train bearing Davis and the Confederate government had already passed to Danville, but Lee was now forced to seek another route. Without the supplies waiting at Danville, he could no longer fight unless he succeeded in reaching the depot at Lynchburg.

On 5 April Lee abandoned the railroad and departed from Amelia Court House, marching northward and then westward across rolling fields toward Farmville. He could not hope to outrun Sheridan's cavalry, which interposed between the gaps that developed in the long column. The roads were bad,

and Sheridan's attacks on the wagon trains caused constant delays.

On 6 April, when the wagons began moving through the bottomlands of Sayler's Creek near the Appomattox River, a lengthy gap developed when General Gordon veered north with the wagons to

Below: *Confederate prisoners on the way to the rear, captured at Five Forks.*

Above: *Fire engine number 3, Richmomd, would have been busy – or perhaps little more than useless – when the flames reached the arsenal.*

Right: *View of the burned district. In limited areas the destruction was total.*

236

EVACUATION OF RICHMOND

On the morning of 2 April General Wright's VI Corps broke through Lee's attenuated line four miles southwest of Petersburg. In an attempt to recover the line, A.P. Hill lost his life, and Lee lost one of his ablest corps commanders. While Confederates continued to fight in broken masses, Lee turned to Colonel Venable, and said, "It has happened as I told them at Richmond . . . The line has been stretched until it is broken." Then he sent a courier to Breckinridge stating that Petersburg would be evacuated that night, and so must Richmond.

Breckinridge received the message around 10:40 A.M. and immediately dispatched it to President Davis, who was attending Sunday services at St. Paul's Church. Davis departed immediately, ordered the evacuation of Richmond, and with his wife and cabinet began packing personal belongings. Late in the afternoon he received a message from Lee: "I think the Danville road will be safe until tomorrow." Davis settled his family into one of the last cars reserved for the government, handed his wife a loaded pistol for protection, and returned to the city.

Frantic citizens converged on the railways, trying to wedge themselves on board with their bundles of belongings. Soldiers guarding the government train fended them off, for the cars were already overloaded with government officials, baggage, boxes of official documents, and the last of the Confederacy's specie.

As Richmond emptied of soldiers, agents, brokers, and government employees, the city's natives remained behind and witnessed the exodus. They hid what little they owned in cellars,

Above: *A damaged locomotive at the Richmond and Petersburg Railroad depot. Davis was lucky to escape.*

attics, or yards to keep it sheltered from looters. They stayed off the streets where traders were buying and selling stolen goods at bargain prices, including slaves for five or ten dollars in gold.

Richmond's city officials did what they could to save the town. When looting became uncontrollable, they broke open whiskey and rum kegs and let the liquor pour down the street. One eyewitness observed, "The rougher elements of the population, white and black alike, were dipping up the vile stuff with their hands and pouring it down their throats."

At dusk Davis' engine pulled from the station. His farewell to Richmond was bright. Fires set in cotton, tobacco, and food warehouses illuminated the skies. Flames reached the city's arsenal and touched off thousands of shells, hurling red-hot fragments and chunks of glass across the city and setting buildings ablaze in commercial and residential districts. At dawn on 3 April more explosions shook the city when sparks touched off a powder magazine.

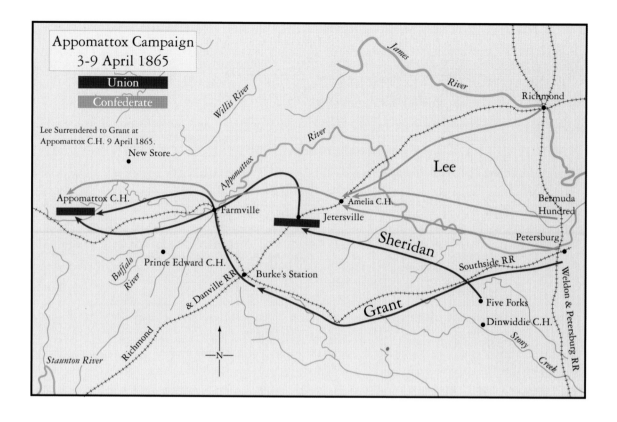

Appomattox Campaign
3-9 April 1865

Union
Confederate

Lee Surrendered to Grant at
Appomattox C.H. 9 April 1865.

avoid attacks and in doing so left the rear of Anderson and Ewell's corps unprotected. Sheridan and elements of the VI Corps pounced on Anderson and Ewell but were checked. Encouraged by early success, the Southerners launched a disconnected counterattack that ended in disaster. Lee had no artillery in the vicinity and watched as Federal shells cut the Confederate ranks to pieces. Entire brigades collapsed and surrendered. Meanwhile, Gordon's wagon train bogged down along Sayler's Creek. Humphreys' II Corps struck Gordon's rear guard, rolled over the Confederate defenders, and captured 8,000 men, including General Ewell, Joseph Kershaw, G.W. Custis Lee, and several brigade commanders. When Lee received the disheartening news, he groaned, "My God! Has the army dissolved?"

The remnant of Lee's force, after living on parched corn for four days, entered Farmville and found a small supply of bread and meat. They could not dally and again made a wide detour north of the Appomattox River to get back on the road to

Lynchburg. Lee's dwindling command tried to move around Grant's 120,000 pursuing Federals by way of the old Richmond and Lynchburg stage road, but could not outrun Sheridan's cavalry. Instead of following Lee's route, Sheridan took cavalry and two infantry corps on a fast-paced, direct route to Appomattox Court House, where he expected Lee to attempt to connect with the Lynchburg railroad. Sheridan reached Appomattox first and blocked Lee's only viable escape route.

On 7 April Grant sent Lee a message asking that he surrender to avoid any further "effusion of blood." Lee probed the Federal lines for weakness but found them too strong. On 8 April Lee admitted, "There is nothing left but to go to General Grant, and I would rather die a thousand deaths." With his army surrounded, Lee had finally exhausted his options and on 9 April accepted Grant's invitation to surrender.

The Army of Northern Virginia had withered away. On the day Lee surrendered, he had 7,892 infantry with arms, 2,100 cavalry, and 63 pieces of artillery. Federal units brought in more Confederate prisoners than Lee's entire army. When the process of issuing paroles began, more stragglers and deserters drifted in from the countryside because they needed written passes to return home unmolested. By 13 April 28,231 paroles had been issued, and the Army of Northern Virginia passed into history.

MCLEAN'S MISFORTUNE

Wilmer McLean, by all accounts a loyal Virginian, lived on a hill near Manassas Junction. During the Battle of First Bull Run he claimed a shell smashed through his window, and this induced him to move the family to a place "where the sound of battle would never reach him." At first, McLean's relocation to Appomattox Court House proved providential because in 1862 part of the Second Battle of Bull Run occurred in his front yard. McLean bought a 2-story brick home in a small village located in a remote part of Virginia having absolutely no strategic importance. But on 7 April he went outside and discovered thousands of Federal troops descending upon the quiet meadows and making noises like Bull Run all over again. Late morning, 9 April, Lee decided to surrender and sent Colonel Charles Marshall into the village to find a suitable place to meet with Grant. Marshall encountered McLean, who wanted to avoid his second encounter with field armies. McLean pointed to an abandoned and dilapidated building some distance from his home. After Marshall explained the purpose, McLean relented and offered his parlor and porch.

Early in the afternoon Lee prepared to parlay with Grant at McLean's home, which Marshall described as a "fine place for a meeting." He put on

Below: *Confederates taking the oath at Richmond, sketched by Alfred Rudolph Ward (1828-1891).*

Above: *Federal soldiers outside Appomattox Courthouse.*

his finest uniform and wore his best sword, but he brought only a colonel and a sergeant to the meeting. Grant entered the parlor accompanied by Generals Sheridan, Ord, a bevy of staff officers, and captain Robert Todd Lincoln, the president's son. Lee rose to his feet and shook the general's hand.

The two men were a study in contrasts: Lee, tall and elegant in a clean gray uniform and black polished boots: Grant, short and slouched with untrimmed reddish whiskers and wearing a mud-splattered sack coat. Grant observed the dissimilarity in dress and became embarrassed by his shabby appearance, confessing later that he was "afraid Lee might think I meant to show him studied discourtesy by coming so." Lee paid no attention to Grant's dress. He wanted to finalize the surrender agreement

and leave. Grant's terms were lenient and acceptable. Three hours later Lee signed the document and departed, leaving the formal surrender ceremony to take place on 12 April. Neither he nor Grant would attend the ceremony.

On the afternoon of 9 April, as Lee returned to his headquarters, hundreds of soldiers surrounded him, asking, "Are we surrendered?" Lee could barely speak, and in a trembling voice, his face wet with tears, replied, "Men we have fought through the war together. I have done the best I could for you. My heart is too full to say more."

The war was over for Lee and his threadbare legion, but not for Wilmer McLean. As soon as the meeting ended, hundreds of relic-hunters charged McLean's home looking for souvenirs. Some offered

to pay, but McLean refused them all. In the end the looters carted away anything they could carry, including furniture, shreds of drapery, pieces of wood, and left McLean with the shattered remnants of his once elegant sanctuary from the war.

THE CAPTURE OF JEFFERSON DAVIS

On the morning of 2 April, warned by General Lee that the Confederate government must evacuate Richmond, President Davis put his family, the cabinet, the archives, and the government treasury on the last train to Danville. Cabinet members were George Davis (Attorney General), George A. Trenholm (Treasury), Judah P. Benjamin (State), Stephen R. Mallory (Navy), and John H. Reagan

(Postmaster). Breckinridge, the secretary of war, was in the field, and Alexander Stephens, the vice president, had long ago lost confidence in Davis. The government's departure from Richmond initiated a two-month chase for the capture of Davis and the Confederate bullion.

The presidential train arrived at Danville the morning of 3 April and waited a week for the army to arrive. On 10 April, when Davis learned of Lee's surrender, he took the train to Greensboro, North Carolina, to be with General Johnston's army. Breckinridge located Davis at Greensboro and told him that Johnston was about to surrender. He urged Davis to do the same. Davis refused and on 15 April began traveling south by carriage. As the Confederate cabinet passed through North Carolina,

Above: Wilmer McLean's house at Appomattox.

Above: *The 15-inch Rodman at Fort Monroe that became known as the "Lincoln gun."*

members began to debate the pros and cons of surrendering. At Charlotte, George Davis resigned and on 26 April surrendered with Johnston to General Sherman. George Trenholm traveled on to Fort Mill and on 27 April did the same.

Davis and the others had ample opportunity to end their flight in a similar fashion, but they had enough gold to escape from the continent and start new lives in England.

The cavalcade of carriages continued through South Carolina and on 4 May crossed the Savannah River into Georgia. Federal cavalry picked up Davis' track and began searching along the same route. President Andrew Johnson announced a $100,000

LINCOLN IN RICHMOND

Abraham Lincoln waited at City Point with his 12-year-old son, Todd, and Rear Admiral David D. Porter for Grant to notify him that Richmond had fallen. When on 3 April a dispatch arrived announcing that the city was in the possession of Major General Godfrey Weitzel, Lincoln departed on a gunboat with Todd, Porter, and an escort of Marines for an unannounced visit to the Confederate capital. The gunboat ran aground, and Lincoln made the rest of the trip by barge, protected by only a crew of sailors armed with carbines.

He stepped ashore in a remote part of Richmond not yet occupied by Federals. The only people in the area were black laborers at work nearby. They immediately recognized the president, dropped their shovels, and clustered around him. Some knelt and tried to kiss his feet, but Lincoln protested. Word spread fast. "They seemed to spring from the earth," Porter recalled. "They came, tumbling and shouting, from over the hills and the waterside, where no one was seen as we had passed." The sailors formed around the president and fixed bayonets to stave off what they feared would develop into an overpowering lunge.

Lincoln calmly waved them off, saying, "You are free, free as air." Then he moved into the city, followed by an ever-increasing mob of reveling blacks. Upon reaching a residential area, Porter spotted a Federal cavalryman, hailed him, and asked for a presidential escort. Several minutes later a troop of horsemen arrived, pushed back the crowd, and escorted Lincoln through two more miles of dusty streets to Weitzel's headquarters in Jefferson Davis' former executive mansion.

Above: Lincoln thoroughly enjoyed his stay in Richmond. On 5 April he conferred with Confederate Assistant Secretary of War John Campbell, another old acquaintance, on the subject of peace. They parted amicably, though Lincoln remained adamant on the abolition of slavery and the reunification of the nation.

Lincoln discussed the latest news with Weitzel, and feeling much better after a short rest said he wanted to visit other parts of the city. Weitzel provided him with a carriage and a cavalry escort, and the president toured the town visiting the Confederate Capitol, Libby Prison, and a few old acquaintances. He made one unexpected stop at the home of General Pickett, whose young wife came to the door holding their 10-month-old son. Mrs. Pickett recalled that upon opening the door she found "a tall, gaunt, sad-faced man in ill-fitting clothes standing outside." When he said, "I am Abraham Lincoln," she gasped, "The President!" "No," he replied, "Abraham Lincoln, George's old friend." Mrs. Pickett did not know the two men had been friends. Lincoln took the baby in his arms, and said, "Tell your father I forgive him for the sake of your bright eyes."

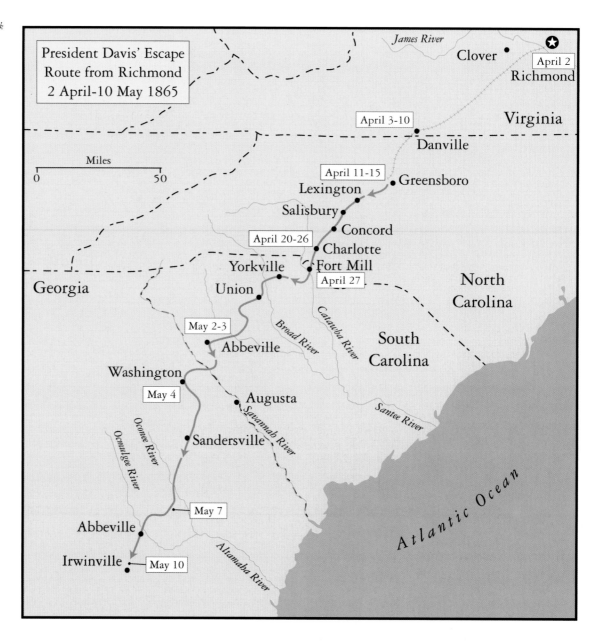

President Davis' Escape Route from Richmond 2 April–10 May 1865

Right: *Jefferson Davis' six-week flight southward. What did he see on that journey, and what effect did it have on him?*

Far right: *Jeff Davis "reaping the harvest," a wood engraving in Harpers magazine from 1861. Despite the heroism and sacrifice of the men who answered his call to arms, it is difficult not to see this image as prophetic.*

reward for the capture of Davis and $25,000 for the lesser officials. A group of disaffected Confederate soldiers escorting Davis' entourage lost interest in the getaway, mutinied, and demanded their wages. Breckinridge dipped into the shrinking treasury and paid them.

At Washington, Georgia, other members of the cabinet decided to part. Mallory went west and on 20 May was captured at Lagrange. Breckinridge departed on horseback, jogged down the length of Florida, crossed to Cuba, and sailed to England. Benjamin reached Tampa, hired a ship, and also reached England. Davis continued south into Georgia with the last of the Confederate treasury and on 7 May reunited with his wife near Abbeville. He now hoped to join forces with Lieutenant General Richard Taylor in Alabama, not knowing that Taylor on 4 May had also surrendered.

On 10 May the 4th Michigan Cavalry and the 1st Wisconsin Cavalry finally caught up with Davis' party at Irwinville, Georgia. They searched the carriages for the reputed $15 million in gold specie but

Above: *Davis in prison in the casemate, Fort Monroe.*

Right: *3rd Pennsylvania Heavy Artillery on parade at Fort Monroe, December 1864. Images such as this imply that the southern cause was doomed from the beginning. But it should not be forgotten that the standing US army was relatively tiny at the beginning of hostilities.*

found nothing other than a few thousand dollars in the pockets of their prisoners. The captors packed Davis off to Fort Monroe, where he remained for two years without being charged or brought to trial.

Unlike Lee and Johnston, who surrendered with honor, the same could not be said for Davis.

EPILOG FOR THE VIRGINIANS

Without Robert E. Lee and Joseph Johnston, two able Virginians and generals, there could never have been a viable Confederacy. Neither man brought the war to Virginia but both men ably fought it. Former Governor Henry A. Wise initiated the breach in 1861 when he addressed the convention and persuaded them to vote for separation from the Union. Governor John Letcher widened that breach beyond repair by eventually succumbing to Wise's demands. Letcher served as governor until 1864, succeeded by Major General William "Extra Billy" Smith. When Davis evacuated Richmond, Smith took the state government to Lynchburg and then to Danville, but he returned to Richmond after Lee surrendered. Letcher remained a private citizen during the last

year of the war and eventually became a member of the state legislature until his death in 1894.

Ex-Governor Wise joined the Confederate army to fight a war he helped start. He became a brigadier general but never distinguished himself, though he commanded coastal defenses and did fight in battles around Richmond and Petersburg. Captured at Appomattox and always a diehard rebel, he never applied for the pardon that would have restored his U.S. citizenship.

Right: *Confederate and imported cavalry carbines and artillery musketoons; while the Confederates ware obliged to import lomg arms and to take them from the enemy, it is not true to say that they were outgunned for most of the War. Quite a few contractors fabricated guns such as these under contract to the Confederate Ordnance Department, including J.P. Murray (left, third from top, and top right). Most Richmond Arsenal carbines and musketoons were modeled after the British Pattern 1853 Enfield (right, third from top, carbine version).*

General Robert E. Lee, perhaps the most revered man in Virginia and one of the ablest commanders in American history, demonstrated some of the finest attributes of his character after the war. He rejected prestigious job offers that would have made him wealthy and became the president of Washington College in Lexington, Virginia, at a modest salary of $1,500 a year. He revolutionized the curriculum, added departments in business, commerce, and journalism, and soon young men from the North and

Above: *Robert E. Lee in civilian clothes, photographed on 15 April.*

South began filling the college's rolls. Though deprived of his citizenship, Lee became the South's outspoken advocate of putting the bitterness of war aside. The conflict had taken a huge toll on Lee's health, and he died at the age of 64. He was buried at the college, and in recognition of his distinguished life, the trustees changed the name of the institution to Washington and Lee University.

The commonwealth of Virginia had a history of producing great men. George Washington was among them. So was Robert E. Lee. (There was even a family connection between the two: Lee's wife, Mary Custis, was the great granddaughter of George and Martha Washington.)

The number of Virginians lost in the Civil War, great, potentially great, or humble, will never be known.

TIMELINE: 1865

16 January: The Confederate Congress passes resolution advising President Davis to name Robert E. Lee general-in-chief of all the armies of the Confederacy. On 19 January Lee accepts the post.

28 January: Peace talks are initiated between the Confederate and Union governments.

31 January: The U.S. Congress passes the 13th Constitutional amendment abolishing slavery.

3 February: Peace talks between the Union and the Confederacy fail.

6 February: Fighting resumes south of Petersburg at Hatcher's Run (also Dabney's Mills).

9 February: General Lee assumes the position of general-in-chief of the Confederate armies.

18 February: Lee endorses the idea of arming slaves to fight the war.

21 February: Lee warns of the possible necessity of abandoning Richmond.

2 March: General Early's army in the Shenandoah is destroyed at Waynesboro.

4 March: President Lincoln is inaugurated for a second term.

13 March: President Davis signs a bill providing for the recruitment of slaves into the army. None ever serve.

19 March: General Sheridan completes the destruction of the Virginia Central Railroad.

25 March: General Gordon's Confederate assault on Fort Stedman in the Petersburg area is repulsed.

26 March: General Lee warns President Davis that the abandonment of Richmond is imminent.

30 March: The Union flanking movement south of Petersburg begins.

30 March-1 April: Confederate forces are defeated at the Battle of Five Forks.

2 April: General Lee informs President Davis that Richmond must be evacuated. At Petersburg,

Left: *A Confederate boy-soldier, aged 14, lies outside a bomb-proof in the trenches of Fort Mahone in 1865.*

General Ambrose P. Hill is killed. Lee begins withdrawing to Danville, Virginia.

3 April: President Davis and his cabinet escape to Danville, Virginia. Federal troops enter Richmond. Union troops occupy Petersburg.

4 April: President Lincoln enters Richmond.

5 April: Lee moves army toward Farmville, Virginia.

7 April: At Appomattox, Grant sends a latter to General Lee asking that he surrender.

9 April: Lee attempts to breach the Union cordon, and when the effort fails, he surrenders at Appomattox Court House.

10 April: President Davis flees Danville.

12 April: The official surrender of the Army of Northern Virginia takes place at Appomattox Court House.

14 April: Lincoln is shot by John Wilkes Booth and dies the following morning.

15 April: Andrew Johnson of Tennessee takes the oath of office.

20 April: Lee advises Davis to end the fighting.

10 May: President Davis and elements of his cabinet are captured near Irwinville, Georgia.

22 May: President Davis is imprisoned at Fort Monroe, Virginia.

29 May: President Johnson issues a proclamation of amnesty to those who fought in the rebellion, but with exceptions that include Lee, Davis, and several other leading figures.

Below: *Lee's slouch hat.*

BIBLIOGRAPHY

Alexander, E.P. *Military Memoirs of a Confederate.* Dayton,
   Ohio: Morningside Press, 1977.

Allan, William. *The Army of Northern Virginia in 1862.*
   Boston: Houghton, Mifflin & Company, 1892.

Barry, Joseph. *The Strange Story of Harper's Ferry.*
   Shepherdstown, W.V.: Shepherdstown Register, 1959.

Bearss, Ed, and Chris Calkins. *Battle of Five Forks.*
   Lynchburg, Va.: H.E. Howard, 1985.

Bigelow, John, Jr. *The Campaign of Chancellorsville.*
   New Haven: Yale University Press, 1910.

Blackford, W.W. *War Years with Jeb Stuart.*
   New York: Charles Scribner's Sons, 1945.

Boatner, Mark M. *The Civil War Dictionary.*
   New York: Daviud McKay Company, Inc., 1959.

Boney, F.N. *John Letcher of Virginia.* University, Ala.:
   University of Alabama Press, 1966.

Bridges, Hal. *Lee's Maverick General: Daniel Harvey Hill.*
   New York: McGraw-Hill Company, 1961.

Butler, Benjamin F. *Autobiography and Personal Reminiscences of
Major General Benjamin F. Butler: Butler's Book.*
   Boston: A.M. Thayer, 1892.

Casler, John O. *Four Years in the Stonewall Brigade.*
   Dayton, Ohio: Morningside Press, 1981.

Catton, Bruce. *A Stillness at Appomattox. Garden City,*
   N.Y.: Doubleday & Co., 1953.

_____. *Gettysburg: The Final Fury.*
   New York: Berkley Books, 1974.

_____. *Grant Takes Command.*
   Boston: Little, Brown, 1969.

Chesnut, Mary. *Mary Chesnut's Civil War.*
   New Haven: Yale University Press, 1981.

Coddington, Edwin B. *The Gettysburg Campaign:
A Study in Command.*
   New York: Scribner's, 1968.

Davis, Burke. *Jeb Stuart: The Last Cavalier.*
   New York: Rinehart & Company, 1957.

_____. *The Long Surrender.*
   New York: Random House, 1985.

Davis, William C. Battle of Bull Run: *A History of the
First Major Campaign of the Civil War.*
   New York: Doubleday & Company, Inc., 1977.

_____. *The Battle of New Market.*
   Garden City, N.Y.: Doubleday & Company, 1975.

Dabney, Virginius. *Richmond: The Story of a City.*
   New York: Doubleday & Company, 1976.

Douglas, Henry Kyd. *I Rode with Stonewall.*
   Chapel Hill, N.C.: University of North Carolina Press, 1968.

Downey, Fairfax. *Clash of Cavalry: The Battle of Brandy Station.*
   New York: David McKay Company, 1959.

Dowdey, Clifford. *Lee.* Boston: Little, Brown and Company, 1965.

Early, Jubal Anderson. *War Memoirs.*
   Bloomington, Ind.: Indiana University Press, 1960.

Evans, Clement A., ed. *Confederate Military History: Virginia.*
   Vol. 3. Secaucus, N.J., Blue and Gray, n.d.

Fox, William F. *Regimental Losses in the American Civil War,
1861-1865.*
   Albany, N.Y.: Albany Publishing Company, 1889.

Freeman, Douglas Southall. *Lee's Lieutenants:
A Study in Command.*
   3 vols. New York: Scribner's, 1942-44.

_____. *R. E. Lee.*
   4 vols. New York: Scribners's, 1934-35.

_____. *The South to Posterity.*
   New York: Scribner's, 1939.

Gordon, John B. *Reminiscences of the Civil War.*
   New York: Charles Scribner's Sons, 1903.

Grant, Ulysses S. *Personal Memoirs of U.S. Grant.*
   New York: Charles L. Webster & Co., 1984.

Hassler, William Woods. *A.P. Hill: Lee's Forgotten General.*
   Chapel Hill, N.C.: University of North Carolina Press, 1962.

Hearn, Chester G. *Six Years of Hell: Harpers Ferry During
the Civil War.*
   Baton Rouge, La.: Louisiana State University Press, 1996.

_____. *When the Devil Came Down to Dixie:
Ben Butler in New Orleans.*
   Baton Rouge, La.: Louisiana State University Press, 1997.

Henderson, G.R.R. *Stonewall Jackson and the American Civil War.*
New York: Longmans, Green, 1909.

Jackson, Mary Anna, ed. *Memoirs of Stonewall Jackson.*
Louisville: The Prentice Press, 1895.

Johnson, Robert U. and Clarence C. Buel, eds. *Battles and Leaders of the Civil War.*
4 vols. New York: The Century Company, 1887-88.

Jones, J.B. *A Rebel War Clerk's Diary at the Confederate States Capital.*
2 vols. New York: Old Hickory Bookshop, 1935.

Jones, Virgil C. *Eight Hours before Richmond.* New York: Henry Holt & Co., 1957.

_____. *Ranger Mosby.* Chapel Hill, N.C.: University of North Carolina Press, 1944.

Lee, Robert E., Jr. *Recollections and Letters of General Robert E. Lee.*
New York: Doubleday, Page & Co., 1924.

Livermore, Thomas L. *Numbers and Losses in the Civil War in America 1861-1865.*
Boston: Houghton Mifflin Company, 1901.

Longstreet, James. *From Manassas to Appomattox: Memoirs of the Civil War in America.*
Bloomington, Ind.: Indiana University Press, 1981.

McClellan, H.B. *The Life and Campaigns of Major General J.E.B. Stuart.*
Boston: 1885.

Moore, Edward A. *The Story of a Cannoneer under Stonewall Jackson.*
New York: Neale Publishing, 1907.

Mosby, John S. *The Memoirs of Colonel John S. Mosby.*
Millwood, N.Y.: Kraus, 1981.

Official Records of the Union and Confederate Armies, War of the Rebellion.
128 vols. Washington: Government Printing Office, 1880-1901.

Official Records of the Union and Confederate Navies in the War of the Rebellion.
30 vols. Washington: Government Printing Office, 1894-1922.

Patrick, Rembert W. *Jefferson Davis and His Cabinet.*
Baton Rouge, La.: Louisiana State University Press, 1944.

Pember, Phoebe Cates. *A Southern Woman's Story: Life in Confederate Richmond.*
Richmond: Mockingbird Books, 1974.

Robertson, James I. *The Stonewall Brigade.*
Baton Rouge, La: Louisiana State University Press, 1963.

Schaff, Morris. *The Battle of the Wilderness.*
Boston: Houghton Mifflin Co., 1910.

Simkins, Francis Butler, and James Welch Patton. *The Women of the Confederacy.*
New York: Garrett and Massie, 1936.

Sommers, Richard J. *Richmond Redeemed: The Siege of Petersburg.*
Garden City, N.Y.: Doubleday, 1981.

Stackpole, Edward J. *From Cedar Mountain to Antietam: August-September, 1862.*
Harrisburg, Pa.: The Stackpole Company, 1959.

_____. *Chancellorsville: Lee's Greatest Battle.*
Harrisburg, The Stackpole Company, 1958.

_____. *Sheridan in the Shenandoah: Jubal Early's Nemesis.*
Harrisburg: The Stackpole Company, 1961.

Starr, Stephen Z. *The Union Cavalry in the Civil War.*
3 vols. Baton Rouge, La.: Louisiana State university Press, 1979-85.

Strode, Hudson. *Jefferson Davis.*
4 vols. New York: Harcourt, Brace, 1955-66.

Tucker, Glenn. *High Tide at Gettysburg.* Dayton: Morningside Bookshop, 1973.

Turner, Edward Raymond. *The New Market Campaign: May, 1864.*
Richmond: Whittet & Shepperson, 1912.

Warner, Ezra. *Generals in Blue: Lives of the Union Commanders.*
Baton Rouge: Louisiana University Press, 1964.

_____. *Generals in Gray: Lives of the Confederate Commanders.*
Baton Rouge: Louisiana University Press, 1959.

Wise, John Sergeant. *The End of an Era.*
New York: Thomas Yoseloff, 1965.

INDEX

ACKNOWLEDGMENTS

R = Right   L= Left   C = Center T = Top   B = Bottom

All images © Chrysalis Image Library apart from the following:

Library of Congress, Geography and Map Division pg 26, pg35, pg36, pg60B.
Library of Congress, Prints & Photographs Division: pg7 Civil War Photographs, [LC-B811-2449], pg8 Civil War Photographs, [LC-DIG-cwpb-02711], pg9TL [LC-USZ62-38891], pg9TR, Civil War Photographs, [LC-DIG-cwpb-01471], pg10 [LC-USZC4-11787], pg11 [LC-USZ62-115350], pg12 [LC-USZC2-2703], pg13 [LC-USZC4-7997], pg14 [LC-DIG-cwpbh-04775], pg16 [LC-BH824- 5391], pg 17 [LC-USZC4-2439], pg18-19 Civil War Photographs, [LC-DIG-cwpb-03739], pg20-21 Civil War Photographs, [LC-USZ62-119128], pg23 Civil War Photographs, [LC-DIG-cwpb-04106], pg29 Civil War Photographs, [LC-DIG-cwpbh-03115], pg30 Civil War Photographs, [LC-DIG-cwpb-03739], pg34 Civil War Photographs, [LC-DIG-cwpb-00768], pg37 [LC-USZ62-105557], pg38 [LC-USZ62-33456], pg39TR [LC-USZ62-9911], pg39B [LC-USZ62-13955], pg41 [LC-USZ62-132759], pg43 Civil War Photographs, [LC-DIG-cwpb-07453], pg47 Civil War Photographs, [LC-DIG-cwpb-03748], pg48, pg49 Civil War Photographs, [LC-DIG-cwpb-01510], pg50-51 [LC-USZ62-126960], pg56 [LC-USZ62-7001], pg60T [LC-USZC4-1796], pg64TL [LC-USZ62-83277], pg64CL [LC-USZ62-71781], pg64BL [LC-USZ62-99838], pg67TR [LC-USZC4-2040] , pg70 Civil War Photographs, [LC-DIG-cwpb-01400], pg72BL Civil War Photographs, [LC-DIG-cwpb-04942], Civil War Photographs, [LC-DIG-cwpb-00200], pg83 Civil War Photographs, [LC-DIG-cwpb-01002], pg94 Civil War Photographs, [LC-USZ62-106283] pg97 Civil War Photographs, [LC-DIG-cwpb-00222] , pg109 Civil War Photographs, [LC-DIG-cwpb-03870], pg111CR Civil War Photographs, [LC-DIG-cwpb-01085], [LC-USZC4-9829], pg118T [LC-USZ62-163] pg 125 Civil War Photographs, [LC-DIG-cwpb-03686], pg129 Civil War Photographs, [LC-B813- 6408], pg133T Civil War Photographs, [LC-B811- 342], pg135 [LC-USZC4-7943], Pg136 Civil War Photographs, [LC-DIG-cwpb-01152] pg139 Civil War Photographs, [LC-B817- 7139] pg140 Civil War Photographs, [LC-B813- 6583], Civil War Photographs, [LC-DIG-cwpbh-03240], Pg144 Civil War Photographs, [LC-DIG-cwpb-03856] pg145 Civil War Photographs, [LC-B817-7516], pg147B Civil War Photographs, [LC-B817- 7131], pg159 Civil War Photographs, [LC-DIG-CWPB-03915] pg161 Civil War Photographs, [LC-GID-CWPB-03787], pg163T Civil War Photographs, [LC-DIG-CWPB-03856], pg168 [LC-USZC4-5983], pg174 [LC-USZ62-104043] pg178B Civil War Photographs, [LC-DIG-cwpb-07612], pg180 Civil War Photographs, [LC-DIG-cwpb-01199], pg183 Civil War Photographs, [LC-DIG-cwpb-03965], pg189 Civil War Photographs, [LC-DIG-cwpb-05088], pg190 Civil War Photographs, [LC-DIG-cwpb-01721], pg194 Civil War Photographs, [LC-DIG-cwpb-01218], pg195L [LC-B813-6770], pg195R [LC-USZ62-139760], pg197 Civil War Photographs, [LC-DIG-cwpu-00492], pg208T [LC-USZC4-5797], pg208B [LC-USZC4-5789], pg212 [LC-USZC4-9828], pg217 [LC-USZ62-57018], pg219 [8184-4794], pg220 [LC-B8171-3194], pg224 Civil War Photographs, [LC-DIG-cwpb-00468], pg226 [LC-USZ62-109737], pg227 Civil War Photographs, [LC-DIG-cwpb-05341] pg229, [LC-B8171-3197], pg234 Civil War Photographs, [LC-DIG-cwpb-07523], pg235T Civil War Photographs, [LC-USZC4-1759] pg235B Civil War Photographs, [LC-DIG-cwpb-02581], pg236T Civil War Photographs, [LC-DIGcwpb-02760] pg236B Civil War Photographs, [LC-DIG-cwpb-02673], Civil War Photographs, [LC-DIG-cwpb-02704], pg239 [LC-USZC4-8106], pg240 Civil War Photographs, [LC-DIG-cwpb-03908], pg243 [LC-USZ62-6931], pg245 [LC-USZ62-115352], pg246 [LC-USZC401157], pg247 Civil War Photographs, [LC-DIG-cwpb-03674], pg250 [LC-USZ62-10865], pg251T Civil War Photographs, [LC-B8184-3187]

Courtesy Author's Collection pg138 / © Frank & Marie T Wood Print Collection pg128

© US Army Photograph pg66B (B1575), pg133R (SC107402)

© U.S. Navy Photograph (NH-82533) pg74

Maps on pages 22, 42, 60, 63, 75, 88, 99, 108, 141, 146, 188, 196, 209. 233, 238, 244 by Mike Marino © Chrysalis Image Library

"Let me tell you what is coming . . . Your fathers and husbands, your sons and brothers, will be herded at the point of the bayonet . . . You may after the sacrifice of countless millions of treasure and hundreds of thousands of lives, as a bare possibility, win Southern independence, but I doubt it. I tell you that, while I believe with you in the doctrine of state rights, the North is determined to preserve this Union."
GOVERNOR SAM HOUSTON, TEXAS, 1861

"In firing his gun, John Brown has merely told what time of day it is. It is high noon."
WILLIAM LLOYD GARRISON, MASSACHUSETTS, 1859

"Little did I conceive of the greatness of the defeat [at Bull Run], the magnitude of the disaster which it had entailed upon the United States. So short-lived has been the American Union, that men who saw it rise may live to see it fall."
WILLIAM HOWARD RUSSELL, 1862

"Get there first with the most men."
STRATEGY OF CONFEDERATE LIEUTENANT-GENERAL NATHAN BEDFORD FORREST

"In glades they meet skull after skull / Where pine cones lay – the rusted gun, / Green shoes full of bones, the mouldering coat / And cuddled up skeleton; / And scores of such. Some start as in dreams, / And comrades lost bemoan; / By the edge of those wilds Stonewall had charged – / But the year and the Man were gone."
HERMAN MELVILLE, FROM "THE ARMIES OF THE WILDERNESS"

"If the Confederacy falls, there should be written on its tombstone: DIED OF A THEORY."
(JEFFERSON DAVIS, REFERRING TO SOUTHERN SLAVEHOLDERS' INTRANSIGENCE, 1864)